First Big Crush

The Down and Dirty on Making Great Wine Down Under

Eric Arnold

SCRIBNER

New York   London   Toronto   Sydney

SCRIBNER
A Division of Simon & Schuster, Inc.
1230 Avenue of the Americas
New York, NY 10020

First Scribner hardcover edition September 2007

SCRIBNER and design are trademarks of
Macmillan Library Reference USA, Inc., used under license
by Simon & Schuster, the publisher of this work.

For information about special discounts for bulk purchases,
please contact Simon & Schuster Special Sales:
1-800-456-6798 or business@simonandschuster.com

Designed by Kyoko Watanabe
Text set in Minion

Manufactured in the United States of America

1   3   5   7   9   10   8   6   4   2

Library of Congress Control Number: 2007008740

ISBN-13: 978-1-4516-1327-8

For the family I already had and the second one I gained.
Amazing neither of them has killed me yet.

Cut the crap. Gimme a drink.

—MARION WORMER, *ANIMAL HOUSE*

Contents

PART I

Harvest

How I Wound Up in the
South Pacific with Grape Skins
in My Underwear

Let's get one thing clear right away. You're not reading this book because I'm some kind of wine expert. You're reading this book because at the time I set out to write it, I was just like you: I liked drinking wine even though I knew relatively little about it. Actually, I'm embarrassed to admit that for years I was the worst kind of wine drinker: the kind who *thinks* he knows something about wine. Carlo Rossi's mattress stains could've taught you more about wine than I could have.

I declared myself a wine expert, wrongly and assholishly, during my senior year of college, for a simple reason: because I was in college. College students think they're experts in everything, and my circle of friends was no exception. We didn't just think the world would be different if we were in charge—we *knew* it would be. Because we were drunk.

But we weren't just regular drunks; we thought we were so much cooler. In lieu of dank frat-house basements and warm Coors Light, just about every Saturday night my friends and I would pile into a jazz bar that sold Washington-made Hogue Cellars Fume Blanc by the bottle for about thirteen dollars. Early on I figured out that it didn't make sense to spend thirty or forty dollars on gin and tonics if I could get just as drunk by ordering a bottle of Hogue with one glass. Everyone else in the group quickly caught on to my line of thinking. One night we drank every last drop of Hogue in the place and still left with money in our pockets. (A brief word to the wise: Well-meaning as it may be, the compliment "I used to get *so* wasted on this stuff in college" does not go over well when you visit Hogue, now one of the biggest and most reputable wineries in Washington state.) From this experience I somehow convinced myself I was a wine expert when all I really knew was how to get drunk on wine for less than twenty bucks.

After I graduated my thoughts on wine didn't change, but my alcohol-consumption habits varied depending on what job I had or where I lived or whether I had a sex life. For example, when I had my first—and worst—job, at a public television station, I drank giant gin and tonics when I got home every night. You would, too, if you had to spend each workday assembling direct-mail pieces for a Nazi devil woman with dried saliva caked on the corners of her mouth. Because I wasn't getting laid I switched to whiskey, since one bottle can get you through long periods of unintended celibacy. And after the dried-spit Nazi devil woman fired me I went with the cheapest beer I could afford. I did, however, order wine when and if I went out for dinner courtesy of the Department of Employment. But I always ordered Hogue, or something similar.

Around 2000 I joined the dot-com boom in New York, and for a while I dated a French girl. However, I'm afraid this isn't the part where I tell you that she took me back to France and taught me everything there is to know about Bordeaux, Burgundy, and Champagne (and the Paris sex clubs in which the wines are served). Actually, we barely ever left her apartment. We ordered in, because at the time I could only cook two things (mac and cheese, and mac and cheese with Cheez Whiz), and she couldn't cook at all. She had so little interest in food and wine—plus she didn't smoke *and* she shaved her armpits—that they must've kicked her out of France for not being French enough. It wasn't long before we went our separate ways and I was back on the whiskey. I needed to get away for a couple of weeks, and a friend passed along to me a magazine article about a camping and mountain-biking tour around the South Island of New Zealand. I decided to do it even though at the time I couldn't have pointed to the country on a map, but the article made the tour sound like a great way to see a new country *and* get laid. The first part turned out to be exactly what I'd hoped for, but the second, well, I was still drinking whiskey.

For a short time, that is. I met two Germans and a British guy named Spencer—no, we didn't have an orgy. What did happen was Spencer suggested we all take a day trip to wineries once the tour was over. I saw it as an opportunity to get drunk for a day, but Spencer, a longtime wine drinker, was informed enough to know that wine isn't just France, Italy, and California. He knew that with some science, some tradition, and a little luck you can make good-tasting wine just about anywhere.

By the mid-1970s, New Zealanders of European descent had been growing and making wine up and down the country for about a century. But it was little more than a few people growing this variety here or that variety there and maybe having enough booze to talk a couple of girls into a threesome. New Zealand winemakers eventually started making grape-flavored, bag-in-a-box rocket fuel on a commercial scale. Then someone, somewhere along the line about thirty years ago, figured out that the Marlborough region—with its three-hundred-plus days of sunshine; low annual rainfall; nutrient-rich, stony soil; and cool, maritime climate—would be perfect for growing Sauvignon Blanc. Around the same time someone else figured out that the warmer weather of Hawkes Bay on the North Island would work well for Merlot, Cabernet Sauvignon, and Syrah. A little later someone else figured out that the rugged, arid, mountainous Central Otago, at the bottom of the South Island, would be ideal for Pinot Noir. And so on. New Zealand's winemakers, generally educated in botany, biochemistry, or even food science, then began traveling to California, Europe, and South America to learn the traditional tricks of the trade. By the mid-1990s, with their scientific knowledge and study-abroad experience, New Zealanders were making wine that was just as good as or better than anyone else's—and selling it for a fraction of the price. In less than three decades New Zealand had done what the French, Spanish, and Italians needed two thousand years to do. Connoisseurs, like Spencer, knew that the Kiwis had caught the traditionalists with their thumbs up their asses.

And from my very first sip of Marlborough Sauvignon Blanc at ten-thirty or so on that morning, I knew it, too—I was tasting something special. My mouth zipped and zinged, and though I couldn't describe the flavors I was tasting, I was sure of only one thing: I wanted more. I was hammered by noon, with five wineries still to go. At one point I stole the tour guide's microphone in the van and started singing karaoke—"The Tracks of My Tears" by Smokey Robinson—even though I didn't know the words. I might've taken off my shirt, too, but I don't remember. From winery to winery and sip to sip, the wines just got better and better. From the time I got back home to Brooklyn, whenever I was in a wine shop I either bought wine from New Zealand or asked for something similar. Marlborough Sauvignon Blanc was my new Hogue.

The difference, though, was instead of drinking just one wine from one place I was drinking the same type of wine from several different Marlborough producers, so they all tasted slightly different from one another. Because the wines were all different I assumed there had to be something different about each of the winemakers. I assumed that what's in the bottle says as much about the winemaker as, say, what the food on the plate says about the chef. It never occurred to me that there might be other elements involved, some completely beyond human control.

For a few years after that trip I was still guzzling whatever New Zealand Sauvignon Blanc I could find at night, and spending my daylight hours working the copy desk at a small business magazine. It was better than working for the Nazi devil woman at PBS, but the same could probably be said for cleaning up monkey shit at the zoo (which, I imagine, is very similar to working at PBS). So out of a desire to drink more, work less, and maybe satisfy a little curiosity, up sprang the idea of just throwing myself into the lifestyle: getting a job at a winery and writing a book about it. I mean, how hard could it all be? Only thing to figure out was where to go.

I thought about France and California, but I couldn't imagine a winery would let an idiot with no training anywhere near their facilities. Plus, a quick Amazon search showed that the world needs another book about French or California wine about as badly as it needs another Starbucks. I had my heart set on returning to New Zealand, but had no idea where to begin.

I got some help when I attended my ten-year high-school reunion. One person I considered a friend back then, a guy named Jim, told me that he'd just returned from New Zealand, where he did forestry work. He explained the ins and outs of getting a one-year work visa. Right then I knew I had my one-way ticket to the good life, strolling through vineyards, having three-hour lunches, and gulping the wine I already couldn't get enough of.

I got the visa, then cold-called a guy in San Francisco named David Strada, who does marketing work for New Zealand wines in the United States. I pitched him the idea of working at a winery and writing a book, and though he had to have known right away that I had no clue what I was talking about, he was nice enough not to hang up on me or call me a moron. What he told me was that I couldn't have called at a better time.

It just so happened that New Zealand was about to enter the most pivotal time in its brief winemaking history. David said that the grape volume of the 2004 harvest in Marlborough was projected to be 50 percent higher than ever before. I think he was trying to tell me that I was asking for trouble, but all I heard was that there'd be 50 percent more wine for me to drink. Despite the disconnect, however, he agreed with my basic idea of getting an up close look at the people and the process, and that in order to do so I needed a winemaking family to welcome me into its home and workplace. And put up with me, of course. But I also needed them to put me to work. Just as no one would have trusted Bill Buford to write about English soccer thugs if he hadn't become one, I reasoned, I knew I had to make wine in order to tell the story of the largest wine region in New Zealand (not to mention one of the most prominent in the southern hemisphere). I couldn't imagine that the work would be all that difficult, though to remain completely objective and open-minded (and make my credit-card company panic), I made it clear that wherever I worked, I needed to do it for free. Allan Scott Wines & Estates gladly accepted my offer.

This was actually the first winery I approached, because I had a good feeling about the place when the two Germans, Spencer, and I stumbled in there for a tasting toward the end of the day way back in early 2001. For whatever reason, I remembered liking the wine from there more than any of the others. Even though I'd never written anything informed or coherent about wine (or anything else, some would argue), convincing Allan to let me into his world proved easier than I thought. This is pretty much how the first phone conversation went:

Me: Hi, Allan. This is Eric Arnold calling from New York.
Allan: I already told you I fuckin' hate aluminum siding. Stop
    calling.
Click.

Okay, not really. But the call was nearly as brief. I asked if he could put me to work at his winery while I wrote a book, and he said sure, no problem. He never asked if I was a serial killer, planned to smuggle heroin up my ass, or both. He just told me to show up whenever.

Easy. Good life, here I come. I quit my job and a few weeks after our brief conversation, I was on a plane to New Zealand, timing my arrival for mid-March (just before harvest). On the last leg of the journey, from Auckland to

Marlborough (the northeastern tip of the South Island), I stared out the window of the little propeller plane—as it bounced over row after endless row of green vines stretching across the valley—since it was all I could do to keep from throwing up. My nausea only increased once the plane was safely on the ground, because the enormity of it all had just begun to sink in. I'd landed in a country I didn't know, to work with people I didn't know, in an industry I didn't know, and then write a book about it. Which was something I'd never done. It quickly became clear that it wouldn't get any easier.

Allan picked me up at the airport, only a couple of miles from his home, vineyards, and winery. Calling the area desolate on that late-afternoon weekday would've been like calling Dean Martin a bit tipsy. We didn't pass a single car as Allan drove me past some small homes, a couple of vineyards, and a sheep paddock . . . and that was pretty much it. We turned onto Jacksons Road and passed Allan's winery on the left and the Cloudy Bay winery on the right, both embedded in large vineyards. We then pulled up to Allan's house, which was hidden from the road, surrounded by tall trees Allan had planted himself. The wood and stone two-story house kind of looked like a bed and breakfast, but without the old hippies and stale muffins.

We went inside and sat in the open, airy living room. After a few minutes of get-to-know-you chitchat, Allan, who was slouched on the leather sofa, let out a long sigh. "This year will be the leveler," he said, explaining that many Marlborough wineries would either grow or fold after the 2004 vintage. Hundreds of acres of new plantings were producing a crop for the first time, and a rainy February threatened the quality of the dense crop being carried in established vineyards. This just happened to come at a time when contract growers, who sell grapes to wineries such as Allan's, had raised their price per ton of grapes to their highest-ever levels. In some cases they were delivering grape volumes double what was expected—and therefore collecting double the money from the wineries. Some wineries would be able to maintain a respectable level of quality and sell all their wine, while others would founder and ultimately get acquired or absorbed by their neighbors. It was an incredibly tense time. "I don't want anyone to go broke," Allan said quietly, eyes fixed on the muted television. It could have been showing *Girls Gone Wild* and he wouldn't have noticed. "We just have to make sure *we* survive first."

A few minutes later he fell into an early-evening snooze, lightly snoring with his head leaned back and his mouth gaping open. The guy's industry—his whole way of life—was transforming in front of him . . . and he was passed out with a complete stranger sitting three feet away. The stranger felt pretty awkward (How long do I sit here? Do I wake him up? Flick his ear?), but Allan, even amid tense times, could be totally calm and cool.

Maybe it's because Allan's been in Marlborough pretty much since the beginning, and he's seen and done it all. In the 1970s Allan was planting large vineyards for Montana Wines, the largest producer in New Zealand. He started at less than a dollar per hour, and by the end of the summer he was a vineyard manager making NZ$14,000 per year. Years later he was poached by Corbans, which would also become part of the Montana empire, but by 1990 Allan was ready to venture out on his own. It was small potatoes at first, since Allan and his wife, Cathy, only intended to make a few thousand cases a year, and would spend long evenings pasting on labels by hand in their living room. Today the country has more than five hundred fifty wineries producing more than 14.5 million cases a year (exporting about 1.5 million cases to the United States). Allan Scott Wines grew with everyone else. Allan and Cathy's operation now produces more than sixty thousand cases of multiple varieties every year, and has several large vineyards. It's a full-time job for many—especially Allan, owner and operator of the company. The vineyard manager is Cathy's brother-in-law Brian, an old curmudgeon, and the head winemakers are Jeremy McKenzie and Allan's son, Josh—two guys who work hard and play hard, often at the same time. Not necessarily sober, either.

So if Allan was calm, cool, and snoring, I figured maybe I should be, too. After all, I thought as I went to bed that night, I just showed up to relax, get some sun, and help make some wine, right?

Wrong. From the very next morning, my first at the winery, there was no question that what I'd signed up for was getting wet, cold, dirty, sunburned, sore, scraped, bruised, broken, and completely shit-faced. And then doing it all again the next day. As if to emphasize the point that this year was gonna be a doozy, a local farm-supply company handed out free, ugly red T-shirts with the bold, black words THE BIG ONE stamped across the front. Making wine in a faraway land might sound romantic, but even in a normal year it's a grueling lifestyle embraced by some extraordinary as well as frighteningly ordinary people. It's every bit as exciting and fun at some times as it is boring and exhausting at others.

Wine in general, and New Zealand wine in particular, took on a lot more meaning after my work at Allan Scott Wines and the countless hours I spent meeting and speaking with other winemakers in the region, sitting in their cluttered offices and around the kitchen tables in their homes. Turn the page and you'll learn how wine is made in Marlborough, who makes it, why they make it the way they do—and why it tastes the way it does. Just as I did. Beyond that, it's up to you to decide if you like New Zealand wine or any wine at all. You've always relied on your experiences and instincts to figure out what you like to eat, where you should live, or whose pants you want to try to get into. So by the time you've finished reading, you should be informed enough to undergo the same kind of trial and error to figure out what kind of wine you like to drink. Certainly you can figure it out if a miserable, undersexed idiot scarred by abuse at the hands of a Nazi devil woman at PBS eventually can.

And the best part is, unlike me you won't ever have to pick grape skins out of your underwear.

Australia

U.S.A.

New Zealand

Auckland

Gisborne

Hawkes Bay

Nelson

Blenheim

Wellington

Marlborough

Queenstown

Christchurch

Central Otago

Dunedin

South Pole

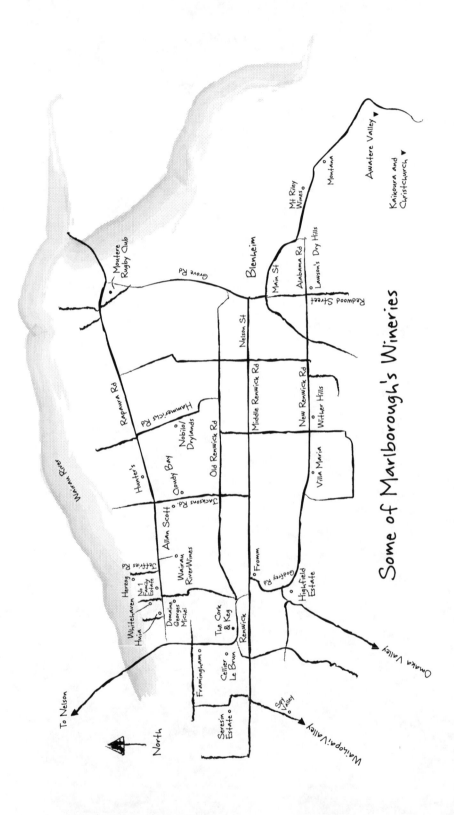

Some of Marlborough's Wineries

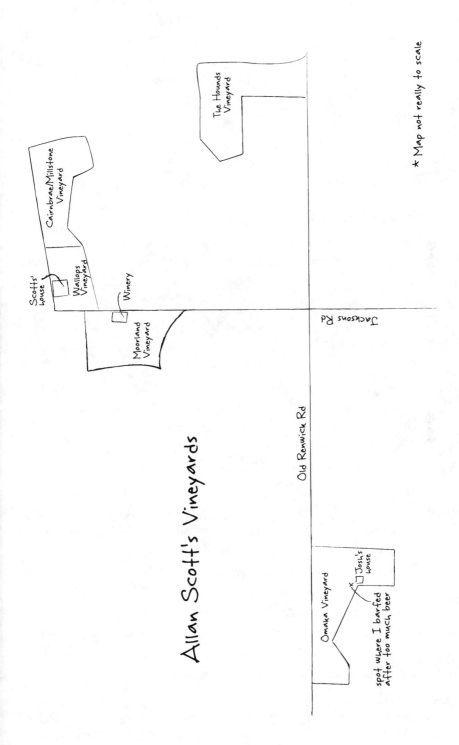

Allan Scott's Vineyards

Scott's House

Wallops Vineyard

Cairnbrae/Millstone Vineyard

Winery

Moorland Vineyard

The Hounds Vineyard

Jacksons Rd

Old Renwick Rd

Omaka Vineyard

Josh's House

× spot where I barfed after too much beer

* Map not really to scale

Author's Note

My interviews for this book were restricted, for the most part, to wineries that have their own bricks-and-mortar winemaking facilities. There are several noteworthy Marlborough brands that make their wine at massive contract facilities, such as Rapaura Vintners, Marlborough Valley Cellars, and South Pacific Cellars. These are giant wineries where you pretty much just show up with grapes, and the winery handles all the winemaking for you, from start to finish. And while there's nothing wrong with the several brands of wine made at each of these places, the operations themselves are large, impersonal, and, with a few exceptions, uninteresting. Furthermore, a winery's having its own facilities is a pretty good sign that its products will be available on store shelves for years to come, whereas brands produced at contract facilities often come and go with changes of the wind. I wanted to make sure that any wine you read about in this book is available for you to try.

In fact, I highly recommend that you drink wine as you read this book. Because that's certainly what the author did as he wrote it.

—*Eric Arnold*

PART I

Harvest

It's important not to just view this as wine and winemaking, but part of your total life. You work with people, you work with the land, markets all around the world, and you live in a place that enables it all to happen.

—MIKE ALLAN, OWNER/WINEMAKER OF HUIA VINEYARDS

1

A Family Affair

Three metric tons of Chardonnay grapes fell with a crash into the giant stainless-steel bin below the huge dump truck, landing with a loud boom that drowned out any conversation in the vicinity. As the back of the truck tilted, another four tons of grapes slid into the bin, the wet, juicy, plump berries landing on top of one another, making an arrhythmic slapping noise. Ironically, it kind of sounded like drunk people fucking.

"Seal up the tank," Jeremy, one of the two winemakers at Allan Scott Wines (ASW), instructed me.

A hose had already been laid between the thirty-five-ton-capacity press (an imposing steel cylinder on stilts) and one of ten 20,000-liter stainless-steel tanks huddled together, each reaching more than twenty feet into the air. I affixed the seal—about the size of a bike tire—to the door of the tank and pulled it shut, twisting the clamp tight. Of course, I'd done it incorrectly, since I'd never worked at a winery. Hell, I could barely replace a bike tire, much less use something that looks like one to seal up a wine tank correctly. Jeremy was kind enough not to roll his eyes as he unscrewed the clamp on the door, pulled the seal off, attached it properly, and secured the door in place again.

"You got the one on top?" he asked, and I nodded. Why he trusted me after the debacle I'd made out of exactly the same simple task twenty feet lower to the ground, I'll never know. He really shouldn't have, because only a couple minutes earlier I'd closed the lid on the top of the tank and twisted its clamp tight. Sure, the thought occurred to me that there would be juice flowing in and 20,000 liters of air would have to get out somehow, but I thought, *Hey, he told me to seal it up. He's the winemaker, and I'm the wine drinker.*

After the truck had rolled down the ramp and driven away to retrieve more grapes, the bin began to rise high in the air on its hydraulics. As it did, bright-green grapes, juice, stems, leaves, and twigs began to spill out of a hole in the end of the bin, pushed through by a giant steel corkscrew-looking auger, and into the crusher-destemmer.

"It's all happening!" Allan said excitedly, and gave me a gentle punch on the stomach before walking off briskly, having witnessed the beginning of a vintage for the thirty-somethingth time.

The crusher-destemmer was rattling and rumbling as it let a green, slushy mixture of grapes and juice fall below into the must pump, while it spit all the leaves, twigs, branches, and perfectly clean stems out the other side.

"I'm mesmerized as to how this works," I told Jeremy, once I realized I'd been staring at it like a stoned housecat.

"You'll figure it out," he said confidently, "'cause you get to clean it later." This, I'd discover, is essentially how you learn how everything works at a winery. Clean it, get it dirty, take it apart, clean it again, put it back together. Repeat. Just make sure the American guy doesn't fuck it up somehow.

The must pump continually pushed the grapes and juice through a long, four-inch-diameter hose, into the end of the press, a giant steel cylinder about the size of most overpriced studio apartments in New York. Juice then ran out the other end of the press and into a small stainless-steel tub from which Jeremy and Josh, the second winemaker and Allan's son, regularly dipped glasses and pulled out juice to swirl, sniff, and taste. From the tub the juice ran to a pump, which then pushed the juice through a long, one-inch-diameter hose, into the bottom of the tank.

Josh was answering one of many idiotic questions I'd ask him about his job when the pump, which had been at work for about half an hour, started to make a rattling noise. It was a subtle-enough sound that my untrained ear didn't notice a difference, but it elicited a near-Pavlovian response in Josh. Only without the drooling.

"Is the lid open?" he asked me, gesturing in the general direction of the tank.

I looked at him confidently and said, "Shouldn't be. I closed it," my tone of voice conveying, *I'm cool. I've done what I've been told. Jeremy told me to seal it up, and I did. I may never have worked at a winery, but I can follow instructions. He told me to seal it up, and I sealed that thing so frickin' tight it—*

As if the roof of his house were on fire, Josh sprinted up the ladder to the catwalk and began furiously twisting at the clamp on the lid of the tank to defuse the ticking time bomb I'd inadvertently created. If he hadn't heard the pump struggle when he did, well, this book would've ended right after this sentence. A pocket of air that had been under ever-increasing pressure escaped as Josh got the lid open, thus keeping the tank from exploding and sending grape-juice-coated steel shrapnel in every direction, which would have made the winery look like your average neighborhood in Baghdad.

When Josh came down from the catwalk, his hair was blown back as though he'd been driving a Formula One car in a wind tunnel. He was smiling because he could see the humor of the situation, but the accompanying shake of his head spoke volumes. "When Jeremy said seal it," he told me, "he meant just put the seal on. Not seal it shut! Fuck, I got a huge blast of air in the face there." (This was Kiwi slang for, "Are you tryin' to fucking kill us all?")

He proceeded to give me a brief lesson in junior-high-level physics, a class I'd obviously slept through. "And when you let juice out," he concluded, "you have to open the lid or the whole thing will collapse in on itself. It'll look like an empty beer can when you crush it with your hand." Of course, for the remainder of the harvest whenever I was asked to seal a tank, the request would be quickly followed by, mockingly, "Not the top." (This, translated from Kiwi slang, meant, "Please don't try fuckin' killing us all again.") I felt like the Scottish guy in that joke who says, "I laid every brick in this town, but do they call me a bricklayer? No! But I fuck just *one* goat . . ."

I managed to make it through the rest of the day without causing thousands of dollars' worth of damage—or any gruesome deaths. We crushed seventeen tons of Chardonnay grapes that would later become sparkling wine, but for the time being was called "bubbly base" in the local lingo.

Indeed, as Allan said, it was all happening. My new life as a professional drunk/winery bitch had begun—fortunately, not with a bang.

* * *

It would make my job a hell of a lot easier if I told you that was my first day at the winery, that I arrived just in time for the start of the crush, and that everything was just peachy and incident-free from then on out. But I'd be lying, and this book would be indistinguishable from any one of Andrea Immer's perky collections of wine commentary. I should point out, too, that I have nicer tits.

Anyway, I had landed in Auckland about two weeks earlier, when *Lord of the Rings* mania was still in full swing, even though the excitement over the final installment had died down months earlier throughout the rest of the world. I never got the sense that Kiwis, a normally underappreciated people, were overly enthusiastic about the Peter Jackson movie and the attention it brought them, but they certainly seemed enthusiastic when it came to capitalizing on it. I saw a health-food stand called Gandalf's Pantry and a Middle Eastern take-out place called Lord of the Kebab. I wouldn't have to worry about Marlborough, though. No *Lord of the Rings* shit there. Unfortunately, however, it was like stepping into the movie *Boys Don't Cry,* only with a different accent.

Okay, maybe I'm being a bit harsh. Really, Blenheim, the main town in Marlborough, is just a farm town, and farm towns have a lot of farm people (and sheep with some of the biggest testicles you've ever seen—I swear, they're like fuzzy basketballs). People in a small farm town look, think, and act differently. And sometimes they, too, have the biggest testicles you've ever seen.

One night when I was in a bar drinking with one of the ASW vineyard guys Ra, I was introduced to a dude named Clint.

"Hey, Clint!" Ra yelled at him. "Come here and show Eric your ball!"

Clint walked over and started to unbuckle his pants, even though I pleaded with him not to show me his balls.

"No, his ball . . . just one of 'em. You gotta see this," Ra told me.

"Please, keep your pants up," I begged him. "I don't wanna see your . . . holy SHIT!"

This guy had one testicle the size of a grapefruit, and the other one was the regular size. Seriously, this guy made Picasso subjects look normal.

"What do you feed that thing?" I asked him, but he just shrugged his shoulders as he zipped up his fly. There was nothing I could say about his giant ball that this guy probably hadn't already heard. He left before I could encourage him to run off and join the circus, but I suppose the thought's never occurred to him since the town pretty much seemed to be a traveling carnival that just never went on the road. This guy was right at home.

However, I wasn't exposed to any of this at first—I was busy at the winery pretty much from the get-go. Even though I flew down to Marlborough after a couple of days in Auckland—timing my arrival for the middle of March and the start of harvest—the fruit wasn't ready when I arrived at Allan Scott Wines, situated halfway down Jacksons Road in the heart of the region. No one's was. February had brought one of the coolest and rainiest summers ever experienced in Marlborough, throwing everything out of whack as far as what grapes would be ripe for picking when. But there was still enough work to fill a day. Wine from the previous year, still sitting in tanks, needed to be bottled, though most of the preharvest weeks were filled with cleaning. And lots of it. "Ninety-five percent of winemaking is cleaning," Josh told me, and after two weeks of cleaning tanks, power-washing everything in sight, and hosing off everything within reach, I believed him.

It was during this time that I started to get to know the people who make Allan Scott wines. Allan's appearance matched everything I'd heard about his personality: unassuming. He doesn't look like the kind of guy who's involved with any type of alcohol—drinking it or making it. Allan stands out in a crowd only because of his size, but I wouldn't be surprised if women constantly tell him he's a big teddy bear.

What he is, though, is a farmer. Granted, an exceptionally intelligent and well-traveled one, but a farmer nonetheless. Spend any amount of time with him, and the first thing you'll notice is how massive his hands are. His fingers are puffy and his knuckles worn, and his handshake, though gentle, feels a bit like sandpaper. Maybe it's genetics, or maybe years spent shearing sheep and, later, planting and tending to vines throughout Marlborough. Perhaps both. But no matter how fancy the visitors' entrance to the winery, or even Allan's sunny, spacious office above it, look at his hands and you'll know instantly that any amount of luxury he enjoys is purely a result of hard work.

In other words, behind the complex business that is Allan Scott Wines is an uncomplicated man. He always wears jeans and a button-down shirt, which would suggest a near constant state of relaxation if his normal expression weren't one of worry and concern. After all, much of the hair on the top of his head left long ago, perhaps having been tugged away with each early frost or late fall of rain. But he's smart, steady, and calm, taking things as they come and refusing to make decisions before all the facts are in.

Nevertheless, it was mid-March, and harvest should have been under way, so if Allan was experiencing any anxiety at all, it was only because everyone else was, and unloading it on him.

"To be honest, I hate this time of year," he told me across the table as we waited for our food in a Thai restaurant in Blenheim one night. The *only* Thai restaurant in Blenheim, actually (and I think the people who work there are Korean). "I can't go anywhere without people I don't know asking me, 'How's the harvest?' " Sure enough, only fifteen minutes after we sat down, at least four people had waved hello or come over to ask that very question. "It's not that I don't want to talk about it, but so many people ask me, and it's just such a stressful time of year. I'd like a T-shirt that says, 'Don't fucking ask me about the harvest!' "

Allan often changes subjects when he speaks, or gazes into the distance at odd moments. He's also a neat freak, picking up even the smallest piece of trash lying on the grounds of the winery. What it all adds up to is a man who doesn't at all seem like someone who would have his name splashed on more than 600,000 bottles of wine every year.

"It was Cathy's idea," he told me over dinner in the Thai restaurant, "and it was the right one. I was a little nervous about it at first, since we only ever intended to make five thousand cases a year. But as we grew, the brand developed on its own, separate from me."

It's evident simply by looking at the winery's public entrance or even the Scotts' house. Their driveways, across Jacksons Road from each other, feature arching iron gates and stone pillars adorned with small, perched lions. The winery's high-end reserve label is even called Prestige.

"That doesn't quite fit with Allan," I said as I pointed at the lions when Allan's son, Josh, and I drove up to the house one night. "Your dad's such a mild-mannered guy. He isn't flashy in the slightest."

Josh gave a little chuckle. "That's the dragon lady at work," he said of his own mother.

Cathy's reputation precedes her. I never saw her completely lose her cool, but I'd heard the stories. She's a confident woman who never needs to think about what she's going to say or who she's going to say it to, and her wit and honesty cut to the bone. Seriously, this lady could bring a statue to tears. She enchants some people instantly and terrifies others. Me, I'm enchanted . . . and a little terrified, I admit. I never want to piss her off. One time when an employee complained to Cathy that the toilet paper in the bathroom wasn't soft enough, let's just say that he quickly wished he hadn't. He barely got a word in, possibly because the discussion itself was proof, in Cathy's mind, that the guy spent too much time worrying about his ass and not enough worrying about his job. Needless to say, he doesn't have one at ASW anymore.

"I'm the one who takes risks and tries new things, and Cathy's the one who makes sense of them all. She's the practical one," Allan explained to me. I asked for an example of a time when either one of them was flat-out wrong when it came to a business decision, but he couldn't put his finger on one. "We always work on an idea together, so it's never just me or just her," he said. "Sometimes one of us is more right than the other," he confessed with a wry smile.

Allan and Cathy have three children, all of them involved in the wine business in one way or another. Their oldest daughter, Victoria, twenty-nine, has two children of her own, and helps run the winery's restaurant alongside her mother. Middle child, Josh, twenty-three, is one of the winemakers at his parents' operation, and youngest daughter, Sara, twenty-one, is a winemaker in training. In 2004 she was working as a cellar hand at Spy Valley, one of the newest and fastest-growing wineries in Marlborough if not all of New Zealand.

Sara has short, shaggy blond hair, is broad-shouldered, and has thick legs, as if she spends nearly every waking minute exercising. And she does. The times I saw her in the morning on my way to the winery she'd either already swum for an hour or ridden twenty kilometers on her bike. Most days she also runs, and it's a wonder that she even considered winemaking as a career since she makes the people in those Bowflex infomercials look like your average muumuu-wearing audience member on *Jerry Springer.*

I refrained from asking her too much about her life or winemaking career plans, because if you haven't grown up in New Zealand, she's impossible to understand. My notes would have been just squiggles.

One night that I happened to be at the Scotts' house, her phone rang, and she got more and more excited as the conversation continued. Finally, when she ended the call, she turned and said to me, "Gointa Chryse-shurch tatheh Medlef kahn-sit! J'no Medlef?"

"Uh, no," I responded. "Medlef? What's Medlef?"

"Meatloaf," Allan interjected before Sara could answer. "Christ, Sara," he said. "I spent all that money on your education, and you can't even speak properly."

"Meeeeeeeeaaaaaaat . . . loooooooooooaaaaaaaf," she said mockingly, and soon thereafter left the room.

"Both Sara and Josh," Allan said as he shook his head. "Their diction is just terrible."

I learned this all too well, having spent most of my time with Josh, as I not only worked under him at the winery, but lived in his house. It's a good thing I did, since the more time I spent around him the less time it took to comprehend the Kiwi accent and the slang. It helped, too, that our third housemate, a well-spoken Air New Zealand pilot named Timur, could act as an interpreter. (Our fourth housemate was Josh's dog, Billy, a Jack Russell who's extremely adept at licking his own penis.)

Josh's small den of alcohol consumption, er, I mean, tin-roofed house is set at the end of a long gravel driveway, behind what's known as the Omaka vineyard—ASW's largest, situated about a mile southwest of the winery. The other vineyards are Moorland, which surrounds the winery; Wallops, which surrounds Allan's house across the street; and the Hounds, which sits about two kilometers east of the winery.

"I rather liked living at home," the twenty-three-year-old told me. "But my parents kicked me out."

"Why?" I asked as we bounced along in Josh's Jeep toward his house, between rows of vines, as opposed to on the even bumpier gravel driveway.

"Because I kept eating all their food and drinking all their wine," he said, as if such things were beyond his control. (They may very well be considering how much food and wine he and I would consume over the next year.) Josh is a beast of a guy. He's as big as his father and shares most of his features—despite retaining his hair (for now) and sweating the small stuff now and again. He plays on the local rugby team, Moutere (pronounced *mo*-tree), and never shies away from a task at the winery that involves brute force.

"Come on, you dirty bitch!" he'll scream as he wraps his long, sausage-link fingers around hose connections, trying to untwist them from the valves, refusing to use a wrench. "You fucking whore!" And sure enough, he usually manages to complete the task with his bare hands. Similarly, I found the word "cunt" helped me . . . but I still usually needed wrenches.

Josh was never a particularly good student, and more or less stopped attending school by the time he was fifteen years old. He grew up around the winery, and learned everything inside out simply by doing it all. Like his father, he's proof that ruggedness and wine expertise can find a home in one body. Though he lacks the refined sensibilities of what most people probably imagine is the archetypal European winemaker (or anyone else for that matter, since he chews with his mouth open, curses like a sailor, and makes crude jokes whenever the opportunity presents itself—much like the author of this book, except for the openmouthed-chewing thing), Josh is European in his approach, relying on what he sees and tastes rather than what a teacher or textbook ever told him. He trusts his instincts before the results of a lab test.

When he was working in Sancerre, France, for a year, he was out walking through the rows with the owner of the winery, who plucked a grape from a vine and popped it into his mouth. "It's ready," he told Josh.

"'Bullshit,' I said to him," Josh recalled. "He didn't have a lab, so I borrowed some equipment from a winery up the road, and sure enough, he was right on the money. They know their vines so well and have so many years of tradition. In New Zealand we have no fuckin' tradition."

They do, but it's called science. And that half of the ASW winemaking duo is represented by Jeremy McKenzie. Allan calls the team of Josh and Jeremy "the brawn and the brains." Jeremy, twenty-seven, has also worked in France, but he has degrees in forensics and biochemistry, and even spent time working crime scenes in Auckland before he decided to settle on winemaking as a career.

Jeremy is a very by-the-book winemaker. "He's the theoretical one and I'm the practical one," Josh told me before I'd even met his colleague. But that doesn't mean Jeremy is a geek. Far from it. Not only does he play on Moutere with Josh (he's one of the team's best players), he stays in shape by running in the mountains, and he won't so much as touch a cigarette. He hunts wild boar in the forest with his three dogs, which chase down the pig and clamp their jaws onto its ears until Jeremy can catch up, jump on the pig's back, and slash its throat. He's a wall of muscle and an absolute pit bull on the rugby field, yet he's mild-mannered, and often sports his straight, white grin when he speaks.

Jeremy and Josh are close friends, and spend as much time together away from work as they do at work, much of it on the rugby field. (When I went to watch them play a preseason match one night in the lead-up to harvest, I learned that the most important element of the sport is stomping on the other guys with your spikes when they're on the ground, then buying each other beers afterward.) Everything about them is contradictory when it comes to winemaking, however, and it's why they work so well together even if they do often butt heads. Nevertheless, Jeremy is more or less treated like family by the Scotts. That's just how the Scotts are, really. Treat them well, and they'll treat you well. Fuck with them, and . . .

In other words, gaining the Scotts' trust isn't easy. Among those who have, to varying degrees, are assistant winemaker, Jemma Funnell, an Australian who's made wine as far away as Crete and as nearby as Cloudy Bay (the winery right across the street), and Geoff Hopkins, manager of ASW's bottling hall. Even though she's only twenty-five, Jemma has a round, wise-looking face, which I saw a lot less of than her ass, since she gets plumber's crack whenever she bends over to mix a bucket of yeast or pick up a wrench. Which is often. "She knows it, but she just doesn't care," Geoff told me. Geoff is as pleasant and good-natured as Jemma, but he's probably one of the hardest-working—yet most easygoing—people I've ever met. When someone has to get to the winery at 5:00 A.M. or needs to stay until 4:00 A.M., Geoff's your man. He's a blue-collar guy through and through, and seems to like working in the wine business, having done so for more than a decade. But he's also a guy who can have a beer with his colleagues as easily as he can with college professors after a long day on the job.

Also on hand for the vintage were Tim, a Kiwi who more or less bounces from job to job, but returns to ASW every year to work as a cellar hand, as well as two French harvest workers. Marine, twenty-three, was pretty, blond, petite, and friendly. She reminded me a bit of the exchange student in high school every guy wanted to be the first to bang. The other, well, I'll call him Frenchie. Of course, I know his name, but for one, Frenchie is the name Jeremy and Josh used for him as well as for Marine, and two, Frenchie could be a total dick to work with. In a word, he's French. In truth, Frenchie actually proved to be a really nice guy away from the winery. Unfortunately, it wasn't until after the harvest that he told me that one of his favorite things to do is get stoned and watch *The Big Lebowski* (so if not for Frenchie, I never would have learned that the Dude is known as Le Mec in French). I have no doubt that would have scored him at least some cool points with me and, more important, everyone else, if he'd mentioned this at the very beginning. But instead he had a holier-than-thou attitude on the job that did him no favors.

So aside from Frenchie, ASW was a group of nice, well-adjusted people, passionate about what they do. But not the complete antithesis to the boorish farm-town life. The person at the winery I have to thank for introducing me to that side of Blenheim is Kosta, the chef in ASW's restaurant. At first I thought Kosta was the life of the party, but at some point I came to realize that he was just insane. (I therefore bonded with him very quickly.) For starters, no one I met ever actually knew how old he was, since he just told everyone he was nineteen, even though he was clearly inching toward thirty. And it would only take about half a beer before the guy would drop his pants and tuck his stuff between his legs à la *Silence of the Lambs*. For his birthday, Cathy gave him a pencil holder that was a plastic naked guy, bent over, and when you put the pencil in his ass, he'd scream, "Ohhhh! That feels goooood!" Kosta thought it was the best gift he'd ever received. If that isn't enough for you, he once called out my name when he was getting a blow job from a nineteen-year-old girl (she corroborated this), though somehow I think he did it just so he'd have a funny story to tell. I'll never know for sure, though, since he just sort of disappeared one day, kind of like D-Day at the end of *Animal House.*

Long before he split, though, Kosta moonlighted as manager of a tacky, Native American–themed bar in the center of town called Bar Navajo, which, of course, had a couple of stuffed Indians in the corner, dream catchers hanging on the walls, and other odd touches obviously chosen by someone who'd never actually been anywhere near a real, live Native American. After the harvest, sometime in May, I needed some time away from the winery as well as a way to earn some cash, so Kosta happily offered me a job behind the bar on Friday nights. And since this bar happened to be the hangout of choice for Blenheim's not-so-elite (such as a retarded guy with no teeth, known as Dangerous Dave, whom the other bartenders seemed to have no moral qualms about serving copious amounts of alcohol), it was never a question of if there was going to be a brawl, but when and how many. The other joys of the job included finding a used condom as I cleaned up for the night; two of the female bartenders deciding to fuck each other in the bathroom out of pure boredom; a patron getting thrown out, only to return and smash the bouncer's face with his steel-toed boot; and another patron giving me the brown eye (wow, those things do get wide when you've spent time in prison). Anyway, these were just a few of the things that made me wonder what I'd done wrong in a past life to deserve being punished while trying to earn an extra buck in this one.

Fortunately, I wasn't exposed to any of this until after the harvest. If I had been before or even during that time, I'd have probably tried to swim back to North America, perfectly at ease with the fact that I'd be shark bait inside of a mile. However, the harvest would turn out to be as thrilling and captivating as it was insanely goddamn busy, so I was under a spell. No matter how completely bizarre I found the town to be, or how mentally and physically exhausting the work got, from day one at the winery I was hooked.

* * *

On that first day of crushing, while the bubbly base Chardonnay grapes were in the press, Jemma was holed up in the lab, where she'd spend much of the vintage. She was testing the Pinot Noir from three different vineyards for sugar levels, acidity, and pH. The three samples all had different colors, but all smelled like a freshly mowed lawn and tasted, well, like grape juice. The sample in the middle was red, while the outside two were brown.

"You probably got the sugar and ripeness from the second one, and acidity from the third," Josh guessed as I tasted each one, but I just nodded because I didn't have a fucking clue what wine-quality grape juice was supposed to taste like in the first place. "Which Jemma's tests will now confirm," he joked with a slight hint of cockiness. Like it or not, Josh's instincts were usually right. Sure enough, the second sample was closest to picking, about two weeks away. Two weeks late as far as anyone in the room at that moment was concerned, but two weeks nonetheless.

These were all the same type of grapes from the same valley, in some cases from blocks or rows right next to each other—but all of them had developed differently. In 2003, Josh told me, the same variety at a block just up the road from another reached ripeness four weeks later, and was picked accordingly.

Farming rules.

So much so, that one can't help but wonder just what sort of consideration Allan put forth before purchasing his land all those years ago. In 2003, when Cloudy Bay across the street and Allan's neighbors to his left and right all lost 50 percent of their crop due to a spring frost, ASW was relatively unaffected. At least that's what they told me. It could have been bullshit, although in the couple of weeks leading up to harvest it was downright freaky how often I noticed an overcast sky—with a break in the clouds just over the winery, sunshine pouring onto the Moorland vines.

But after crushing that first load of grapes, the next day the clouds were covering everyone in Marlborough, and there was relatively little to do. Josh took a phone call in the car on his way home, and the tension over The Big One was clearly setting in.

"I just don't feel right about it, and I can't put my finger on what it is," he told his mother as he pulled the car to the side of the road to complete the conversation. "I'm nervous about this harvest since it's gonna be late. I'm not sure if it's the grapes or how the whole crop looks. Maybe I'll calm down once we get into it."

Maybe not.

Vintage is a binge work period, but I know that it only lasts six or eight weeks, and after that I get a chance to chill out. I like that I can work hard, and then not work hard.

—ALISTAIR SOPER, WINEMAKER AT HIGHFIELD ESTATE

2

Wine 101: The Crush

Before I tell you how the rest of the harvest went, it's helpful to learn a little about how it all works, just as I had to (though in my case it was mostly so I could avoid injury or death). I hate to abuse the restaurant analogy, but every chef has essentially the same equipment at his or her disposal in the kitchen: knives, pots, pans, amphetamines, and so forth. It's the quality of the ingredients they choose and what they do with all that equipment that makes them different from one another, and much the same goes for winemakers. However, if you don't understand the tools of the trade and the processes employed, it's a little harder to understand what makes one wine or winemaker different from the next. This is the first of a few chapters that are as much designed to help you learn about winemaking as they are to help you appreciate just what an extraordinary pain in the ass it is to make wine in the first place.

Now just to warn you, this is gonna get a bit technical. But hang in there. Nothing too complicated, and it's only a few pages. And besides, by the end of this chapter you'll know how wine is made as well as the people who sell it to you—maybe even better. Plus, I'd kinda hope you'd be grateful that I went

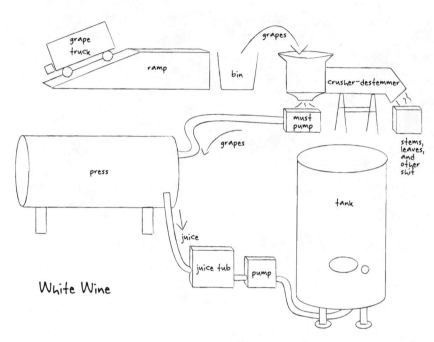

White Wine

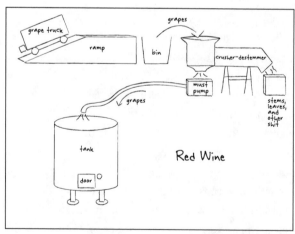

*nothing is to scale

all the way to New Zealand, lived off my credit card, and did all this shit so you don't have to.

First things first, get that image of Lucille Ball stomping on grapes out of your head. It's not quite as simple as rolling around in some grapes and havin' a few laughs. If it were, I'd make my own and probably never leave the house. Instead, the grapes are grown over several months in large vineyards. At the moment of perfect ripeness, they're picked and brought to the winery facility. It's there that a series of processes are employed—among them, crushing the grapes and letting the juice ferment—to turn the grapes into wine.

Where it starts to get tricky is that different varieties ripen at different times, as do different vineyards or even parts of vineyards (called "blocks") of the same variety. It also depends on how many bunches of grapes the vines grew—the heavier the crop load, the harder it is for the vines to ripen all their grapes by the end of the season. So the idea isn't to grow as many grapes as you possibly can. The vine ripens the grapes by capturing sunlight and absorbing nutrients from the soil. But if the vine's carrying too many bunches, it can't give the grapes all the nutrients and energy they need to ripen fully, so they won't have fully developed flavors . . . which means crap wine. And in 2004, Marlborough's crops were generally much heavier than in past years. So think of the harvest as a marathon, but with no starting gun to announce its beginning, and no finish line with a screaming crowd and tape to break through at the end. Sometimes you even want to wait at the starting line, letting the grapes hang out as long as possible to fully develop their flavors, and then make a mad dash to harvest them all. Wine may have an air of sophistication, but it's based almost entirely on agriculture (the dirt, the sun, and the rain) and all the other nuances—and nuisances—that go with it.

How do you know when the grapes are ready? Good question. In Europe, so I'm told, winemakers simply go by taste. As I mentioned in the previous chapter, a winemaker will often just walk through the rows, eat a few grapes here and there, and make his decision. Taste trumps everything in Marlborough as well, but most of the winemakers always try to be one step ahead, relying on lab tests as a guideline.

"In Germany I worked for five different wineries, and not one of them had a lab," I was told by Mike Just, the winemaker at Lawson's Dry Hills. I have to admit, Mike was tough to take seriously at first since he wears an eye patch and an earring and has the longest mullet I've ever seen. Seriously. He's also really into medieval sword-fighting, and owns a full set of armor, which I would have found scary if he weren't one of the friendliest winemakers in Marlbor-ough, not to mention one of the most passionate; the guy was making fruit wines in his bedroom even when he was a kid. "When someone's drinking the wine, they're not worried about pHs and acids," he went on. "Either they like it or they don't. To me the numbers just help with the parameters—help you see what's happened previously, and see what sort of zones we're working in."

Matt Thomson, a consultant who makes the wines for St. Clair, Mud House, Lake Chalice, Cape Campbell, and Delta and has a master's in bio-chemistry* (he was going to be a vet, but "decided I didn't want to have a hand stuck up a cow's ass for the rest of my life"), relies even less on science. "Ninety-nine percent of it is on taste, just tasting grapes," he said to me in the middle of harvest. "Science sets the borders, and if you don't know where those are, you tend to stray outside them and make some silly wines."

The three main things winemakers measure with lab tests are Brix, acid-ity, and pH. Brix is a measure of the natural sugar content of the grapes, and different varieties have optimal levels of sugar and acidity. Actually, every fruit does. When you eat an apple, orange, pear, or whatever, the reason it tastes good when it's perfectly ripe is that its natural sugar and acidity are in balance with each other. It works the same with wine grapes. In Sauvignon Blanc, for example, you want about 22 Brix. In Chardonnay it should be any-where from 23 to 24.5, and in Pinot Noir you want it as high as 25. You mul-tiply that number by ten, and that's roughly how many grams of sugar you have per liter of juice. So 25 Brix is 250 grams of sugar per liter. The trick, though, is that in waiting for your Brix to rise, the level of acidity can drop, which means the grapes don't taste quite right, and neither will the wine. If the sugar and acidity are out of whack, the winemakers have to weigh their options: Either add sugar to compensate for the lower Brix, or add tartaric acid if the natural acids have dropped during the wait for the Brix to rise. Neither is really a great solution, but by and large you'll find winemakers more willing to add sugar than acid. In Marlborough, sugar is usually only added to Sauvignon Blanc when the Brix level is lower than 18 or 19. Small amounts of tartaric acid are added only to a variety like Pinot Noir, because if there's one thing Sauvignon Blanc almost never lacks, it's acid.

---

*Winemaking consultants working for more than one winery are pretty common, just like it's accepted and understood that sorority girls have more than one boyfriend in the same frat house.

The best way to collect a sample, as Josh showed me, is to simply walk through the rows with a bucket and randomly grab fistfuls of grapes—near the post, between posts, high on the vine, low on the vine, some bunches with rot, some bunches without. Essentially you're simulating the work of a machine harvester, which doesn't discriminate, ripping everything off like it just got out of prison and the vine is the dress on a twenty-dollar whore. When you get the bucket back to the lab you stick your fist in and pummel the living crap out of the grapes, then use a piece of cheesecloth to separate out the juice. You then fill a cylinder with juice and put in a hydrometer that looks more or less like a thermometer, only the level at which it floats in the cylinder of juice tells you how many Brix are in the sample. The tests can be as simple or complex as you like, employing the few simple, aforementioned tools or expensive, high-tech equipment that looks like it should also be able to download and play adult movies on demand. More in-depth tests that require a working knowledge of high-school chemistry can confirm your findings, as well as tell you what your acid levels and pH are. I barely managed a C in high-school chemistry, so I'm not qualified to tell you how those tests are performed. And to be honest, they're not very interesting. Which is why the assistant winemaker usually gets the job of working the lab.

Now, let's say you have a block of grapes ready to be picked because the Brix and acids are right, and the flavors in the grapes taste good. You have two choices: Use the machine harvester or hire people to pick the grapes by hand. Both have their advantages and disadvantages.

Handpicking is pretty much standard in both Europe and California, especially the latter, because they have Mexico right nearby and more than enough of its citizens willing to pick shitloads of grapes for incredibly small amounts of money. Handpicking is very gentle on the fruit, so the way it comes into the winery is pretty much the way it looked on the vine. In Marlborough, however, pickers are really only used for the more sensitive varieties like Pinot Noir, though there are some wineries in Marlborough—such as Seresin, Dog Point, and the Fromm Winery—that rely on handpicking for everything. But here's the catch: Not only is it expensive (Mexicans are in short supply in Marlborough), but the pickers generally aren't very experienced and don't know what they should and shouldn't pick.

When ASW needed to bring in a couple blocks of Pinot I went out with the pickers, a group assembled by a labor contractor and so random that it should have been used for polling and surveys rather than picking grapes.

Bored grandmothers. Hippie kids with pierced lips, tattoos, and dreadlocks. Frenchie's girlfriend, who didn't have a work visa, which I guess now makes her an honorary Mexican. There were even some Japanese backpackers who clearly thought they were going to a wine tasting but were given shears instead, and were too polite to say anything so they just sucked it up and worked. At least that's what they looked like to me. Every half hour or so Brian, the vineyard manager, would show up and bark orders based on what Jeremy told him about the fruit that had come in so far. But it didn't matter because the pickers just kept on picking through the monotony and boredom, knowing that the faster they worked the sooner they'd be able to go home and attach hoses to their tailpipes to put themselves out of their misery.

I was working with two guys from the full-time vineyard crew, Terry and Ra (short for Raymond, "Because Ray sounds gay," he claims), picking up the 12.5-kilogram bins into which the pickers dropped their grapes. We'd dump the grapes into a half-ton bin, then redistribute the small bins along the rows for the pickers to refill. Picking grapes is sticky, messy, and boring (and worst of all, you have to start at 7:00 A.M.). The pickers would look at us as though we had the easy job, but working the bins is actually dirtier and stickier. Within five minutes of lifting the bins your back is sore and you give up trying to keep your hands clean. You've also made a clear-cut decision to burn your clothes rather than try to wash them, and the edges of the bins are sharp, so you wind up with more than a few scrapes, cuts, and blisters by the end of the day.

With handpicking you get fruit in good condition, but it comes at a higher price. The machine harvester, on the other hand, is a major initial investment at about NZ$400,000,* but is far more cost-effective to operate over the long term. It's a huge piece of equipment that actually drives over the top of a row of vines and shakes the grapes loose. The grapes are then carried along a series of conveyers, either collected in a gondola on the harvester itself or spit into a bin being pulled along by a tractor in the next row over, driving at the same pace as the harvester (every so often Ra chucks a fistful of sulfur into the gondola to help prevent the juice from oxidizing). Either way, machine harvesting is pretty rough on the fruit, so by the time it comes into the winery much

---

*All money amounts throughout this book are preceded by "US" or "NZ" to indicate American or New Zealand dollars. Exchange rates rise and fall all the time, meaning very generous before and after I lived in New Zealand, and outright sodomy while I did. But the conversion is usually about sixty-five American cents for every New Zealand dollar.

of it is not only already crushed, but has leaves, stems, and twigs along with it. Machine harvesting is mostly done on white varieties like Sauvignon Blanc, which can take tons of physical abuse and still make for perfectly good wine. But if you're in a pinch and need to get the grapes from other varieties off the vines quickly and for far less money than it would cost to hire a picking crew, you go with the harvester.

While most winemakers believe that you should always handpick Pinot Noir, there are some—like Josh and Gary Duke, winemaker at Hunter's—who believe that any variety can be machine-harvested so long as the fruit is of good quality on the vine, and it doesn't take too long to truck the fruit from the vineyard to the winery. Not all of a winery's vineyards are necessarily right nearby—they're often several miles away. Which I didn't know since I was drunk on my previous visit. When I was packing for my trip, I didn't realize that wine companies are basically massive farms separated by acres and acres of other people's vineyards, so I lugged my mountain bike halfway around the planet, thinking that could get me anywhere I needed to go. After laughing at me for a while, Allan was kind enough to loan me a car he bought for general winery errands, a 1980 Japanese-made Ford Laser with pink interior. It got me from point A to point B reliably and even had a tape deck, so I went to the Warehouse (New Zealand's version of Wal-Mart, only much smellier, since no one realized they should put the garden department *outside* the building), and got myself some music. Unfortunately, the only album they had that I recognized was a Duran Duran greatest-hits tape, so I now know "Hungry Like the Wolf" by heart.

Anyway, whether handpicked or machine-harvested, at ASW all the grapes are dumped into a huge truck driven by Gerald, one of the vineyard workers. In fourteen years, few have ever seen Gerald wear long pants, even in the dead of winter. He's in his mid-sixties, has a shaggy white beard, and usually wears a hat like that of an Australian outback tour guide. Rumor is that he's also a nudist on the weekends, and wears a thong under his work clothes. If that's not true, well, Gerald won't mind my saying so, because the other rumor is that he's got a dick big enough to choke a moose. That might be how he pushes the clutch on the truck for all I know.

Speaking of which, when Gerald gets back to the winery, he backs the truck up a concrete ramp. Once he's at the top, he dumps the fruit into a large stainless-steel bin below. From the bin the grapes go through the crusher-destemmer, and what comes out is a slushy combination of crushed grapes and juice, called "must." It all falls into the appropriately named must pump, a small steel tub that contains a corkscrew-looking auger that pushes most of the must through a long hose, up into the press (the rest, a few grapes here and there, shoots out of the pump and splatters onto just about every inch of your clothing over the course of the day if you happen to be the one operating the crusher). The press doesn't start working right away, though. As the grapes run in, the sheer weight of them all pushing down on one another naturally presses out juice—this is called the free run, and is the best-quality juice from any load of white-wine grapes. The juice falls into a tray underneath the press and runs out a hose into another steel bin, called a juice tub, about a cubic meter in size. From there it flows out another hose connected to a pump, which then pushes the juice into a tank.

When the free run has all come out, the hose is connected to a different tank for the juice from the pressings, which is of lower quality than the free run, and is therefore dealt with separately. The pressings juice is usually brown from oxidation, just like when you cut an apple in two and leave half of it on the kitchen counter for an hour because you couldn't pull up your pants and get off the couch during the *Baywatch* marathon on cable.

The press has a giant air bag inside it, which it inflates to push and push on the grapes until it gets every last bit of juice out of them. The press also rotates frequently, shifting around its contents and pushing ever harder on the grapes. The whole process can take up to three hours, depending on how many tons of grapes were loaded in and how old the press is—kind of like how a new VW Beetle performs better than one of those old ones that reek of pot smoke and BO.

When the press finishes, all the stuff left inside—mostly skins and seeds—is called the marc. It's brown and clumpy, and looks like a high-fiber cereal or the sort of stuff that's fed to cattle—which is what ASW does with it. To get the marc out of the press, four half-ton bins are pushed in beneath it, and the door to the press is opened. The marc spills out, and is so heavy that the bins have to be dragged out with a forklift and then dumped into the truck. The farmer who owns the truck shows up at the end of every day and drives the truck back to his farm for the cows' dinnertime. (Some wineries have much more advanced ways of getting the marc out. Big operations like Montana can actually back a truck under the press, while newer wineries have a conveyer belt underneath it that takes all the marc away.) At the end of the day someone has to jump inside and hose out the press, which is a job that gets you soaking wet.

If the press is fully loaded, the bins will have to be moved under and emptied at least three or four times, which is the last thing you want to do at 11:00 P.M., toward the end of a long day at the winery. Especially when it's cold and rainy.

So you have to try to make things fun when you're cold and miserable. Which is why Josh decided to convince Frenchie, whose English was weak at best, that the marc is actually called the "poos." For weeks he'd go around saying things like, "Where do we take the poos?" and, "Wow, that's a lot of poos." The French accent made it especially funny, but even better was the fact that when Frenchie didn't understand something, he'd just say, "Yes, yes." So Josh would greet him every day by saying, "G'day, mate. Did you shave your balls this morning?"

"Yes, yes."

I tried to get in on the act by telling Marine, as we were cleaning a line of hose, that when it sprays you in the face that's called a "money shot." But she wasn't as gullible as Frenchie.

Anyway, after the free run and the pressings, there's still one more place to get juice, and that's from the juice solids, also known as the lees. After the juice has been sitting in the tank for a few days, the solids start to fall to the bottom of the tank, forming a cloudy, brownish-green substance that looks and smells like the rug in your grandmother's bathroom. This is the juice lees. Disgusting as it looks, however, it still contains a hell of a lot of flavor.

First you pump the juice sitting above the lees to another tank—this procedure is called racking. To get an idea of what this is like, go buy yourself some fresh apple cider, shake up the bottle, and fill up a clear glass. After a few hours, you'll see that the solids have fallen to the bottom, and the clearer juice will be sitting on top of it. In a racking you take all the juice off the top and leave the solids—the lees—behind. The lees are then pumped to another tank full of lees from other batches of the same variety (all the Sauvignon Blanc lees are collected in one tank, all the Chardonnay lees in another, and so forth).

How you get juice out of the lees involves the single coolest piece of equipment you'll ever see at work at a winery, the rotating-drum vacuum filter, better known as the RDV. The RDV is complicated to operate, much less understand, but in layman's terms it's a rotating cylinder that operates under pressure to make the lees stick to the outside of it. It sucks the liquid inside while keeping the solids stuck on the outside, slowly cutting them away with a large blade as the drum rotates. The juice inside the drum is then pumped to a tank. The RDV is an expensive piece of equipment, but it more than pays for itself when you consider the fact that it's responsible for 8 to 10 percent of ASW's total juice volume in a given year. It's an amazing machine, even more so once you taste the juice as it comes out the other end, as clear and almost as fruit-flavored as the free run.

All of the stuff I just explained about the free run, pressings, and the RDV is completely different for red wine, because you need the skins of the grapes to make red wine, well, red. So while you do run the grapes through the crusher-destemmer, you skip all the steps involved with the press and push everything, skins and all, into the top of the tank. So what this should tell you is that while a machine-harvested white variety is easy on the vineyard crew, it's more time-consuming for the winery. A red variety like Pinot Noir, however, involves hard work by the vineyard crew and pickers, but is easy for the winery because the workers there just have to push everything into one tank, and not worry about so many additional steps.

At first, anyway.

The juice and skins sit in the tank, kept at low temperature, for six to eight days or sometimes even longer (some go as long as twenty days, and the winemaker at Mount Riley decided to let one tank sit for a few months, just to see how it would turn out). This is called the cold soak. After that, once yeast is added and fermentation has begun, the skins rise to the top of the tank, forming a layer called the cap. It's pretty dry because all the juice is below it, so the cap sets like concrete. To keep the wine consistent and the skins moist throughout the fermentation process, someone like Frenchie usually gets the job of plunging the tank. This involves taking what looks like a giant toilet plunger, standing on top of the tank, and pushing the skins back down into the fermenting juice several times a day. And it gets harder as fermentation goes on, because the cap gets thicker and tougher to break through with each passing day. Really, it's just like plunging a giant toilet. If King Kong were potty-trained and on a high-fiber diet, I imagine this is what it'd be like to work as his personal plumber.

Some big wineries have automatic plungers, and some also prefer pumping over, which is less time-consuming and involves considerably less physical labor, to plunging. All there is to pumping over is running a hose between a valve on the tank and a pump, and then running another hose from the pump back to the top of the tank. If you're like me, you forget to secure the top hose in place, so when you turn on the pump the hose comes flying out like a coked-up python and douses Frenchie with red wine. If not, and you do it correctly, all the juice is pumped from the bottom onto the cap, hence "pumping over," until the cap breaks up under the weight of the juice.

Though it's open to debate, true Pinotphiles claim that pumping over harms the wine. Because the more you pump and push around the grapes, the more tannins are extracted from the skins and the seeds.

"If you get a bunch of grapes and just pick the berries off and eat them, and then stand on a bunch and eat them, I bet the ones you picked tasted better," Mike Just of Lawson's Dry Hills explained to me. "Every time you put the berries through some kind of pump, there's a lot of maceration going on. Pinot is very fragile—the color is fragile, the skin is fragile, the chemical makeup of the juice is fragile. So you have to treat it carefully."

Mike practices the less-is-more philosophy at his own vineyard, Clayridge, a twenty-acre plot of Pinot that he and his wife, Paula, planted themselves— down a long dirt road at the ass end of the Omaka Valley, in the far southern part of Marlborough—and got their first crop from it in 2004. There's no irrigation; friends helped the Justs handpick all the fruit; and every part of the process is environmentally friendly. "We managed to work it all by gravity— it hasn't seen a pump," he told me proudly. In other words, the bunches of grapes are destemmed very gently, and the grapes then fall from the destemmer into a bin. That bin then gets raised in the air with a forklift, and the grapes tipped directly into the top of the tank. "My whole approach is do it once, do it properly."

Proper care for safety is equally important around a fermenting tank of Pinot Noir. Fermentation in any wine comes from adding yeast, which converts the sugar to alcohol, and produces carbon dioxide (CO_2) as a byproduct. So CO_2 is more or less yeast fart, and that's what pushes the skins to the top of the tank, forming the cap. You have to be careful whenever you open the top of a tank or even stand over a Pinot tank as you plunge it, because prolonged exposure to CO_2 will make you dizzy at first, then completely rid you of your interest in wine. Because you'll be dead. I heard a rumor once about a winemaker in California who looked into the top of a tank of fermenting wine, passed out from inhaling too much CO_2, and fell in. People don't float in wine; they sink. And I'm sure at least half the people at ASW were convinced this would happen to me by the end of the harvest.*

---

*The other half probably wanted it to.

There are all sorts of different types of yeast to add to different varieties, and you've probably heard of "wild" or natural ferments. All that means is that rather than add yeast, the winemaker let the yeast that was sitting on the grapes and naturally blowing around in the air do its job once the grapes were crushed and in the tank. You're probably even breathing yeast right now as you read this sentence. Freaky, huh? But no one does a wild ferment willy-nilly without extensive testing on small batches, because there are all sorts of bad yeasts out there that will make the wine taste like that lees-colored rug in your grandmother's bathroom.

With Pinot Noir, you know that fermentation has stopped once the sugar level has dropped to less than two grams of sugar per liter, and that means it's time to separate the wine (not juice anymore—because fermentation is complete) from the skins. Every winery does this a little differently, but at ASW they set up the juice tub in front of the tank and put a metal sieve on top. They connect a hose to the tank's valve and let the wine run out through the hose and into the juice tub, and any skins that make it through the hose will be stopped by the sieve. From the juice tub the wine is pumped to another tank.

Once the wine has all run out, the door to the tank is slowly opened, and the juice tub is replaced with one of those half-ton bins I mentioned before. The top of the tank is opened, and someone jumps in and starts scooping out the skins with a shovel into the bin (this is how you wind up with grape skins in your underwear). The bin is then pulled away with a forklift, and the skins are dumped into the press for a quick squeeze to get any last bit of wine out of them.

Assuming no other adjustments are necessary, which we'll get to later, the wine can then get pumped from the tanks into barrels. Most white wines, like Sauvignon Blanc, spend all their time in stainless-steel tanks, but with a white wine like Chardonnay you actually get the fermentation started in the tank and let it finish in the barrels, or even pump the juice into barrels before the fermentation has started. Red or white, though, the wine might be kept in the barrels for a few months, a year, or sometimes even longer. It all depends on philosophies, ideas, or even attitudes.

Marlborough has plenty of all three.

One of our workers got stuck in the press. It was late, and he thought it was off and he had the key in his pocket, but the press was on wash cycle when he got inside. He was bloody lucky.

— BEN GLOVER, WINEMAKER AT WITHER HILLS

3

A Rough Start

In the northern hemisphere, at least in the United States, they teach schoolchildren that March comes in like a lion and goes out like a lamb, an expression you need to reverse if you're in the southern hemisphere. And if you're in New Zealand in general, a lamb is pretty appropriate for describing the beginning of March because the weather is indeed gentle, but also because sheep in fact outnumber people in New Zealand by about eleven to one.* But if you're in Marlborough working the harvest, well, a lion's not an appropriate animal for describing the end of March. Tyrannosaurus rex is more like it. Maybe even a sixty-foot disemboweling slob monster from the distant planet Zaltria 6. Because not only can it be extremely cold and rainy, but you have to work through it all outside for hours and hours.

Now, I didn't know the first thing about farming when I landed in New

---

*Seriously. They're *everywhere*. On several occasions I got caught in sheep traffic jams when the animals were being walked along the road from one paddock to another. Traffic jams suck in general, but when they smell like sheep shit they're that much worse.

Zealand. But I can tell when people are stressed out, and the buildup to the 2004 harvest was ushered in by chain-smoking, an increasing dependence upon coffee, and gray hairs forming at the temples. And snow, lots of it, covering the Richmond Range on the northeastern side of the valley, frighteningly close to hundreds of acres of vineyards with grapes still hanging.

In a normal year, harvest is already in high gear by mid to late March (remember, the seasons are opposite south of the equator). But March had been extremely warm following an atypically cold and rainy February (normally summer). Fall in Marlborough doesn't arrive until early May, so snow shouldn't have lingered beyond morning on the hillsides for at least another month. It was nearing the end of March, and very few blocks had been harvested to this point.

That was just one sign that 2004 wouldn't be business as usual. As the day warmed up and the snow disappeared, the vineyard crew was out harvesting a grower's small block of Sauvignon. I tagged along with Josh as he went out to see how things were coming, and we climbed onto the harvester with Ra so the two of them could shoot the shit while Josh looked at the quality of the grapes as they splashed into the harvester's gondola. He didn't look especially pleased, but I wasn't sure why. Whether or not they're healthy, to an untrained eye such as mine machine-harvested grapes look like a blender cocktail gone awry, with all sorts of strange textures. But by this point I'd already come to know that if Josh was terribly upset about something he'd speak his mind. After we jumped down from the harvester at the end of the row Josh pulled a couple of grapes off a bunch and popped them into his mouth.

"Macca might be wrong about this," Josh said as he swallowed the grapes, referring to Jeremy.

His last name is McKenzie, so he's Macca for short. I have no idea why, but it seems just about every Marlborough winemaker—even every Kiwi—has a nickname of some sort. Allan is "Scotty." Brian, the vineyard manager, is Uncle Brian or Uncle B for short. Kevin Judd at Cloudy Bay is "Juddy." Bill Hennessey at Mount Riley is "Digger." Hell, by the end of the vintage I was known around ASW as Eric the Eel—probably because it was as clear to the crew as it was to me that I was out of my element, much like the 2000 Olympic swimmer from Equatorial Guinea who'd never seen a fifty-meter pool.

Josh was concerned that the sugar levels might be too high. Plus, some of the grapes were turning purple with botrytis, a kind of rot that looks as though someone ate strawberry jam on toast, pounded six beers, and then barfed on the grapes. Strangely enough, this can be a good thing if you're making late-harvest or dessert wine, since botrytis sucks the water from the grapes and concentrates the sugars. But botrytis is a bad thing if you're just trying to make regular table wine. The extra sugar means more alcohol, and not necessarily well-developed flavors. It's the same as having more gin than tonic, more Jack than Coke or too much tequila in your margarita. Actually, too much tequila in your margarita means waking up in Vegas with a tattoo on your ass, a ring on your finger, and a strange itchy, burning sensation. But you get the idea.

When we got back to the lab, Josh's suspicions proved correct. The Brix level was at 23.2, as opposed to the rough target of 22. But what no one predicted was how thin the crop would be off that particular block, especially in a year when everyone was expecting massive grape tonnages. They had estimated twenty tons, but what came in weighed just over seven—a huge miscalculation. As the grapes were spilling into the crusher Allan walked by, and Jeremy gave him the news. "Shit," Allan muttered, and stomped back to his office.

Jeremy disappeared into the lab for a few minutes and then returned with a bucket half full of liquid, and began adding it to the must pump as it churned and pushed juice and grapes into the press. Jeremy gave me the usual grin he gets when it comes time to explain something about making wine, after I asked him what he was adding. I could never tell if it was the grin of a bullshitter or of someone who enjoys his work so much he's excited when someone bothers to ask about it.

"I'm adding tannins, just to balance it out," he said as he poured them in. He later explained that this addition would help drop out unwanted proteins, and not actually give the wine a tannic taste or texture. "Josh doesn't want to, but he doesn't like change. But I know from looking at the rotted and split fruit that it needs it."

Josh, the if-it-ain't-broke-don't-fix-it winemaker, shook his head as Jeremy emptied the bucket into the slushy must.

They walked off in separate directions, obviously annoyed with each other, and perhaps even wondering what lines were drawn where in terms of their responsibilities. About half an hour later, as I jotted down my account of their disagreement in my notebook, Jeremy and Josh came back to look in the juice tub and check on the pressings flowing in. Neither had to guess what

I was writing down, and they both saw it as an opportunity to make sure I got the story straight.

"It's not a whole lot," Jeremy insisted of his addition of tannins. "Only about five parts."

"I trust Macca," Josh added. "He only wants to make good wine."

True as that may be, I didn't buy the charade for a second. And I wouldn't have to. Later in the afternoon, as about seven tons of Chardonnay grapes harvested from the block in front of Allan's house were being crushed, Josh dipped a glass into the juice tub and brought it to me as I operated the crusher. I took a sip.

"Now *this* needs tannins," he said. I could feel a bit of grittiness on my tongue, almost like the juice was a little dirty. "*That's* how you know you need them. Told you I didn't think we needed them before."

Josh and Jeremy have this kind of back-and-forth every day, on issues small and large, rugby being one of the most important. The conversation always moves on to rugby at some point (then to sex, then back to rugby—these guys would be in heaven if they ever found a way to combine the two). But when it gets back to winemaking, somehow they always manage to meet in the middle and come out with decisions that they both can live with, even if they don't seem immediately satisfied after such an argument is resolved.

The debate about tannins was forgotten only moments later, when a loud boom brought everything to a halt. "Did Eric the Eel just blow up a tank?" was probably at the top of everyone's thoughts, but a two-by-four that serves as a stop for the truck's tires as it backs up the ramp to drop off its fruit had become wedged between the receival bin and the four-inch-thick layer of concrete on the top of the ramp. As Geoff raised the bin to tilt more grapes into the crusher, the two-by-four acted as a lever and snapped the top concrete layer of the ramp in half.

To you and me, well, it would just look like a broken slab of concrete, and nothing more. A crack in the sidewalk, so to speak. People in the wine business, however, not only are extremely paranoid (and justifiably so in some cases), but look at things differently, daisy-chaining events and consequences together into a final result. This thing happens and has that effect. Rain means more water in the grapes, which means dilution of the flavors, which means crap wine. In this case, a damaged ramp means the truck can't back up it safely, which means there's no way to get the grapes into the bin, and therefore no way to get them through the crusher, which means no wine can be made. And a winery with no wine is about as viable as a restaurant with no food or a brothel with no hookers.*

Allan stood atop the ramp surveying the damage. He seemed calm as his son explained to him how it happened, and he nodded as though he understood. No big deal. These things happen. As he descended the ramp and walked around the presses, back toward his office, calm quickly turned to fury. "Get everyone together, and explain it!" he yelled toward Josh, drowning out the everyday background noise at the winery, which to that point I didn't think was possible. "No fuckups! This is NOT a good start!"

No one spoke for the next several minutes, instead choosing to focus on their assigned tasks with an elevated level of attention. I got the impression that no one had ever seen Allan angry, and no one wanted to now. (Actually they had, but I guess they were used to it. It scared me shitless.) Luckily, the ramp would still be usable for the rest of the harvest, which probably calmed everyone a little. But the situation was far from ideal, and the ramp would require extensive—and possibly expensive—repair work in the off-season.

At the end of the day on the drive home, Josh brushed off the incident. "There's always a big fuckup each year, and you just hope it's not too bad. But one always happens."

You hear about most fuckups from rumors that fly from one winery to the next, and as they're carried across the valley plains they get more and more exaggerated, ranging from the downright disastrous to the hilarious. One I heard later in the harvest was that a cellar hand had accidentally blended 20,000 liters of Sauvignon Blanc with 20,000 liters of Pinot Noir, of course ruining both batches. For argument's sake, say the Sauvignon retails for fifteen dollars a bottle and the Pinot for twenty dollars. That calculates to just under $1 million worth of wine lost, so I hope that story isn't true.

Another rumor, which did turn out to be true, involved an Australian vintage worker getting a caustic burn on her ass when she slipped into the bucket she was sitting on. (Caustic is a toxic cleaning agent used by just about every winery, and it's most easily neutralized with citric acid, another cleaning agent that most wineries have on hand.) Though I couldn't confirm the accident the way a good reporter should, by finding the girl and asking her to show me the damaged goods, an eyewitness told me that the winemaker had

---

*Prostitution is legal in New Zealand, in case you're on the fence about whether to book a ticket there, and need to break a cold streak.

to tug on the belt of the girl's pants so he could reach in with a fistful of cit- ric acid and start rubbing it on her butt to stop the burning. (I'm applying for a job at that winery next year on the chance that she's working there again, and I'll just follow her around all day with a bucket of citric.)

And sadly, ASW has had its fair share of "cock-ups," as Kiwis call them, in addition to the ramp incident. In 2003, Jeremy's first vintage at the win- ery, one thousand empty bottles fell off the back of the truck he was driving, and he and Josh had to spend the next few hours dodging traffic as they swept up the broken glass scattered on a stretch of road. Essentially, no one's immune from cock-ups during harvest, much less any other time of year, no matter what the people at any winery tell you. Every winery, every year, has someone to blame for something.

"You just hope it's not you," Jemma told me as we were finishing up for the night.

I took her advice and mustered as much hope as I could. But since I still didn't know what the hell I was doing, I'd get my chance.

I like to have a look at the wine list, but I prefer someone just dish it out. If it's a ten-dollar whatever or a two-hundred-dollar whatever, if it's drinking well on that night, I don't mind.

—GARY DUKE, WINEMAKER AT HUNTER'S

4

The Big One, a Bloated Wine Critic, and Battle Scars

When you're one of the hundreds of people from all over the world who descend upon Marlborough to work the kind of hours required to get thousands of tons of grapes off the vines, crushed, pressed, and into tanks, you're getting your ass kicked too hard to notice what the weather's like. That is, unless it gets really bad, and you're stuck outside in it doing the sort of task that someone higher up the food chain passed down to you.

For example, one of my regular jobs was to drive the forklift. Notice that I didn't say "operate the forklift." I did that, too, to a lesser degree (and much more slowly and cautiously than Josh or Jeremy, once they taught me how to use it*), but whenever the forklift was needed at one of the vineyards for

---

*I did once lose control of the thing, but managed to hit the brakes and stop just before the forks rammed through a wall that had three pallets of wine stacked on the other side. As nice a guy as he may be, Allan wouldn't have even hesitated to kill me. Slowly. With electrodes clamped to my nuts and rabid possums chewing off my fingertips.

dumping half-ton bins of grapes into the truck, I usually either got nomi-
nated to drive it over there and wait for someone to come pick me up or got
dropped off at the vineyard to drive the forklift back to the winery at the end
of the day. Even though a golf cart running on AA batteries goes faster, it was
fun at first, when it was sunny and warm, and as I was going along I was
thinking about that scene in *Footloose* when Kevin Bacon drives the tractor
in a game of chicken (even though I probably looked worse off than the old
guy in *The Straight Story*—a forklift has no suspension, so when you go over
a bump you feel whatever flab you have jiggle violently for the next twenty
feet). However, a forklift has no roof, so if it was cold and wet out, well, so
was I, for the long, slow, bumpy ride back to the winery. Über-cool city kid
in the otherwise backward farm town? Not even close. I was the errand boy
doing the bullshit jobs no one else wanted to.

And there's a good reason why. Take the last day of March, which was the
first full day of crushing at ASW—sixteen tons of Chardonnay. Now, if you've
ever been around a winery during harvest, you should be saying to yourself,
"Sixteen tons? At a winery where they machine harvest? That's it? What's he
complaining about? That's nothing!"

That's absolutely right. At the beginning of harvest, though, when people
like me, Frenchie, and Marine weren't yet clear on how things worked, sixteen tons took all day because Jeremy and Josh essentially had to do everything, and assign the rest of us minor tasks that were relatively simple to
understand and nigh impossible to screw up. They had to turn on and set the
press. Connect the hose between the press and the juice tub. Connect the hose
from the juice tub to the pump. Run a hose from the pump to the tank. Measure out the sulfur additions for each load of grapes. Get the crusher started.
Move the hose from one tank to the other to keep the free run and pressings
juices separate. And on, and on . . .

It all sounds simple, and it is, but it's absolutely daunting for your first
couple of weeks if working at a winery is something you've never done before.
The hoses are long and heavy, and tangled in a web of other hoses being used
for other jobs. The tanks are huge. The press, though relatively easy to operate once you understand how it works, at first looks like a piece of equipment
used by NASA. I still feel that way about the RDV, no matter how many times
Tim explained to me how it works.

The leap from growing tomatoes in your garden (or pot in your basement) to the daily grind at a winery during harvest is similar in size and scope

to pumping gas into your car every week, and then all of a sudden becoming a full-time auto mechanic. You just don't do it overnight. But by hanging around the garage every day you start to pick up bits and pieces. It was a couple of weeks into the full swing of harvest when I finally noticed that immediately after my arrival every morning I was hooking up the hose to the juice tub, setting up the pump, and running a hose to a tank—essentially getting the winery ready to receive and process fruit without even thinking about it.

"We might have to give you a promotion," Josh joked, words that, I should add, I've never heard anyone say to me in my entire life. Once I and everyone else had reached such a point with various tasks, crushing sixteen tons of grapes took just over an hour and not the entire day.

That warm feeling of understanding is quickly demolished, however, the instant that you become lazy and let your mind wander, because something bad usually happens as a result. There I was, thinking I had the easiest job of the day, working the crusher. This, I figured out pretty quickly, is the task they give to the guy who's smart enough to flip a light switch (since you just have to watch the flow of grapes and keep them coming at a steady pace without overflowing the must pump), but not experienced enough to complain about being asked to do little else. And because it's an easy job, I didn't bother to put on my gum boots or even the sturdy hiking shoes I'd lugged halfway around the world. I never made that mistake again.

Josh was on the forklift, getting ready to pull backward on a half-ton bin full of skins and seeds that had come out of the press. He asked me to push from the other side for momentum, but since a forklift is a tad more powerful than I am, it was pretty much like a game of tug-of-war when one person just lets go of his end of the rope to see the other person face-plant. I put the sole of my left foot up against a wall to give me even more pushing strength, and when the bin went zooming backward my left foot slammed into the ground, creating a jagged crack across the distal bone in my left big toe (as the X-ray later revealed).

"Eel, what was that?" Josh asked of the shriek I'd made when my toe snapped in half.

"Ahhhh," I said as I limped toward him. "I think I just broke my toe."

"Oh . . . I thought it was worse," he said. "You sounded like a girl."

Getting complacent at a winery and not doing something so simple as wearing the proper footwear results in: (a) sounding like a girl, (b) walking with a limp for the next few weeks, and (c) people laughing at you when you do.

To ease the pain, after work Josh brought me to the Cork & Keg, a tiny pub situated near ASW. It's a favorite watering hole of cellar hands year round, and quickly became a favorite watering hole of mine. We sat at the bar for a couple of hours, me drinking beer after beer to help suppress the throbbing in my toe. Josh and I spent much of the time discussing what about wine is bullshit and what isn't. Like the fact that if you're a wine expert (or if people assume you to be one), the power of suggestion can make someone taste whatever you want him to taste.

For example, say that because my name is on the cover of this book, you therefore believe me to be a wine expert. One night I have you over to my undersized/overpriced apartment in Brooklyn, and I kick out my roommate for the night on the chance that you'll get drunk enough to do the sorts of things you wouldn't do sober.* I open up a bottle of dry Riesling. After we each take a sip I say, "You probably tasted a bit of apple, and maybe even a little pear," even if the wine tastes like the water in the tank behind my toilet. But because I'm a so-called expert, chances are you'll believe that you in fact did taste apples and pears, even though I was completely bullshitting you. (Weeks later when I was in the pub talking to the owner, Bill, as I sucked down a pint or two, he asked me, "When they talk about wine, why don't they ever just say that it tastes like grapes?" Wish I knew.)

After we headed home from the pub that night, I thought about wine-geeky topics like this even more: whether wine really can taste like tobacco, and whether that's actually a good thing. Whether the critics actually help us learn about wine or are doing us and the industry itself a complete disservice by keeping wine unapproachable and intimidating, and therefore a less risky and profitable venture than it could be. The belief that the wine critics/writers have such a high level of education and understanding that we must therefore take as God's truth everything they tell us. The notion that if they taste cherries and green pepper when they're drinking something made out of *grapes,* then we must taste those things as well—and if we don't, well, then we should just give up and go back to doing whippits and drinking Schlitz out of a can.

Fortunately, I got my chance to explore this issue a little bit further the very next day. I had just limped back to the winery from the emergency room

---

*Assuming, of course, that you're a girl. Sorry, I'm not a switch hitter.

in Blenheim, where getting your big toe X-rayed and bandaged up takes a little less than an hour, because if there does happen to be another patient, odds are he's just drunk. I noticed that the door and windows to the tasting room on the second floor of the winery's main building were open. I could see Allan, Jeremy, and Josh in there with some other people, so I decided to be nosy and gimp my way up the stairs to see what was going on.

"Come on in, Eric," Allan said as soon as he saw me. He introduced me to a plump, thick-bearded man sitting at the head of the table with an empty glass, a spit bucket, and a small notebook. "Eric, this is Keith Stewart, the wine writer for the *Listener.*"

The *Listener* is basically the *Time* magazine of New Zealand, and is well known for its straight shooting and solid reporting. Keith not only has written several books, but has a very strong reputation for telling it like it is when it comes to wine. "When it's shit, he says it's shit, and when it's good, he says it's good," Allan later told me, which I found surprising given what happened when I decided to start a dialogue with him based on the conversation I'd had with Josh the evening before in the Cork & Keg.

"So, are you writing about wines that you think people will like, or wines that you think they *should* like?" I asked him.

A fair question, I think. How often do you go to a movie because the critic told you that it's good or even Oscar-worthy, and you wind up hating it? Ever been to a restaurant that the critics raved about, and after dessert and coffee you thought it was all pretty mediocre? We trust movie and restaurant critics, but not implicitly. They get it wrong occasionally, and we understand that as part of our relationship with them. But so many people assume wine to be so complicated that they take what the wine critic writes as gospel when it's the same as liking Coke more than Pepsi or Burger King more than McDonald's. Even with all those years of experience, wine writers are no better than or even different from the movie critic who gave a thumbs-up to *Speed 2: Cruise Control* or the reviewer who gave three stars to the restaurant that's serving up cold cuts on fancy china. What they say is simply a matter of opinion. So as far as I'm concerned, it was a fair question to ask of someone who's a so-called expert in his field. It would have been perfectly fair to ask the same question of Roger Ebert about movies or of Molly O'Neill about restaurants.

"I'm thinking about entertaining my audience, first and foremost," he replied, "and keeping my column interesting and fun every week. My audience is my top priority. I have one million readers every week."

He then turned his attention back to his glass, and resumed sipping and spitting.

Now just what the fuck was that supposed to mean? Just for argument's sake, let's say he conjured up this response to avoid giving the wrong answer: what he *thinks* people should like, not what they actually stand to enjoy. Sometimes these two things are one and the same and sometimes they're not, but with the answer he gave, Keith essentially said that his audience isn't his top priority at all. If it were, he would see himself as an informed expert who can help guide his readers—much the way that Dorothy Gaiter and John Brecher of *The Wall Street Journal* do every Friday—not treat them like idiots. (Or, in my case, lie about how important he is. The *Listener* had one million readers in its heyday in the seventies, and produces only 73,000 copies a week today—never mind that half or more of the magazine's readers may skip over Keith's column entirely.)

What's "entertaining" in wine writing, really? A guy telling you about a wine that's so wonderful and largely inaccessible because it costs $800 a bottle, or a wine that's not only wonderful, but accessible to everyone? Certainly the former. It's the same reason so many people (myself included, I humbly admit) watch the pre-Oscar show to see what all the celebrities are wearing. Never mind that most of them look ridiculous. It's entertaining *because* it's inaccessible. You and I can't afford a $3,000 tux or a $15,000 Versace gown, and we're therefore entertained when we see such items—especially when they're worn by drunk celebrities with eating disorders.

But we're not talking about a $3,000 piece of clothing, are we? We're talking about wine—stuff that, with some obvious exceptions, you and I can indeed afford. Though he should be, a writer like Keith Stewart is not here to help you. He's here to intimidate you because he thinks you'll find it "entertaining." Personally, I just find that to be arrogant.

To confirm my suspicions about Keith, I bought a copy of the *Listener*—dated May 22, 2004, if you want to go check for yourself in the magazine's online archives. When I first started reading his column in that particular issue, I thought I might have to bite my tongue, and maybe not be so harsh. I thought I might've had him figured all wrong:

> Food and wine matching is not a sport, it is a fact of life. And it's one that far too many poseurs are ruining for the rest of us, because they're making such a production out of that most simple of marriages. They

introduce rules of engagement and silly words to enhance a sense of self-importance among the initiated.

Good start. *You might be a man of the people after all, Keith,* I thought to myself. Then I read further. The next paragraph compliments the wineries of Marlborough that have restaurants that focus on simple food to go with their good wines. He mentions that they're unpretentious and welcoming. But does he go on to write about one or more of those fine establishments that you and I can so readily enjoy?

Of course not! The rest of the column is a three-hundred-word ass-kissing of Herzog, whose winery restaurant is considered to be the best in Marlborough. It's also one of the most expensive. And guess what? So are the wines. Surprise, surprise. And this sentence in the middle of the article really got to me: "The only disappointment is that there are no other wine regions with a restaurant to match it."

A pretty bold—not to mention idiotic—statement considering the existence of the French Laundry in Napa and a host of Michelin-star establishments dotting France's winemaking regions much the way McDonald's is spread across the United States. But the closing sentence was the kicker: "If any New Zealand winemakers want to know the environment in which their finest wines will show off their best, perhaps it is time they all visited Herzog." I'm surprised he didn't just round it off by writing, "But *you* certainly can't visit there because it's too expensive. Until you can afford to eat and drink at Herzog, you just will not understand the way that food and wine are supposed to match, the way that I do." He's simply saying that you can't experience or taste good wine if you don't taste the expensive stuff. Herzog may very well be the best restaurant in Marlborough, if not all of New Zealand, but nowhere in the column does Keith mention what exactly he ate and what wines paired well with those foods, and why.

The worst part of all this is that Keith is not only extremely knowledgeable, but a talented writer—he sucks you in with that first paragraph, pretending that he's your friend and that it's all so simple. That he's one of *us*. But by the end of the article he's made you feel like you just aren't good enough because the one example he points to of a perfect pairing of wine and food is a restaurant that normal people can't afford (and one he likely didn't have to pay for since either the *Listener* or Herzog was probably footing the bill). Can't say that I'm very entertained by that, Keith.

I guess he gets the last laugh, though, since the very next day as he was swirling and swishing free wine at God knows how many wineries throughout Marlborough (a few days later I saw him dining at Domaine Georges Michel), I was out picking Pinot Noir with the vineyard crew. After a couple of hours I could feel my neck slowly turning red in the southern-hemisphere sun and my back aching from constantly bending over and picking up bins of fruit.

"Swing looooooooooow . . . sweet chaaaaaaaaaaariot," I began to sing.

I was expecting at least a few chuckles from the pickers, but since I was about 6,000 miles from Alabama, people just asked me what song that was, as if it was a Top 40 hit in America. Oh, well.

Josh called me back to the winery to help crush the fruit, and once I got there I noticed that he and Jeremy weren't speaking to each other. It turned out that they'd again clashed over the work at hand, this time over how many tons of which variety should be picked the following day, and how many liters of which juices should be distributed among which tanks. Though I didn't witness this particular argument, I eventually figured out that all their work-related arguments could be condensed into something like this:

"Fuck you, you're wrong."

"Fuck *you. You're* wrong."

"Dad's going to agree with me."

"No, Allan's gonna take my side. I did the numbers, and you just wanna wing it."

"I fucked your girlfriend last night."

"I fucked yours. And you know I'm right."

"All right, fine, but I'm gonna fuck you up at rugby practice tomorrow."

"Yeah, you'll fuckin' try. Oh, and by the way, *fuck you.*"

Minor disagreements just seem to be the nature of the job during harvest. I'm sure this wasn't their first or their last argument, especially because tank space would become a logistical nightmare as more and more loads of grapes arrived each day. Later, at the Cork & Keg, Josh let his mature, professional side show when he recounted the argument for me.

"I knew Macca was right, and I was kind of embarrassed about it," he admitted to me. "But we went away and talked it out privately, so no one else could see the tension between us, and we got it sorted."

What surprised me about this admission was not just that a twenty-three-year-old would have such a strong handle on professional decorum—making sure that the other employees didn't hear him fighting with Jeremy—but that he could talk about something so calmly and rationally only an hour or so after nearly lopping off two of his fingers.

Yes, you read that correctly.

Earlier, after the last load of Pinot was pumped into the tank for the start of its cold soak, Josh was helping clean the crusher-destemmer and was moving quickly since Frenchie, who'd been assigned the task, was moving too slowly. The back portion of the machine lifts up on hydraulics so a person can reach inside, but somehow the hydraulics failed, bringing the lid, all hundred or so pounds of it with its sharp edges, crashing down on Josh's hand. At first he didn't make a sound, so I just assumed that he was okay.

"Mother*fucker!*" he uttered with a strange blend of calm and excruciating pain after a few seconds of silence. He later told me that the instant it happened he simply thought, "That's it, I've lost my fingers."

And he came close—lucky for him he has his father's beefy hands. As he freed himself and walked over to the hoses to clean his wounds, I could see blood streaming down his hand, leaving a crimson trail behind him. He'd lacerated two of his fingers to the bone, and one of them is now more crooked than a spoon that took a couple turns in the garbage disposal.

Now, remember my mentioning something about Josh being a fix-it-yourself kind of guy? Did he go to the emergency room? Hell no. He wrapped up his hand and drove home, and spent the next half hour stitching himself up with a needle and thread, drove back to work, and then wanted to go have beers at the Cork & Keg. The next day the pain was so unbearable that he went to the accident clinic, where they drilled holes in his fingertips to relieve the mounting pressure. And a month later, after the bandages were off but the fingernail still cracked and torn, he just squinted and ripped the whole fingernail off as if it were an old Band-Aid.

I won't sit here and tell you that every winemaker in Marlborough is as resistant to pain as Josh. Call him an ogre, call him too macho, or even call him crazy. But the reason he stitched himself up was so he could get back to work and see to every small step of the process, ensuring that the wine would be made the way he and Jeremy wanted it made.

Now *that's* the sort of thing that tells me that a wine is probably going to be good. It's also pretty entertaining. It's just too bad they couldn't put a picture of Josh's finger on the label . . . it's certainly a better sign of quality than anything critics like Keith Stewart have to say.

Because we spend more time in the vineyards, we have a better understanding of what happens in those vineyards. We taste the fruit, look at the vines, and make a decision. That's done on gut feel and experience on what was done in the past.

—MATT THOMSON, CONSULTANT WINEMAKER FOR ST. CLAIR, LAKE CHALICE, MUD HOUSE, DELTA, AND CAPE CAMPBELL

5

Learning the Ropes

During harvest there's really no such thing as a weekend, because at eight o'clock Monday morning things will never be the same as you left them Friday afternoon at five. Which means that unless there's a major change in the weather, the grapes just keep on doing on Saturday and Sunday whatever it was they were doing on Friday: ripening, splitting, rotting, whatever. So if you skip Saturday and Sunday you can find yourself totally screwed by Monday.

"The most important winemaking decision you make is the day when you pick the grapes," I was told toward the end of the harvest by Digger, the winemaker at Mount Riley. "We're about capturing fruit flavors, and they can change so quickly that if you're not out in the vineyard keeping an eye on it, you can miss it . . . which I have done on a few occasions."

Not many winemakers would openly admit that. One other who did, though, was Andrew Hedley, winemaker at Framingham, who told me, "You get one shot at your picking decision, and if you've got it wrong, you can't go back and stick it back on. Picking is a lot about compromise, unfortunately—

I don't suppose anyone else would say that because everyone else makes perfect picking decisions, of course," he said as he rolled his eyes.

So the first Saturday in April was a normal day at the winery, the only difference being Jeremy's midday absence to play rugby, followed by his limping back to the winery a couple of hours later with torn ligaments in his ankle. Between his ankle, Josh's finger, and my toe, I half expected somebody to lose a nut by the end of harvest. Jeremy's injury kept him sidelined from the team for another six weeks or so, but he had no time for rugby anyway. With harvest in full swing he wouldn't get more than a few hours off from the winery each day, which was the time he used to sleep—if he was able to, considering the ever-increasing pressure he and Josh would come under as the winery inched closer to full capacity with several hundred tons of grapes still hanging on the vines. If the previous two days' loads of Pinot Noir—and the accidents and injuries that came with them—tested the winery's resilience, the first working weekend in April would be the beginning of an extended test of everyone's perseverance.

The morning started simply enough, with a crush of five tons of hand-picked Sauvignon Blanc. No sweat. Josh and Jeremy were more or less happy with the fruit that was coming in, although it also contained a fair amount of rot. This meant that either the pickers weren't told what to take and what to leave on the vine, or the contract grower told his crew to just pick everything they could to raise the total volume and, in turn, his own paycheck. So really all that Jeremy could do that particular morning was send Uncle B over to the vineyard to yell at the pickers. Even though he's good at that sort of thing, it probably didn't help much since, as I mentioned before, the pickers would rather pick than think—doing both at the same time is usually very difficult for them. Ask them to rub their stomachs and pat their heads, and they might start crying in despair.

Actually, despair is probably the right word for how we at the winery felt by late morning, as seventy tons of Chardonnay showed up in about ten loads, one after another. (I imagine this is what postal workers feel like: No matter how many annoying J. Crew catalogs they deliver, more frat-boy bibles just keep on coming.) Some wineries are built to process seventy tons in the blink of an eye, but ASW has only one bin, one crusher-destemmer, and two presses (which is one more than most have), so seventy tons takes about twelve hours from start to end-of-the-day beer. The old press can take about fourteen tons of grapes, and the new one, only two or three years old, is designed to take thirty-five (though on a few occasions throughout harvest we were able to squeeze in forty or even a little more). What all this means is that a winery the size of ASW can't just take seventy tons of grapes, press them all off together, and call it a day.

In this case, we started by pushing as much as we could into the large press, and once it got going we began to fill the small press. The large press, because it's newer, can squeeze a full load in less than two hours (the small press takes three hours or more), so in a situation such as this the hope is that the big press will be done by the time the small press is full. The large press can then be emptied and cleaned, which takes about half an hour to forty-five minutes, then closed up and filled again for another pressing.

In between the changeover, however, there are a couple of procedures that have to be followed fairly closely. Once the press is full, its siren wails to let the crusher operator (me) know to turn off the must pump. The thing is, though, at this point there are still a few hundred pounds of crushed grapes sitting in the hose between the must pump and the press itself. If you're a beast, like Josh, you can disconnect the hose from the press using your bare hands instead of a wrench, and then drag the heavy hose full of crushed grapes twenty or thirty feet to the nozzle of the other press, hook it up, and get going again. But sane—and normal-sized—people like me and Geoff do what's called "pushing through," which just means using water to push the grapes still sitting in the hose into the press. Since the hose between the must pump and the press is partially transparent, you can see when the water reaches the press, and as soon as it does, you stop the pump and close the valve on the press so all that gets in is grapes, and not water. If a little water does get in it doesn't make much of a difference, but that's when someone like Geoff or Josh gets the opportunity to joke, "Eh, we'll send this load to the Americans"—for my benefit, of course. Once the valve is closed off, the hose is disconnected, the water drained out, and the now-much-lighter hose dragged over to the other press so crushing can resume.

It's one of those tasks that's extremely easy in theory, and something you can do in your sleep after a while. But the first time is often the most embarrassing—in my case, extremely so, because I didn't understand that the press wasn't actually turned on until after all the grapes were inside it. I just assumed that if the grapes were running into the press, it was, well, pressing the whole time. I didn't know the difference between free-run juice and pressings.

So there I was, standing at the juice tub and looking at the greenish-gold nectar flowing into it after Josh asked me to watch for water as he began to push through. The whole process only takes about twenty or thirty seconds, but you want to get it just right. After about fifteen seconds of pushing water into the pump, Josh looked up and asked with a hint of panic in his voice, "Is anyone watching that hose?!"

"Yeah, I'm right here," I answered, not realizing I was looking at the wrong hose entirely, which if water had been coming through, would be ruining all the juice.

"No, not there!" he screamed, which caused Geoff to look up, realize what was happening, run to the end of the press just in time to catch where the water line was, and signal Josh to turn off the pump. This was yet another of those moments when Josh wondered if I'd been dropped on my head as a child or smoked too much pot in college.* It didn't help that Allan was standing right there the whole time. Fortunately, he just laughed it off.

Though I probably shouldn't have, every time Josh made a crack about a screwup of mine such as this, I'd say, "Well, part of the deal of my coming here was that I promised your dad you'd have to come back to New York and learn how to write."

Such a thought was as funny as it was horrifying to Josh, because he's not the type of person who can sit at a computer for more than ten minutes without going nuts.† But it was also my way of reminding him that if he didn't want things to get screwed up, I'd have to be taught pretty much everything in detail far more explicit than he was used to providing. Three words: "Treat me like a moron."

He would get his chance to do so again later the following day which, in terms of the weather, was a major change from the previous two weeks of warm sunshine. Just like the saying that uses lions and lambs to describe March, there's that other one, "April showers bring May flowers." Catchy, but April showers in Marlborough, while they were rare in 2004, were pretty harsh once they did happen to work their way off the South Pole, across the Tasman Sea, and up the South Island. Miserable, in fact. If it's cold and wet when the grapes come in, so are the workers crushing them from dawn to well

---

*It's very likely both.

†Unless it's to forward me a doctored photo of Jessica Simpson blowing a horse.

after dusk. So needless to say, April showers don't bring May flowers in Marlborough. April showers, when they occur, bring misery among cellar hands and panic among winemakers.

Midway through the day Josh and I were pumping some fermenting Sauvignon Blanc juice into barrels. It was a small batch of maybe one thousand liters total, but the small volume doesn't make it any easier to handle. Because the ferment is under way, that means that the wine is essentially carbonated—the yeast is converting the sugar to alcohol, and CO_2 is bubbling off. So you have to go slowly, just as you would if you were pouring Sprite or 7 Up into a tall glass—go too fast and, well, you can see what's coming.

I was peeking down into the barrel to see how much room was left while Josh operated the pump.

"Stop? Stop yet? You sure?" Josh asked me. I told him to keep going because it looked like there was still a ways to go. When I finally gave the stop signal, though, white foam and wine came shooting out the top of the barrel like it was Old Faithful.

"It looked like there was still plenty of room," I pleaded to Jeremy as he swaggered by mideruption, shaking his head.

"It always does," he said.

Either because he felt bad about it or because it was the truth, Josh later told me that it wasn't entirely my fault (fun as it was for him having me think so), as a gas bubble had gone through the hose and into the barrel, causing the eruption. Nevertheless, it would make me extra-cautious any time I had to go near barrels ever again. That may sound silly, but just think about it for a second. How would you feel if I came to your family retail business, and every so often took a few minutes to pull cash out of the register and set it on fire? Even if it's accidental, allowing juice to spill down the drain at a winery is roughly the same thing. Every drop is money.

As if that weren't enough, later in the day as we were cruising the vineyards, sampling grapes from three blocks at three different vineyards—Omaka (near Josh's house), Wallops (near his parents' house), and Moorland (surrounding the winery itself)—I could sense Josh becoming more and more frustrated. He'd mentioned to me several times that he thought the sampling that had been performed up to that point was flawed—that Jemma and Marine only took the healthiest-looking bunches from the vines back to the lab. When we got back to the lab and tested our samples, his suspicions proved correct, even if he knew pretty much the instant that he tasted the grapes—the Omaka and Moorland blocks had good flavors as well as Brix levels ranging from 22.5 to 23.5, meaning that they should be harvested immediately. There was no time to lose, since if the Brix levels kept rising, there would be too much sugar in the juice, and therefore too much alcohol in the finished wine.

Josh called his father, then tossed his phone onto the dashboard of his Jeep at the end of the conversation, disgusted that the vineyards had caught him off guard.

"I knew he'd be pissed," he sighed. "It fucks your whole schedule. You always want to be a little ahead so you can plan. We don't have a hundred illegal immigrants who can pick our grapes."

Surveying the land and the clouds above, he expressed as much concern as he did relief over the rain to come. "It's actually good, because it can lower your Brix," he said. "But it can also cause your fruit to split. You never know."

Either way, there were enough blocks ready to be picked that Josh and Jeremy began to contemplate instituting twenty-four-hour shifts, which had never been done in the history of ASW. But it might be necessary with eight tons of Chardonnay coming later that day, and full days of Pinot Noir picking for the next three days.

There are no ivory towers here, like where the winemaker walks down the aisles and gives everyone a slip of paper in the morning.

—CLAIRE ALLAN, OWNER/WINEMAKER OF HUIA VINEYARDS

6

It's a Dirty Job, but . . .

It was cloudy, with temperatures hanging in the high forties, and though twenty-four-hour shifts weren't deemed necessary, the winery was running at full speed by 6:30 A.M.—for the day Allan had demoted himself to truck driver, since every spare set of hands was needed in the vineyards as well as in the winery. The wake-up call came the day before, when the winery crushed thirty-eight tons of Sauvignon Blanc, twenty-three tons of Chardonnay, and another ten tons of Pinot Noir, all coming in small batches at different times. At one point the small press needed to be emptied and refilled, but all the bins were being used by the pickers. So the fourteen tons of marc inside the press was just dumped onto the ground and shoveled up by hand later. (Next time you have a bad day at work, think about the fact that you likely didn't have to shovel up anything, much less fourteen tons of it.)

Allan drove several loads of Sauvignon Blanc to the winery in quick succession, totaling about fifty tons. We filled the small press and then the big press, and by the time we'd hosed out the bin and cleaned the crusher and must pump, just under ten tons of Pinot Noir arrived. Once it was all crushed and soaking in the tank, Jeremy and I started to clean everything again to prepare for seven and a half tons of Pinot Gris already on the way in from the fields. Once the bin, crusher, and must pump were cleaned, we emptied the small press and quickly crushed and pushed in the Pinot Gris (which, by the way, is the exact same thing as Pinot Grigio, because Italians always seem to have to make things sound cooler than they actually are). By the time we were done with that, we had to clean out the big press and stuff in another twenty-four tons or so of Sauvignon Blanc. In total the winery crushed 91.6 tons of grapes in a single day, just under 10 percent of the winery's total intake for the year. A standard, solid day is maybe thirty-five to forty tons.

Working a good day's crush, especially one that's incident-free and runs smoothly, gives you a bit of a buzz. But you still can't get complacent and rush things, as I learned when Jeremy and I were switching from crushing Pinot Noir to Pinot Gris. We'd forgotten that the end of the hose was still sitting in the tank of Pinot Noir, so when we disconnected it from the must pump to clean it for the Pinot Gris load on its way, the grapes began to siphon back out of the tank. Fortunately, we got the hose reconnected the very instant before ten tons of Pinot Noir would've begun to splatter all over the ground. Losing your focus at a winery may hurt you. But if you make a minor mistake and don't catch it in time, the laws of physics will absolutely screw you. So, needless to say, my next book won't be about working at NASA.

As the workday came to a close shortly before midnight, the weather took a turn for the worse, and the temperature dropped to only slightly above freezing. Geoff and I were standing near the presses, hoping that by staring at them we could force them to work that much faster. Cleaning them and the surrounding area is wet work, so once they were finished pressing, the wetter we got, the colder we got.

While we were in the middle of wrapping things up, Jemma came down from the lab to help us, and joked, "This makes for good writing, doesn't it?"

"If you're referring to how cold it is out here and how warm Jeremy's been up there in the lab for the last hour or so, then yes," I said as I shivered.

"You're going to trash him, aren't you?" she asked, and I answered her question with a sheepish grin.

However, that was just a gut response at a moment of discomfort. Though Jeremy was indeed sheltering himself from our cold and wet work, he was plenty busy with work of his own. For every single action that's taken at a winery there's a form that has to be filled out so that if anything goes wrong there's a paper trail that leads to someone's decision. This creates heaps of paperwork, and the more grapes you crush, the more the paper stacks up.

Jeremy was also trying to manage the logistical nightmare that involved what would be harvested when and what juice would go where. This gets harder and harder as more and more tanks are filled, since there's less and less space available to do something as simple as rack juice off its lees and into another tank. The setup was pretty much the way that he and Josh had arranged it—Jeremy does as much as he can in the winery, and Josh picks up the extra work whenever Jeremy has to step away and handle the paperwork. Kind of like how one roommate cleans the bathroom, while the other remembers to pay the bills before the power gets shut off. It more or less has to be that way, since Jeremy is the one who can look at work orders or a diagram of the tank farm and make sense of it all, and Josh is the guy who has his hands in and on everything.

"Never trust a winemaker who isn't dirty," Josh told me around this time. If they're not hands-on, out on the cellar floor as he and Jeremy are every day, then they can't be making the best wine possible. "Look at their hands, look at their clothes," he advised.

That was the first time that I even considered that winemakers could *not* be hands-on—that they could wear jackets and ties, eat fancy lunches every day, and say things like, "Why, this wine reminds me of an '82 Mouton Rothschild! I believe I have a bottle or two in the trunk of my Jaguar. Why don't we take it out for a spin and crash it just for fun? No biggie, I have fourteen others."

Rumor is that's how they are in Bordeaux, and that even in Napa you'll find people with the title "winemaker" on their business cards who never plunged a tank of red grapes, filled a barrel, or drove a forklift, even though these are two of the best wine regions in the world. Before I got to Marlborough I just assumed that if a chef's in the kitchen, a winemaker has to be, well, in the winery making wine. Despite the stacks of paperwork generated during harvest, Josh still contends that other winemakers sit in their warm offices because they can—that they feel they've earned it, and would rather someone else do their work for them. But Josh is young and opinionated, so I decided to ask around about how important it is for a winemaker to be in the cellar getting dirty with everyone else.

Some people rolled their eyes. Others nodded in agreement. But by and large most told me that it's simply an issue of size. The bigger the winery, the harder it is to be out on the cellar floor filling the press, racking tanks, washing barrels, and so forth.

"In a big company, the only way to be the winemaker is to sit in an office and issue work orders," declared Al Soper, winemaker at Highfield. "You've still got to wander around, I guess, to have a feel for what's going on in the winery. However, you won't ever have the need to turn a pump on."

Al's a very hands-on guy, and when I interviewed him he had bags under his eyes and grape skins covering his clothes and gum boots. He also hadn't shaved in at least a week. He looked like he'd been on the run from a bounty hunter.

"As I get older I might want to do less of it, but part of being in this industry is getting caught up in the excitement of the harvest. At some point the adrenaline kicks in, and you realize that you're thriving on the long hours and the inadequate sleep. It wouldn't be vintage if you were sitting in a nice warm office telling other people what to do. I don't think you can be as close to the wines if you're doing that."

One guy who does sit in a warm office, yet still believes he's close to his wines, is John Belsham of Wairau River and Foxes Island. (Both are produced in the same winery, jointly owned by John and the Rose family, who owns Wairau River—John owns Foxes Island. The winery itself is in a nondescript, ugly building that looks like a warehouse Mulder and Scully would come across in *The X-Files* and discover to be a government facility performing tests on aliens.)

"It's about being smart in this business," John told me, and he is indeed one of the smartest winemakers in Marlborough—something even those who don't like him are all too willing to admit. "I know where to use my expertise most effectively and efficiently. It took me a long time to work that out, to be honest. The temptation is to get in there and lead by example. My task is to make sure that only the things *I* can do can be done properly. Like when we pick the fruit. When are the flavors right? Analyzing various results. Do I make an addition or don't I? When do I start plunging? I can't do that if I'm out loading the press. This is a fifteen-hundred-ton winery. If this were a fifty-ton winery, I could do all those things and make all our decisions."

When I asked this question of Matt Thomson, a guy you'll only see dirty after he's been out kayaking (he's one of the best competitive kayakers in all of New Zealand), he threw his head back and said, "Ah, shit," as if he were a CEO and I'd just caught him with his secretary bent over the desk. He's one of the most respected winemakers in the world, consulting for wineries in Italy in addition to the five in Marlborough he works for—but he was very clean.

"Really, I think the bigger picture is more important than rolling a barrel, filling a barrel, cleaning a barrel, cleaning a tank. If you can't let go of some of that and trust someone competent to do that, you miss the important things," he said as we drank coffee at his kitchen table one morning in the middle of the harvest. "If you want to be everything, you won't process more than one hundred tons. You have no economy of scale. Your price point for quality is going to be pretty high, and there will be wines out there that will be better for less money."

I should point out that Matt and John agree on this issue possibly because they both worked at Vintech, a contract winery set up by John and a few other partners several years ago. But Matt and John are not exactly the best of friends; after speaking with Matt I got the impression that these two didn't like working with each other at all. Matt wasn't the first person I heard say that he didn't like John, so I decided to do the really dumb thing and ask John why people don't like him. The answer he gave me not only proved how smart he is, but made me appreciate the way he runs his operation (even though I'd be scared shitless to work for him).

"I've just been around a long time," he said in a relaxed tone of voice, though the look on his face when I asked him the question made me think he was going to throw me out the window—without opening it first. Most journalists only ask him about flavors, oak barrels, vineyard management, and other stuff that they pretend to know something about. Not this. "I'm just an old fart. Because I ran a contract winery, I had interaction with a lot of people—a lot of winemakers who've gone on to be winemakers at other companies who worked for me. I don't make any bones about it. As a boss I've always been very demanding. At this time of year you've got to put your attitude toward wine first. You don't go through life being friends with everybody."

Even Sam Rose, son of the owners of Wairau River and rugby teammate of Jeremy and Josh, admitted to me that he once saw his brother Hamish, the vineyard manager, come to fisticuffs with John. (John won.) They get along well now, but Sam chalked it up to John's having more passion for his work than anyone else in the region—something that really no one in Marlborough doubts in the slightest.

However, I still wasn't sure I agreed with John's belief that once a winery reaches a certain size, the winemaker can't be in the winery. So I asked around even more.

"I think that's to be taken with a grain of salt, really," Digger at Mount Riley said to me of Josh's opinion. "Hands-on for me is actually being in the vineyard," which is probably especially important in Digger's case since Mount Riley's vineyards are scattered all across the valley, several miles apart from one another, meaning that the soils, nutrients, microclimates, and flavors are all different. So he has to be out there monitoring things all the time. "I've got a vineyard out at Renwick where it's really rocky at one end, and really heavy silt at the other. Down that one row the flavor profile changes so much that it means picking something you have to learn to balance. You never get those answers right until you've made a few mistakes. If you get it right in the vineyard and that juice comes in, it's all downhill from there. The less I have to do to the juice, the better the wine I've made, and the easier my job is."

Okay, so to Digger being a hands-on winemaker means being out in the vineyard, and not actually making wine in the winery. Several others I spoke with agreed. Then I thought about it a little more, and I realized that Jeremy and Josh go out to the vineyard all the time, and still also manage to be in the winery racking tanks, filling barrels, and tasting all the tanks a couple of times a day to make sure the juice inside them is fermenting properly. Digger even said to me, "Darryl Woolley is a guy I'd trust implicitly. He probably doesn't get too dirty anymore."

Darryl Woolley is the head winemaker and viticulturist for Nobilo Wine Group (owned by Constellation Brands, a publicly listed U.S. company). He's been making wine in New Zealand since 1978, and the winery he runs processed just over 8,000 tons of grapes in 2004, though it can hold 9,500 tons—part of a NZ$100 million expansion plan instituted in 2000. With Digger's comments in mind, I went ahead and called Darryl and arranged to meet him one morning at his office. Not only was he not dirty, but he had a lot to say about Josh's opinion.

"I agree with him," he said, taking me by surprise. "Up until two years ago I was very much hands-on in this place." He went on to say that the winery is too big for that now, and that he's moved to more of a management job anyway. Nevertheless, when the operation was basically just him and one other person (with seasonal workers, like Marine and Frenchie, on hand for the harvest), they could crush up to 3,000 tons and still be hands-on. (Today, since they crush almost three times as much, there are three winemakers under Darryl who work as a team. "I'm the leader of the band," he explained, "but the band makes the decisions.")

"I worked eighteen-hour days," he said, with a slight grin on his face, like a retired quarterback who misses all those Sunday afternoons. "Don't trust a guy who's never been down in the wine room himself. You can't get a doctorate degree in enology and come down here and start organizing a winery if you've never been down there working at 2:00 A.M., pumping over a red, shoveling out a drainer, or putting a new press bag in, or whatever else happens in the worst parts of a season." Of Josh's idea in particular, he added, "I think it's a very valid comment."

That's not to say, of course, that people like John Belsham and Matt Thomson haven't done all those things. They have, and probably more so than most. Just not in a long time.

"I think there is something extra in the wine if the winemaker did the job," said Ant MacKenzie, winemaker at Spy Valley. His hands were even stained purple from plunging the Pinot tanks when he told me this. Nevertheless, he, like everyone else, seems to trust other people to do certain jobs, "because you end up killing yourself in a vintage trying to do it all."

So at what point is a winery too big for the winemaker to be hands-on? Cloudy Bay crushed probably 2,500 tons in 2004, and I doubt anyone ever saw Kevin Judd turn on a pump or rack a tank during the vintage. "Kevin is the winemaker at Cloudy Bay, but he doesn't make any wine," said Daniel Le Brun, owner of No. 1 Family Estate, when I spoke to him about this and other things. And Kevin himself told me that he sees his role as one like that of Digger: out in the vineyard making picking decisions. But then there's someone like Ben Glover of Wither Hills, a winery that processed 3,500 tons in 2004 (one thousand more than Cloudy Bay). The day I went to see Ben, his hands and shirt were stained purple, presumably from plunging the Pinot tanks—he looked like he'd just jacked off Barney. According to the comments of some other winemakers, Wither Hills is too big for Ben to be working in the winery, and when he is, he's missing what's going on out in the vineyards. But taste his wines, and you'll disagree—they stand up against those of anyone in Marlborough, if not the larger world. "I hope I do stay dirty and trustworthy," Ben confided. One reason he's able to do it is that he hired someone to do data entry and paperwork so he could be out in the winery or the vineyard, rather than do the paperwork himself and hire someone else to, well, make the wine.

Simon Waghorn, who runs Whitehaven's 3,000-ton winery—as well as makes the wine for Tohu and his own label, Astrolabe—manages to rack or plunge a tank a couple of times a year. But to do everything, he'd have to be at a much smaller place. Maybe when he's ready to retire, he said.

That's pretty much how it worked for James Healy of Dog Point. He was a winemaker alongside Kevin Judd at Cloudy Bay for twelve years and gave it up specifically because his job had become too administrative, and was no longer hands-on. Dog Point makes only a few different varieties in small batches, and they handpick everything. The operation is really just Healy and Ivan Sutherland, his partner in the business and owner of the vineyard. If you flip to the map at the front of this book, you'll notice that Dog Point isn't on it. That's because the winery has no fancy restaurant, no tasting room, no nothing—just tanks and barrels in metal sheds off a dirt road. The winery is so well hidden that on a day I was supposed to meet James there, I drove past it twice even though it's off a street I used at least once a week. James and Ivan just want to be left alone to do the best job they can.

"I went out on my own because I did want to do it all myself," James told me shortly after harvest. "We have a general aim of where we're going, and we just want the two of us to be able to do it all."

Similarly, Mike and Claire Allan of Huia wouldn't make wine if they couldn't get dirty every day. "We both get covered in juice," Claire said to me one morning toward the end of harvest as she, Mike, and I sat around their kitchen table discussing this and other things over coffee. "We've cleaned the press forty times," Mike added, "and I've done it thirty-six of those times."

What I learned from these conversations and several others was that Josh's idea that a winemaker has to be dirty to be making good wine isn't entirely right, because there are plenty of aspects to the job that don't involve being dirty. But he or she *does* have to love making wine. The wine won't taste good if they don't, just as this book wouldn't be much fun to read if I didn't enjoy writing it. So as far as I'm concerned, if a winemaker loves making wine, he probably will want to get out there and get dirty as much as he can. The dirtier the winemaker, the more likely I am to trust him or her.

Since I was lower than the lowest man on the totem pole, I was definitely getting dirty. And with the amount of grapes still hanging on the vines and the weather getting colder, things were about to get downright messy.

It was two degrees centigrade, and at seven o'clock at night we were really quite frightened. We'd seen it before. In 1990 we had a frost in the middle of harvest, and it defoliated the whole valley. Losing your leaves before the fruit's ripe is pretty bad.

—KEVIN JUDD, WINEMAKER AT CLOUDY BAY

7

Patience, Young Winemaker

At the end of the first week of April, the morning was greeted by even more snow on the mountaintops, and while the day did warm up a little, muscles were sore, nerves were frayed, and eyes had bags. When I arrived for work the winery was awaiting yet another batch of Pinot Noir, as well as a load of Sauvignon Blanc from a grower in Nelson, about one hundred kilometers away.

While we were waiting for the Pinot to arrive, I was keeping warm in the office as Uncle B and Kevin, ASW's bookkeeper, talked about the weather— a subject that's chitchat to you and me, but is a topic of serious discussion in Marlborough, for obvious reasons. Winemakers discuss the weather the way New Yorkers discuss their soaring careers, tiny apartments, and uncomfortable "social" diseases.

"What about the frost?" Kevin asked Uncle B.

"There wasn't any last night," Uncle B responded as he shuffled papers on his desk.

"No, tonight," Kevin said. "It's supposed to get down to minus three."

"Oh . . . there won't be any," Uncle B said, smiling. "How's that for confidence?" he said as he turned and looked at me.

It's not often that you'll see Uncle B joke about himself or his work. Especially about fall frosts, which tell the vines to shut down for the winter, so they stop ripening the fruit. Brian's as dry as they get—literally. He's a recovered alcoholic, so even though he manages ASW's vineyards, he doesn't drink wine. Before this job he spent twenty-five years in the ranching business, and I asked him if he was a vegetarian back then. "No, I eat red meat every day!" he proclaimed, shocked at the notion. So his sense of humor doesn't kick in very often.

The conversation between Uncle B and Kevin then shifted to the harvest itself, and Kevin asked how many tons had been harvested so far.

"Just over three hundred," Brian said.

"So you're just over a third of the way?"

"Nope," Brian said as he slowly shook his head, conveying mild frustration. I checked with Jeremy and Josh, and the current projection was up to 1,200 tons—three hundred more than they'd expected, much less would be able to find tank space for.

Sure enough, the Pinot arrived, but all the red-wine tanks were already full. So Jeremy and Josh crushed the six tons of grapes and put them in big, open-top plastic bins that had been delivered that morning. Turns out they were actually water troughs for cattle, but would work just fine. Anticipating even more of a space crunch, later in the afternoon a thirty-foot-high, 20,000-liter black plastic tank was delivered, and would from that point forward be known as Black Mamba.

Improvisation under pressure is one thing, but making do on short notice with less-than-ideal materials, such as plastic tanks and water troughs, is something else. After the day's work had ended, I had a silent beer or two with Josh at the Cork & Keg. He was so stressed out that he was having a hard time even forming sentences. He'd also pulled his third late night in a row and was panicked about the inevitable shortage of tank space as well as the high price wineries such as his were paying growers for grapes in this feast-or-famine year.

"One of them is getting a check from us for NZ$500,000. Half a million for *grapes*. It's ridiculous," he said between sips of beer that seemed hard to swallow. "They can't charge these kinds of prices next year. I think we should just start calling them now and telling them that they're getting eight or nine hundred dollars per ton." Of course, it was too late for that, and the growers were getting about three times that.

And the grapes needed to be picked.

Toward the end of the day the weather continued to worsen, and Cloudy Bay made the decision to harvest and crush all through the night to beat out the forecasted frosts. That winery was also one of many to call in helicopters, which hover over the vineyards, blowing the warmer air above the frost down onto the grapes. Some wineries have wind turbines installed to perform the same function. Neither is a particularly cheap option, as the helicopters charge a couple of thousand dollars per hour even when they're on the ground, and installing a wind turbine will run you about NZ$70,000. It's also questionable just how effective either method truly is, because neither can warm up a particularly large piece of land. What it really comes down to, Jeremy told me, is making sure you've planted your grapes on a plot of land that is less prone to frost.

On this particular evening, however, it was Uncle B who was right, as there was only rain and no frost. After the harvest Kevin Judd at Cloudy Bay admitted to me that that night he'd brought in five helicopters that he didn't need, and the winery had spent NZ$80,000 during the harvest on helicopters it never used. So don't be surprised if the price of a bottle of Cloudy Bay Sauvignon Blanc goes up by five bucks.

Rain or frost notwithstanding, Jeremy and Josh worked until 1:00 A.M. They'd waited until 9:30 P.M. for the load of grapes to show up from Nelson, and not only was the quality of the fruit subpar, but they even found rocks scattered in to increase the total weight and, in turn, ASW's payout. Worse, the truck in which the grapes arrived couldn't back up the ramp, so Josh and Jeremy had to make a quick call up the road to Rapaura Vintners, a big contract winery, and have that facility crush the fruit.

"It's nice to watch someone else do all the work for you for once," Josh told me the next day, "but it cost us an arm and a leg."

The next two days brought even more rain to the vineyards and snow to the mountaintops, and even though only thirteen tons of Sauvignon Blanc were crushed in that time, pretty much every other task around the winery involved getting extremely wet and cold, the sort of thing that was only short-term discomfort for me, but sheer panic for Josh and Jeremy as their fruit continued to hang out on the vines during inclement weather.

Just as the bad weather ended I got a chance to sit down with Allan to get his thoughts on how things were going so far. Compared to Jeremy and Josh, he was ice-cool. The nasty weather and threat of frosts hadn't shaken him in the slightest.

"It's farming, at the end of the day," he said as he shrugged his shoulders, just as a farmer would. "You take the good with the bad. You can spend all that money on helicopters and just waste it, and still have the same problem. We can get frost as easy as wank,* but it's got to be a belter to knock everything down. It's a completely different scenario from a spring frost. With that you're protecting your foliage, and it's more crucial to the ongoing development of the vine. Whereas early autumn frosts, the vine is pretty hearty and can take a bit of a knock.

"The critical thing is to be patient," he continued. "I keep saying that we can't make decisions on the fly. Let's talk through them and be as positive as we can. While it's raining, everyone gets nervous. I'm pretty confident that most of the fruit we have out there is pretty good, apart from one or two heavy crops. And the flavor is slowly rising. I don't think there's cause for concern or panic in terms of getting it there."

As for Jeremy and Josh, his faith in them was still unfaltering. "I think they've matured really well," he said. "Both are mindful of the difficulty of managing a vintage like this. I just hope they don't get tired. I'd hoped they'd break up the shifts at this stage, which they haven't done, and two weeks from now the long hours will take their toll."

They were already beating the shit out of me. Even Josh was on a regimen of four cans of Red Bull a day, usually pounding them in quick succession like Popeye sucking down his spinach. With all the early starts and late nights, I was eating at irregular times, sometimes showering only once every couple of days, and shaving only when I had time—maybe once every ten days or so. Just about every morning someone would say to me, "You don't look so good." I'm not a morning person anyway, but spending fourteen to sixteen hours straight outside crushing grapes, then coming back for more the next day was not doing my appearance any good whatsoever. I looked like the Unabomber. On crack.

The only thing that was bothering Allan at that moment, perhaps aside

---

*In case you're American and don't know what "wank" means, it's British slang for a daytime nap. When an English person seems tired or yawns, it's generally considered polite for you to ask him if he could use a good wank. Especially if he's a stranger.

from my generally frightening appearance, was the excess amount of Chardonnay of questionable quality the winery had on hand, hogging valuable tank space. A couple of days earlier Uncle B had used a tractor to smooth out the gravel driveway behind the presses, while Allan sprayed it down with water to help it set. He needed an extension for the hose and asked Josh to get him one. Then he said, "Forget it. We'll just use the Chardonnay." Though it was just a joke, it would certainly solve one problem, since it'd be easier to sell a porno mag to a blind guy than it was to sell juice in New Zealand that year.

The other problem was the weather, which broke in time for Easter weekend, though snow was still lingering on the mountaintops. Saturday saw the winery crush twenty tons of Chardonnay between 7:00 A.M. and 10:00 A.M., and about forty tons of Sauvignon Blanc after that. Everything went smoothly, so I wondered why Jeremy still had a look of concern on his face. I asked him what would put his mind at ease about how things were going.

"Another hundred thousand liters of tank space," he said before walking off.

Once the grapes were crushed, Josh and I went out to sample four different blocks of Sauvignon Blanc, and none of them were even close to being ripe enough for picking. The best was at 19 Brix, which would mean two or three more weeks on the vine at the very least. Fine with Allan, but not with Josh and Jeremy.

"It's about being patient and keeping an eye on it, planning and having a progress chart," Allan told me. "That's probably the most sensible thing you can do. We start firing from the hip, and we create so much more work downstream in terms of deacidifying and sugaring."

It turned out that much of the frustration Jeremy and Josh were experiencing around this time also had to do with the quality of work they were getting out of Marine and Frenchie. Me, well, they *expected* me to be useless. They weren't paying me. And I had no experience. Marine and Frenchie, however, had résumés claiming that they knew how to pump this juice to that tank, wash that barrel, and so forth. But what Josh and Jeremy were getting instead of good work was grief.

Frenchie, in particular, came to New Zealand and ASW claiming to have all sorts of experience, having worked vintages in Margaux, Pouilly, and on a moon orbiting Jupiter for all I know—probably why he was hired. However, his job in France was as a wine consultant, which means he knows what needs to be done, but doesn't have a clue how to do any of it. And we're not talking about difficult stuff here that you or I couldn't pick up after a couple of days—things like connecting this hose to that tank. Even though he'd been working at French wineries for about half a decade (and was very keen on letting people know that), on day one at ASW he was as useless as a writer from New York—only he was actually being paid. He had to be shown how to do everything, just as I did, yet at the end of the day he was still all high-and-mighty, claiming that he knew the right way to make wine.

"He tells other people what to do, but he's never actually done it himself," Josh told me. "I bet he thought he was gonna coast through vintage here," and it was pretty obvious on the first day that Frenchie did not like to get his hands or clothes dirty—he hadn't even brought work clothes with him from France. When he asked Josh for one of the free T-shirts a farm-supply company had dropped off for everyone, Josh said, "Sure . . . after you polish my throbbing member."

"Yes, yes," Frenchie responded.

"You understand *polish*?" Josh asked. "Polish my throbbing member?"

"Yes, yes."

"Good, polish my throbbing member, and I'll give you a T-shirt to work in."

"Okay, yes, yes."

Joking aside, Jeremy and Josh were putting in the extreme hours because they didn't feel confident enough in Marine's and Frenchie's abilities to trust them with crucial tasks. And they sure as hell weren't about to ask me to rack a tank at 2:00 A.M.

That's more or less why Marine and Frenchie were given all of Easter weekend off, as well as the following Monday, a national holiday. In their place was Peter, a thirteen-year-old Kiwi whose parents are old friends of the Scotts, so Allan agreed to give him work for the two-week break from school that came as part of the holiday. Easter Sunday was Peter's third full day on the job, and while I still hadn't graduated much beyond the crusher, Peter was already doing rackings by himself, as well as pumping over and plunging tanks of Pinot. Man, did I feel inferior.

"He's already more useful than the Frenchies," Josh told me, and Jeremy and Geoff nodded in agreement. I even saw Peter using the forklift to move barrel racks, with much greater speed and efficiency than I could. He was practically popping wheelies with the thing.

I'll show him, I thought to myself. *At least I'm old enough to drink*. So when we broke for lunch, I asked Peter what his favorite kind of wine is.

"Sauvignon Blanc," he said without hesitation, crushing my already humbled spirits. "I like the fruit flavors. I'm lucky if I get half a glass a week, though."

Sheesh. At thirteen I was just getting into baseball cards and being excited by the stick of gum (since I had yet to discover *Playboy*). This kid already knew how to rack a tank and drive a forklift with balls-on precision. I half expected him to give me dating advice next, as well as offer to polish up my résumé and reorganize my finances. "I think Pfizer's still a strong stock, even with Cialis hitting the market now," I was waiting for him to say between bites of his PB&J sandwich. "Your portfolio *is* diversified, isn't it?"

The following morning, the Monday after Easter, brought the warm, sunny weather that had blessed the region throughout most of March and the first week of April. Josh and I got an early start and headed straight out to the vineyards to do sampling. A small block of Gewürztraminer at the back of the Hounds vineyard, most of the Hounds Sauvignon Blanc, and a grower's block of Chardonnay were all ready, based on Josh's taste tests and the samples analyzed back at the lab. We then drove to the Omaka vineyard on which Josh's house sits, where the Sauvignon Blanc is broken into east and west blocks.

After we'd picked random bunches and punched them down in buckets with our fists, we tipped the juice into ziplock bags that we'd later bring back to the lab. I took a close look at the bunches as we were sampling, and I also tasted grapes along each row.

"What do you reckon?" Josh asked me.

"I think Omaka west is ready, but east needs more time," I said.

"You're starting to get the hang of this," Josh said as he nodded approval, and sure enough, back in the lab the Brix levels were just right on west, but low on east.

Okay, so I had a fifty-fifty shot of getting it right. And to tell the truth, I was guessing based on the fact that the grapes in the western block looked healthier and just tasted better. They weren't as sour. I didn't detect those tropical gooseberry and passion-fruit flavors everyone always talks about with Sauvignon Blanc, probably because I don't think I've ever had a gooseberry or a passion fruit. I don't think I even know anyone who has, now that I think about it. But the grapes just tasted good. Like grapes should taste. So while Josh may have been convinced for the moment that I was a step closer to learning how good wine is made, that didn't mean I was about to buy a block of land and start planting. I still had a ways to go.

Which is why, back at the winery, I was back on crusher duty. We crushed forty tons of Sauvignon Blanc and all eight tons of Gewürztraminer from the Hounds vineyard. Jeremy and Josh decided to let that load of grapes macerate in the press for six hours before pressing it off—which kept the two of them working until well after 1:00 A.M. that night.

During the day, however, they enacted their contingency plans. For starters, Jeremy and Josh ordered two tons of sugar, as there were two blocks of Sauvignon that Allan wanted picked, since the leaves were beginning to fall off the vines, which meant that the Brix levels weren't going to get higher than they already were. The day also saw the arrival of a new stainless-steel 15,000-liter tank, as well as two more plastic tanks. One was a green 20,000-liter tank, and the other was a 10,000-liter black tank that became known as Septic Steve.

Even though the tanks were made of plastic, getting them off the back of a truck wasn't easy.

"You play rugby?" the driver asked Josh, and he nodded.

"For who?" the driver asked, since rural New Zealand rugby is a lot like high school football in Texas—everyone follows it. It's the local religion, only more violent. I knew of at least two guys who nearly had an ear ripped off during the course of a match.

"Moutere," Josh responded.

"Reckon you can stop this thing as we roll it off?" the driver dared Josh, and started pushing the tank down the ramp off the back of the truck.

Josh was about to meet the dare and throw his shoulder into it (his "golden shoulder," as he calls it after a good game of rugby), but like an animal in a fight-or-flight situation, he bailed, backpedaling and backpedaling until Geoff and Jeremy jumped in to help him. It's a good thing they did, since the last thing ASW needed, with so much work left to do, was a flattened winemaker. It's the last thing I needed, too, since I was hoping to write a book with at least a *reasonably* happy ending.

Just as I was leaving for the night, while the Gewürztraminer was still pressing, Jeremy emerged from the lab and asked Josh, "Guess how many tons so far? Four hundred ninety-six."

"And there's still heaps out there," Josh said.

"I know," Jeremy said, grinning in response to Josh's formal acknowledgment of the increased pressure. "That's what worries me."

For years there's been this bravado thing about stamina and that you have to work horrendously long hours, but that doesn't make you a good winemaker. No one can make quality decisions when they're exhausted. You start to make serious mistakes.

—John Belsham, winemaker at Wairau River and
winemaker/owner of Foxes Island

8

Day of Minor Disasters

As I mentioned earlier, at a winery there's a tendency to get complacent when things are going well. Because there are so many things that can go wrong, you get this wonderful sense of satisfaction when everything's running smoothly, as if you're the director of a big-budget action thriller, keeping multiple yet equally crucial tasks running simultaneously and harmoniously. James Cameron can kiss your ass.

Better yet, I like to think of it as juggling knives. You get three Wusthofs going in the air, catching and flinging them up again perfectly for several minutes. It's going so well that it feels automatic, as if you don't even have to think about it. You look incredibly cool. You are one with the knives. They're an extension of your hands. But the instant that your mind wanders or you accidentally fling just slightly too hard or too high, or try to catch a fraction of a second too early, well, you start to rethink your career choice.

Same goes with winemaking, more or less (only without the emotionally traumatized spectators), and ASW had one of those smooth, sunny sessions in mid-April. The day wasn't entirely without flaw, but nothing happened that Jeremy and Josh couldn't live with. The one thing I did see, though, was another small battle of opinions between the winery and vineyard crews.

Sauvignon Blanc started to arrive at 8:00 A.M., and continued to roll in for the next few hours. Once the big press was full, however, there were still five tons of uncrushed grapes in the bin.

"Fuck!" Jeremy screamed, since he couldn't push the remainder of the grapes into the small press—it was already scheduled to handle ten tons of Chardonnay coming later in the day. What he and Josh would have to do instead was start squeezing what was already inside the press to make room for the remaining five tons. This essentially means mixing a substantial amount of free-run juice with pressings, which Jeremy's expletive clearly indicated he did not want to do.

He wasn't swearing at himself or his own miscalculation, however. He was cursing Uncle B. "He knows how much room we have, and how much is on the block," Jeremy told me, "so he'll try to squeeze in an extra three tons." And this time he'd tried to squeeze in a bit too much.

In other words, the vineyard crew does not like being at the mercy of the winery, and they'll turn the tables if it looks as though they might be inconvenienced in some way. And if you ask any of the vineyard crew, they'll tell you that they work harder than the winemakers. At some wineries that may be true, but it isn't at ASW—everybody works hard. Nevertheless, Uncle B believes it with such conviction that he will do pretty much anything in his power to prevent his crew from working harder or longer than he feels they should. And in this particular case, picking beyond what he'd been asked to meant Uncle B's not having to send his boys back to the same block to pick more grapes later. Instead, the problem was handed off to the winery. You can return the pair of jeans that make your ass look too big, but Josh and Jeremy couldn't exactly tell the vineyard crew to put the grapes back on the vines. Nevertheless, this just seemed to be a regular frustration on an otherwise normal day, similar to the way Eminem and his wife can't seem to live with or without each other.

The Wusthof fell through the proverbial hand two days later.

The morning started innocently enough. Trying to repeat the success of their '03 Riesling (which had received a five-star rating from *Cuisine*—New Zealand's version of *Food & Wine* magazine—and sold out relatively quickly thereafter), Jeremy and Josh decided that to make the wine taste similar in '04 they'd need to let the first fourteen tons of grapes macerate in the large press and give them some good skin-contact time. (What exactly this does to the end product is open to some debate. There are some in Marlborough who swear by it and those who shy away from it. Mike and Claire Allan at Huia pride themselves on making food-friendly wine, which they believe comes from crushing very lightly and avoiding oxidation and maceration in the press. Al Soper at Highfield takes it a step further, and only uses free-run juice; the winery sells off all its pressings to other wineries. Nobilo's Darryl Woolley, on the other hand, discovered several years ago when he worked at Corbans, then one of New Zealand's large wine companies, that the reason his wines developed such strong fruit characters and richness was that the grapes were being trucked to the North Island for processing, and the juice was gaining all its desirable properties from skin contact in the back of the truck during its eighteen-hour journey.)

The first nine and a half tons went into the press without a hitch, and the next five and a half should have been just as easy. But the ports on the press through which the free-run juice normally drains out weren't pointed directly up as they should have been, so juice began to slowly run out and into the juice tub. Jeremy corrected the problem by turning the press's ports up, then disconnected the juice tub so he could bring it around and tip its contents into the must pump so the juice would go right back into the press. The tub only contained about fifty or sixty liters of juice, which wasn't much, but was still heavy enough that he couldn't simply lift the tub and tip out the juice. So Jeremy left the hose connected to the bottom of the tub and decided to let the juice drain out through it and into the must pump—but that wasn't working, either, so I stopped the must pump for the moment. Jeremy realized that he had to come up with a new plan and told me to start crushing again.

Unfortunately, from where Jeremy stood he couldn't see that the hose was still sitting in the must pump, and I thought that he was in the process of pulling it out. So rather than reach down and pull out the hose myself, or turn around to see if Jeremy was indeed pulling the hose out as I suspected, I simply switched the pump on again. Instantly, the pump began to pull in the hose with a ferocity I didn't know the must pump even had. It's such a smooth-running machine that, even when running at full speed, it looks relatively harmless.

Now this heavy, expensive piece of equipment was lurching and flailing around as if it were in the middle of an epileptic seizure, grunting with all its might as it tried to smash a one-inch-diameter heavy-duty hose with a stainless-steel fitting as if it were one bitch of a grape.

I slapped the emergency stop button on the pump's control panel just as

Jeremy screamed, "STOP!" but the damage was already done. The must pump had an inch-long dent on the inside of its basin—amazing considering that it's made of quarter-inch-thick stainless steel. And the pump had worked so hard at crushing and pushing through the hose that it actually managed to contort and twist itself. The pump would make it through the rest of the harvest, but instead of calmly pushing must through the hose and into the press, it would wobble back and forth unattractively with each turn of its auger, and even work a bit slower than before—almost like that guy on the other side of town who hasn't been the same since "the accident." (Marlborough has its fair share of those, and for some reason their debit cards always seemed to get declined when they came into Bar Navajo for a drink.)

The hose was even more unlucky than the pump. Its fitting looked as though someone had taken a giant bite out of it.

"Well, that one's fucked," Jeremy said as he gave it a quick postmortem examination.

"Uh, sorry," I said meekly. Before I could beg and plead to not be thrown out on my ass, Jeremy just shrugged his shoulders and said, "Hey, better a hose than a person."

Never again for the rest of the harvest did I put my hand anywhere near the must pump while it was running. Seeing what it had done to the steel hose fitting—and itself—made me realize that even in its wounded state, the must pump would show me, or any part of my body that got too close to it, no mercy whatsoever. Every time I had to add sulfur or anything else to the must, I was conscious of the power that was built into the pump for it to make a relatively big task look extraordinarily easy. I also hoped that I would be long gone from the winery and New Zealand when it came time for the winery to buy a new must pump, and Allan started looking for someone to blame—and send a bill to—for the unexpected cost.

Shortly after the incident we got the crusher and must pump going again, but before we got too far, the press announced that it was full, not just with the usual wail of its siren, but by juice shooting out of the upward-facing portals. I wondered how this was possible, because it's a thirty-five-ton-capacity press, and we'd pushed in just over ten tons to that point.

"Yeah, but no juice is flowing out," Geoff reminded me. "When no juice is flowing out, a thirty-five-ton press becomes a ten-ton press like that," he said as he snapped his fingers. At this point, Jeremy unwillingly decided to let some of the juice run off and into the tank.

After he'd done that he wanted to make a little more room in the press for the remaining grapes. All that's required to do this is to rotate the press, which Josh and Jeremy did a couple of times, and then ordered me to start crushing again. But they gave me the green light without having reset the press to its fill mode, which opens its intake valve and allows more grapes to flow in. So I turned on the crusher and must pump again, and for a few seconds the pressure in the hose just built up, built up, and built up until—

BOOM!

The hose went shooting off the must pump like a rocket, a stream of green, sludgy grapes behind it like a vapor trail. The repair job and reaffixing the hose to its fitting and the must pump took Josh and Geoff about half an hour, and I was able to get the crusher going and the press filled shortly thereafter. In all, a crush of just over five tons of grapes, which should have taken the winery about twenty minutes, instead took two hours and caused a couple thousand dollars in damage.

I've heard that in pro sports they call it "quicksand." You start to make one mistake after another, and you sink faster and faster until you feel like you can't breathe anymore. I have no idea what they call it at a winery, but I don't care so long as they don't name it after me. Which they probably would've had the right to do, considering that the day was only half over at that point.

In the early evening, it came time to separate a couple of tanks of Pinot from their skins, as they'd finished fermenting. As I explained in Chapter 2, this involves putting a screen on top of the juice tub and resting it just below the door to the tank. A short hose is connected to a valve on the tank so the wine can flow onto the screen and into the juice tub. The screen catches any skins that happen to make it out of the hose, and from the bottom of the juice tub the wine is pumped to another tank. Once all the wine is out, someone jumps into the top of the tank with a shovel and starts scooping the skins out the door and into a half-ton bin. Using the forklift, the bin is brought over to the press and the skins are tipped into the top. Once they're all in, the skins are squeezed to recover any wine they may have soaked up.

Of course, running several thousand liters of wine out of a one-inch hose from the tank can take a while, so to make it all go a bit faster Josh employed a technique that he learned from a cellar hand when he worked in Napa. He took a long piece of cellophane wrap and put it around the edges of the tank door. As he and I slowly loosened the hinges on the door, any wine that slipped out the cracks on the top or sides of the door simply hit the cellophane and drizzled down into the juice tub.

With Marine handling the hose and keeping an eye on the pump, Josh and I began slowly loosening the hinges to the door. I noticed that the hinge on Josh's side was a few turns ahead of mine—almost completely off its bolt. What I didn't notice, however, was that he was using his shoulder to keep the door closed, so as I loosened the bolt on my side to even it up with his, I went a turn too far. And the skins from 8,000 liters of Pinot Noir began to avalanche onto us.

Fortunately, Josh and I didn't back away, and we pressed on the door as hard as we could to secure the bolts back in place and stem the flow. It only took us a few seconds, but Pinot Noir was spilling on the ground the whole time, making that part of the winery look like a South Bronx crime scene.

"Did you mean to do that?" Josh asked me once we got the door closed, almost as if the day's follies added up to a conspiracy in his mind. Then he just shook it off, saying, "Eh, it's one good way to get rid of some Pinot," something the winery had more than enough of on hand, and would likely have trouble selling off. I still felt guilty, however, so I offered to jump in and shovel out the skins. It's not exactly the safest or most popular of tasks, but I actually found it to be pretty fun work. At first the CO_2 gives you a bit of a buzz, and you find yourself working faster and harder. It becomes more and more difficult to breathe, and your lungs will only take in so much air at a time. Eventually, you have to either climb out the top or, once you've shoveled out enough skins, stick your head out the door of the tank to get some fresh air. I won't be surprised if years from now, Josh admits to me that on that night he was tempted to just shut the door while I was inside the tank.

It took me another forty-five minutes or so to clean up the mess I'd made, which Josh assured me was only about one hundred liters of wine lost—less than half a barrel. "Red wine always looks worse than it is," he told me of spills such as this. "And once you've hosed it all down, it never happened."

As much of a relief as Josh's words might have provided, they didn't boost my self-confidence any. I left the winery late and went to bed that night feeling as though I couldn't even order a glass of wine in a restaurant without completely screwing up, much less do the easy jobs around a winery without playing some small part in the day's blunders. The real test, I thought to myself, would be avoiding making any more of them as the hours and workload increased even more.

You start out slowly and sort of build up and build up to this crescendo. Once you get there you just keep going and going for a few weeks, and then all of a sudden it just stops. There's nothing left, and you don't know what to do with yourself.

—JAMES HEALY, WINEMAKER AT DOG POINT

9

High Tensions
and Unexpected Relief

April dragged on, and by the last week of the month the only consolation for me in the daily grind of crushing forty, fifty, or eighty tons of grapes was the warm, sunny weather nearly every day. Jeremy and Josh, on the other hand, no longer noticed the difference between sunshine and darkness, since they'd been working from 7:00 A.M. until about 2:00 A.M. each and every day, including weekends, for three weeks straight. They looked like the backup zombie dancers in Michael Jackson's "Thriller" video. As a result, I thought it best to stay out of their way as much as possible, just do what I was told, and not get involved where I didn't need to be. Gerald learned that lesson for me.

At the beginning of the final week of April, the winery got a late start, since one of the pumps was broken and rackings needed to be done to make room for the grapes on their way to the winery. So the first load of Sauvignon Blanc grapes was already in the bin long before a pump was even available, much less a tank in which to put all the juice. We had just started crushing the first load of the forty tons that would come in that day when Gerald arrived with the second, and made the offhand comment to Jeremy that the winery didn't seem particularly well prepared that morning.

Jeremy went absolutely apeshit in response.

"I've only got two working pumps and I've got rackings to do!" Jeremy screamed at his elder. The rest was drowned out by the background noise generated by the gentle roar of the forklifts and the rumble of the crusher-destemmer, almost like network-television bleeps, but from what I could tell, Jeremy's tirade concluded with something along the lines of, "I've got *roaring* problems here that you know nothing about, so shut the *rumble* up!" I was pretty sure that I made out the f-bomb at least three times. The only other time I saw him that fired up was on the rugby field (actually, fists always seemed to fly just a bit more when he was on the field than when he was on the bench).

Gerald's not a confrontational guy, and he never should have opened his mouth in the first place, but it's easy to see why he felt compelled to do so—and why Jeremy lashed out in response. Gerald's job during harvest is simple: Deliver the grapes and get back to the vineyard for the next load, which is being harvested as he brings in the load he has to drop off. But the gondola chasing the harvester can only hold so many grapes, so if Gerald's running late getting back to the vineyard with the truck, Ra and Terry have to stop picking because they have nowhere to dump their grapes. Gerald gets dirty looks from Ra and Terry for holding them up, and he gets an earful from Uncle B. But Gerald's really caught in the middle, since he can't just dump the grapes on the ground at the winery and go back to the vineyard and get more.

Ugly as the confrontation may have been to watch, at least the winery and vineyard were communicating. I've actually heard of wineries where the winemakers and viticulturists rarely even talk to one another—the "you do your job and I'll do mine" approach. But things would get worse the next day.

The winery started by crushing and pressing forty tons of Chardonnay, the last of it from the 2004 harvest (I asked Jeremy if he was happy to be done with it, and he said, "I'd be happier to see it leaving here on a truck," since the last thing the winery needed at this point was more Chardonnay). I spent most of the morning running back and forth between the crusher, where I was processing the Chardonnay, and some Pinot barrels I was filling. Once the Chardonnay was done pressing and the Pinot barrels were full, forty tons of Riesling showed up, and again, Jeremy and Josh wanted to leave some of it in the press to macerate, which of course meant that it would take longer to process. And then long after the sun had set—and I and most everyone else was excused for the evening—Jeremy and Josh decided to bring in another twenty tons of Sauvignon Blanc.

"Fuckin' assholes," Ra said of Jeremy and Josh the following day, even though the three are close friends. "We were tipping the last bin of the day when they told us they wanted another twenty tons, and the harvester was out of fuel." He and Terry had to go get it gassed up (which takes a while, since a grape harvester doesn't go particularly fast, and the winery isn't exactly around the corner from a 7-11 where you can get a Slurpee and flip through a dog-eared *Penthouse* while you wait for the tank to fill). Terry had also made plans with his kids, and instead had to call his ex-wife and arrange for her to pick them up. "Fucking assholes think we're at their expense," Ra fumed to me.

When I caught up with Ra he was behind Josh's house with a picking crew, harvesting the winery's first-ever crop of Merlot. (ASW had purchased Merlot grapes in the past, but not for a few years.) It was a small load off maybe a dozen rows of vines, and all the grapes were being loaded into big bins. There was no one available to bring the grapes to the winery to be crushed, so I hopped into the flatbed truck and drove it from the winery to the vineyard. When I got there I used a forklift to put the bin on the back of the truck, strapped it down, drove it back to the winery, pulled it off with another forklift, and drove back to the vineyard to get the next load. As I drove the truck back to the winery with the fourth and final load of grapes, I looked at my hands on the steering wheel, and noticed that they were dark and leathery, and that my fingernails had been black for a couple of weeks. It was then that I realized that only two months before I had no idea how to operate a forklift, much less strap a heavy load securely to a flatbed truck or even drive on the left side of the road. For the first time, I actually felt like I knew what I was doing. But by this point I was also smart enough not to congratulate myself, since each new day at a winery during harvest brings bigger challenges and problems I wouldn't have a clue how to handle.

The following morning I arrived at the winery to find big tankers into which Jeremy, Josh, and Jemma were pumping thousands of liters of Chardonnay and Sauvignon Blanc that had been sold off to a large wine company on the North Island. It was only 8:00 A.M., and already Josh and Jeremy were stressed out and yelling at each other. Because there was so much juice to go around, "Selling Chardonnay at this point is like trying to sell someone a dead rat dressed up as high-quality lamb," Josh opined later in the day. "But Sauvignon Blanc *could* be a dead rat, and someone would still buy it."

Once all the juice was pumped and the tanks gone, I asked Jeremy if he and Josh were cranky because they'd pulled yet another late night.

"Nah," he said with a sense of calm and relief in his voice. "They wanted the juice right away, and we needed to clear tank space for the juice coming in and the RDV juice. The logistics make it stressful."

Add to that the fact that one of the sold-off tanks of juice was just starting to ferment, something it shouldn't have been doing until after it arrived at its destination, where a winemaker would inoculate the juice when he or she felt the time was right. So Jeremy was chucking in as much sulfur as he could to make sure the process wouldn't fully kick in. But the tanks got caught up in a series of transit errors and wound up arriving at their destination long after they should have. So fermentation had gotten under way, which didn't make the buyer particularly happy, but because of the juice's accidentally circuitous journey, Jeremy and Josh were able to deflect the blame. And whoever bought the juice obviously wanted it badly enough that it wasn't worth arguing about.

Selling juice and fruit between wineries is very common in New Zealand, and there are countless tangles in this web. But what it all boils down to is each winery trying to achieve a style that reflects its brand or meets its demand. On a large scale, this means that a big winery like Montana or Nobilo can buy juice that's not really up to snuff, not because they make worse wine, but simply because they make more of it. So if Montana has, say, one million liters of Chardonnay and wants more, adding 20,000 liters of Chardonnay that ASW or some other winery isn't happy with won't affect the quality at all, but will increase the volume significantly. It's like making coffee for a big dinner party when you only have five pounds of the premium stuff on hand. So you brew up a pot of instant coffee and add it to the premium stuff so you have enough coffee for everyone. You've blended away the less-desirable coffee, and no one will taste the difference.

At ground level, though, it can get somewhat complicated, with grapes and even entire vineyards being turned over regularly. ASW, for example, buys most of its Pinot Noir from two different contract growers. But ASW also grows its own Pinot at the Omaka and Hounds vineyards and then sells off much of the fruit to other wineries. After the harvest, though, ASW decided to sell the Hounds vineyard, but agreed that it would buy the grapes grown there in the future. The winery then used the money from that sale to buy the Cairnbrae vineyard next to Allan's house. So essentially ASW sold off one vineyard to buy another, but still gets the grapes from both.

It also comes down to marketing and branding. Because the ASW '03 Riesling was so acclaimed, the distributors and even the winery ran out of it practically overnight. Knowing that they couldn't get the '04 wine ready quickly enough to meet demand, ASW found a Nelson winery with some top-quality Riesling of its own that it couldn't sell, because there isn't a big market either for Nelson wine in general or for that particular brand. But it tasted very similar to ASW's '03 Riesling, so the winery bought it, bottled it, labeled it as "vineyard select" instead of Marlborough, and easily sold it all in a matter of weeks because it had the Allan Scott name on the outside of the bottle.

So much juice moves up, down, and around New Zealand every day that I thought I should go see one of the people who manages it all, Lyall Burrows at Tranzlink, one of the country's largest trucking and shipping companies. Tranzlink handles about 80 percent of all wine shipped in and out of Marlborough in a given year and constantly has to change and adapt to the different wineries' needs. In the middle of our conversation Lyall's cell phone rang, and it was Montana asking if he could move 250,000 liters of wine up to Auckland the following day. No problem. "Last week we moved eight hundred thousand liters out of here in four days, which is pretty damn good, to be honest," Lyall proclaimed proudly as he turned off his phone. "So long as we've got the tanks here, someone can ring up now, and we can start moving it out tomorrow.

"You've got wineries that do contract work, that specifically crush grapes for, say, an Auckland winery," Lyall explained to me at his office just a couple days after the last juice from 2004 had been shipped out of Marlborough. "But you've also got wineries, like Allan Scott, for example, that might have more Sauvignon Blanc or more Pinot than they want and will sell it to another winery." They call Lyall, and soon thereafter a Tranzlink tanker truck arrives, the juice is pumped into the tank, and off goes the truck.

Lyall has to be flexible, which probably explains why he looks perpetually tired and stressed, even if he isn't on that particular day. He's a round, gray-haired guy who doesn't look very excitable. But he speaks with incredible enthusiasm for his work, almost like that guy who's just a little too happy about being invited to the cool-kids' party. However, he loves being a part of the excitement of the wine business as much as he does coming up with solutions to the wineries' problems. Lyall can even arrange it so handpicked bunches of grapes are collected in large bins out in the vineyard, refrigerated, trucked to the port, put on a boat, then put on a train. The grapes arrive the next morning at a winery in Auckland (250 miles away), intact and still cold—and ready to be crushed.

But there are also everyday disasters Lyall has to deal with, like the one in 2004, when a train derailed on the North Island, sending a 20,000-liter tank of juice tumbling off the tracks. "The trains stopped behind it because the whole line was blocked," Lyall recalled with a shake of his head. "We had to get a crane in and put the tank up on a truck, and drive it straight to Auckland." Of course, there was a backup of trains behind the derailment, leaving other tanks of juice sitting on the tracks for about twenty hours. "We couldn't get the empty tanks back to Blenheim and we couldn't get the full ones to Auckland. So we had a twenty-four-hour period where it was rather chaotic trying to keep stuff moving."

Fortunately, Tranzlink tanks are pretty sturdy, and not a single drop was lost out of the 20,000-liter tank that derailed.

Sometimes there are delays and accidents, but the reason Lyall is good at what he does is that he, too, makes wine—fifty liters of Merlot per year in his laundry room, something he started doing simply because he wanted to have a better understanding of the winemakers' needs, so he could do his own job better.

"It gives me an understanding that I'm competent enough to know what I'm talking about," he told me. "My father is ninety, and he's been making homemade wine for seventy years. I used to help Dad pick grapes and boysenberries and make wine at home. But it never really rubbed off on me until I moved to Marlborough." When I met Lyall his Merlot was sitting in a small steel keg with a bag of oak chips floating inside it.

"It's average wine, but I'm quite happy with it," he said. "I have a very basic understanding of winemaking and what [the winemakers] require, which I think is very helpful in my job. I know what these guys want from their product, so I make sure that we move their wine in pristine condition."

On that day in late April, just as Jeremy finished explaining why stress levels were so high and the Tranzlink tankers had left the winery, the first load of forty tons of Sauvignon Blanc showed up. Once Geoff and I had filled the last available 33,000-liter tank with juice, there was nowhere to put the rest. There were a few small, 1,300-liter tanks available, but we'd fill each one in a matter of minutes and still have plenty of juice left over. As it happened, however, someone had just finished a racking, freeing a 10,000-liter tank into which we could pump the rest of the juice. Another racking or two was performed, freeing another 33,000-liter tank for the rest of the Riesling, which Jeremy and Josh decided that they wanted to bring in then and there.

As the last of the Riesling was pressing, at about eleven-thirty that night, I asked Jeremy what time he expected us in the next day.

"That's pretty much it," he said, and shrugged his shoulders.

There were still more than one hundred tons of grapes left on the vines of a few different white varieties, but Allan had sold them all off to the Montana winery. The ASW vineyard crew would do the harvesting and dump the fruit into Montana's trucks—it would never come near Allan's winery. A few more small loads would come into ASW here and there over the next couple of weeks, but nothing that the winery couldn't handle without me, much less Frenchie or even Marine (Jeremy told me that Frenchie's work had improved dramatically since a series of screwups, but as the workload died down, he and Josh cut Frenchie loose and kept Marine—who had proven to be a good worker, and was also much nicer to look at—for a couple of weeks to help Jemma in the lab before she, too, would return home to France).

There were some other wineries still harvesting, simply because the soils and microclimates in small areas determine when the grapes in different vineyards will ripen. The leaves were already turning yellow in ASW's vineyards, but when I went to see Darryl Woolley over at Nobilo, only a couple of miles away, he told me that he still had two weeks to go. He even pointed out the window to alert me to the fact that all his leaves were still bright green. In the colder and drier Awatere Valley, just south of the Wairau but still considered part of Marlborough, many vineyards Josh and I drove through still had their fruit hanging. Over the next few weeks many of those grapes would be trucked along the one twisty and windy road to the wineries in the Wairau.

But ASW was done for the year, and I was suddenly hit with a feeling that was more dread than relief. Even though I hated being cold and wet, I'd come to rely on that Sisyphean sense of despair I got each time I'd finished crushing a load of grapes just in time for Gerald to show up with another. My reason for getting out of bed every day hinged on a single thing: crushing grapes.

And with no grapes left to pick and crush, I simply felt empty. It was then that I realized that for the past several weeks I'd been in the zone, caught up in the excitement of the harvest. Though I was drinking relatively little wine during that time (though I probably should have been), the passion for creating it had consumed me. Now I felt as though I'd just been served with divorce papers.

With the 2004 harvest at its end, I didn't feel like drinking wine to celebrate. I actually felt depressed—useless even. I had nothing to do.

The final product has to be the most important thing, but how you get there is not just a destination—it's a journey, too.

—Mike Just, winemaker at Lawson's Dry Hills and owner/winemaker at Clayridge

------

10

The Respected and Admired

With free time all of a sudden in much more abundant supply (in this case, the very day after most of the harvesting was done), Allan and his winemakers took the opportunity to see how their wines stacked up against the competition. But it's not about sitting around staring at sales charts or developing marketing materials. It's about taste.

What pretty much every winery does to evaluate itself is take one or two bottles of its own wines and put them each in a paper bag in a lineup of nine or ten other wines, also in paper bags. At ASW, Allan, Jeremy, Josh, and Jemma sit around a table and try each one and then share all their notes with each other. Once they've all spoken their minds, the bags are ripped off and the labels revealed. And the results are often very interesting.

In a lineup of ten Chardonnays, everyone raved about the first one, and I have to admit, I liked it as well, even though I'm not much of a Chardonnay drinker. It turned out to be ASW's own '03 Chardonnay. So I guess you could argue that they'd made something that suited their own collective taste. But by the time they got to their own reserve Chardonnay, called Prestige, they were shockingly disappointed. It tasted as though it had started to fall apart in the bottle, and Allan just shook his head when the label was revealed.

"They should be improving. That's what they were designed for," he complained. By the end of the tasting he concluded, "We have to go back to the drawing board on viticulture."

The only other wine that truly stood out was the '03 Chardonnay from St. Clair, made by Matt Thomson. And everyone in the room pretty much panned the third wine in the lineup as unexceptional, and it turned out to be Cloudy Bay.

If Cloudy Bay, the most famous winery in New Zealand, got thumbs-down from the people at ASW (and Jemma worked at Cloudy Bay before moving across the street), it made me wonder just what a winemaker has to do to earn the respect of his or her colleagues. So I started asking Marlborough's winemakers who among their colleagues impressed them as exceptional, and why.

There were more than a few names that came up whenever I asked that question of a winemaker, but some came up more than others, like Mike and Claire Allan at Huia, Kevin Judd at Cloudy Bay, James Healy of Dog Point, Mike Just of Lawson's (as well as for his gravity-fed, nonirrigated Pinot project, Clayridge), Matt Thomson, and Brian Bicknell of Seresin. The one who came up most of all, however, was Hatsch Kalberer, winemaker for the Fromm Winery.

Fromm was set up by Georg and Ruth Fromm of Switzerland, who happened to be traveling through New Zealand several years ago as they searched for long-lost relatives of theirs who had emigrated. Somewhere along the way they met Hatsch, who is from the village next to that of the Fromms, and even though Hatsch worked several harvests for a relative of Georg and Ruth's, he had never met them. When their paths did cross, Hatsch was making wine at Matawhero, a small North Island winery.

Hatsch came to New Zealand during the Cold War and took whatever jobs he could find, picking apples or pruning vines. Long before that he'd discovered that the only reason he ever worked was so that he could have enough money to travel and drink wine. So unlike most of Marlborough's other winemakers, who did the extra schooling or studied botany or biochemistry, Hatsch just worked his way up from illegal immigrant to respected winemaker because he had a love affair with wine. Within a year of meeting Hatsch, the Fromms had decided to buy some land in Marlborough and put Hatsch in charge.

"We came to Marlborough with the desire to have a red wine in the middle of Sauvignon Blanc country," soft-spoken Hatsch told me one morning as we sat at the kitchen table in his house, almost smack-dab in the middle of the vineyard, and right next to the winery itself. It's not set up this way purely because Hatsch wanted to be close to everything. That's just one small part of it.

"The property is two hundred meters wide," he explained to me, "and we've got a middle headland rather than just going straight through because a row should never be more than one hundred meters long, because people work better that way. It's demoralizing to work in long rows. The quality goes down. People who are happy and don't feel demoralized in the vineyard work better, and you get better-quality wines. With shorter rows, it's let's just finish it—let's get something done. You see progress. You see you're getting somewhere."

You'd think that such a statement would come from someone who has an MBA or even just looks like he does. Hatsch, on the other hand, looks like he never left Switzerland—or the seventies, for that matter. His legs are pale, long, and skinny, which one can't help but notice because he often wears short shorts and work boots, making his lower extremities look like matchsticks with heads at both ends. He also has long, poofy hair that's straight off the cover of an ABBA* album, and he has a handlebar mustache and pointy goatee that almost look sinister. In short, he's only a costume change away from climbing up a mountain every morning and shouting, "Reeeeeeeee-co-laaaaaaaaa!"

But he's ridiculously serious about the wines he makes. He puts European attention and detail into New Zealand wine, handpicking everything and processing only about one hundred tons of grapes per year (as opposed to more than ten times that at ASW). Any growth the winery considers is aimed only at improving quality, not volume. Fromm is so careful with its fruit that Hatsch's assistant winemaker, Willy Hoare, once joked to me, "When we crush each bunch, it's 'Goodbye, Doris. So long, Fred,' " he said as he pantomimed gently petting each bunch of grapes.

What I really like about Hatsch, though, is how honest he is about his work and the wine being made around him. With the few bouts of rough weather here and there and Josh questioning the quality of ASW's fruit, I

---

*Yes, I know ABBA was Swedish, not Swiss . . . but both cultures are equally funny, for some reason.

wondered how it was possible that everyone else could be telling me what an undeniably great year it was. Hatsch gave me the answer.

"If someone is honest to the press here, sometimes they really get told off by the other winemakers. You don't tell the truth," he admitted to me. "You either say nothing or you say something good. We had a horrible '95 vintage, and one winery here was honest and told everyone exactly what it was, and everyone was up in arms. But you can't fool people that much. It was horrible, and everyone knew it. The public is not all that stupid. I think in the end you're gaining more credibility if you reserve judgment and you say, 'The fruit is clean, and we'll give it time.'"

So he wasn't willing to give me a complete assessment of how he thought the 2004 vintage had gone for Fromm.

"I can possibly say the Riesling is great," he said, and I believed him once I tasted it out of the tank—even though the wine wasn't stable or even filtered yet. "And the rest I don't think we'll be disappointed. But I don't think you should hype it up. If it's good at the end, the wine will sell. If it only sells because we tell bullshit, eventually no one believes you.

"When we got the 2002 vintage in I was very excited—this is better than '01. And after a year or so in the cellar, no matter how dark and impressive they were, it was a bit superficial because a lot fell out in the barrel. It was clearly not as good a vintage as 2001. That's not to say anything bad—just to be realistic."

More than his honesty, one also has to appreciate Hatsch's simplistic approach to making wine. Even the winery itself is pretty bare-bones, with astoundingly less equipment and fewer tanks than you'd find at most others. In fact, the one thing he seemed most excited about at the moment wasn't a new tank, pump, or other expensive piece of equipment. It was simply a metal rack on which the cellar hands could hang tools and valves to keep clutter off the ground.

"We're not trying to reinvent the wheel," he said as he showed me around the small winery. "One of the most important things is knowing when to leave it alone."

But the most important thing to know about Hatsch is that when he makes wine he's never thinking of himself, the Fromms, or his own bank account. He's thinking about you. He's making wines that he wants you to enjoy on a special occasion. Fromm wines are never entered in shows or judging; Hatsch wants your approval, not that of the experts. Fromm wines cost more, but you know that it's Hatsch's blood, sweat, and tears that went into making them (or Willy's—when I mentioned to him that winemaking is what keeps Hatsch awake at night, Willy corrected me: "No, it keeps *me* awake at night, because when Hatsch thinks of something at 2:00 A.M., he calls *me*").

When Hatsch isn't sure about his own wine, he puts it to the test against the best. He puts a bottle of his wine in a paper bag alongside some of the best Pinots from Burgundy and invites over fellow winemakers James Healy or Hans Herzog (who specializes in Merlot-Cabernet blends) to taste the lineup and give him an honest opinion. "If our wine stands out as too this or too that, then we know we've got to do something. But if it's absolutely enjoyable, then you know you don't need to do anything. I always have wine over here"—meaning thirty feet away from the winery, in his house—"before I bottle it in the winery. Have it with dinner to make sure these wines are not just nice when you drink them in the winery. They have to go with food; they have to be enjoyable."

Now why Hatsch invites over Hans Herzog and James Healy, I can understand. A tall, dark, imposing figure, Hans is soft-spoken and shy, possibly because he has wine on the brain 24-7. If you're not convinced of this purely by the fact that Hans is usually impossible to track down, since he's always hidden in the vineyard working (he doesn't even have a cell phone), you will be once you've seen his tiny winery, clearly designed and constructed by a perfectionist who wanted to be left alone for the assembly of his masterpieces. Similarly, James Healy and Ivan Sutherland set up Dog Point a few years ago simply because they wanted to make small batches of good wine and do everything themselves in their small, hidden winery. "What we've done is gone completely to a hands-off style, which is basically just pressing it off, putting it into barrels, and leaving it," James told me of his approach. "To me, making wine is about taking grapes and making a wine that's typical of the region it's grown in and the season it was grown in."

Ask James, however, whom he respects and admires in Marlborough, and while he will mention Hatsch, the first name that comes out of his mouth is that of Kevin Judd, of Cloudy Bay, with whom he worked for more than a decade. "I think the most important thing is that Kevin is still there, because he's been there since the beginning," James said of Cloudy Bay. Hell, ask thirty winemakers in Marlborough, and at least half will tell you that the reason Cloudy Bay is still on top is Kevin. I have no idea why, though, because the remainder either say outright that they don't rate his wines, or simply don't mention Kevin at all as one of Marlborough's best.

This became even more confounding when I actually sat down with Kevin, who, at least upon my first few encounters with him, was about as animated as a two-by-four. Cloudy Bay was the first New Zealand winery to gain international attention, and it put Marlborough Sauvignon Blanc on the map, so to speak. As a result, the price per bottle skyrocketed, and the winery was eventually acquired by luxury-brand holding company LVMH Moët Hennessy Louis Vuitton. Cloudy Bay is to New Zealand wine what Ford is to the Detroit auto industry, yet at the helm of the winery is a man who's shy, doesn't bestow trust easily, says little, and thinks long and hard before he actually does utter a single word. (Listening to the tape after I'd interviewed him, I counted twenty full seconds of silence after I'd asked him a question, before he gave a two-sentence response.) You have to meet him several times before he allows you a glimpse of him smiling or laughing. Yet everyone who works at Cloudy Bay seems to adore Kevin as if he turned water into wine long before that other guy did.

Personally, I think that he was in the right place at the right time and happened to catch on with the right people—which, admittedly, does take as much skill as it does luck. And given the roster of Cloudy Bay employees past and present, Kevin is clearly very smart about with whom he chooses to work. But that doesn't change the fact that when Kevin showed up in Marlborough he admitted to Cathy Scott that he didn't know how to prune a vine (even after a few years of making wine in Australia and three more with Selaks on the North Island). And for a real giggle, check out page 215 of *Wine Atlas of New Zealand,* by Auckland-based wine critic Michael Cooper. Look closely at the portrait of Kevin taken in his office, looking stone-faced and serious, and you'll notice in the background that he neglected to take down a photo of his wife, lying topless on the beach with a couple coconuts covering her boobs. Rumor has it there's also a naked picture of him—taken at a Cloudy Bay party that got a little out of hand—floating around that he offered copious amounts of money to get out of social circulation. No price was high enough—apparently the photo is *that* good. As in, it'd make Tommy Lee blush.

Despite all this, however, one can't deny what Cloudy Bay is: the most famous winery in its corner of the world, one whose products get snatched off store shelves as soon as they become available, no matter the cost. And Kevin's been the winemaker from the very beginning. Cloudy Bay may have an air of prestige to it, but back in the cellar and in the vineyards the people who work there are as laid back as anyone, and have been known to throw some of the sickest parties for themselves and others—because that's the sort of atmosphere that Kevin supposedly provides.*

Sure enough, at the end of the vintage a couple of people from Highfield put together a big party they called Harvest Moon, which featured a concert by popular Wellington funk band the Black Seeds. And there, swaying and rocking back and forth in the middle of a sea of dancing vintage workers half his age, was Kevin Judd, drink in hand, cigarette in mouth. I realized then and there that whatever is said about Kevin, good or bad, is said specifically because he's on top, whether he wants to be there or not. To me, it doesn't matter. If the sole reason that Cloudy Bay continues to produce wine that people like is that Kevin Judd keeps everyone who works there grounded about what they do, then party on, Kevin. Party on.

Two people you won't see partying it up, however, are Mike and Claire Allan at Huia. Nevertheless, they're two of my favorite winemakers in Marlborough simply because they're absolutely obsessed with making great wine. Both are relatively quiet and unglamorous, but no one in Marlborough loves their work as much as the Allans do. They think and act like two halves of the same mind, with Claire handling everything that goes on in the vineyard and Mike running the show in the winery. They often complete each other's sentences.

They went to college together in Australia, and "because we were married at that stage, people thought we were brother and sister. At some times that was a little problematic for them considering we shared the same room," Claire recalled.

However, impressions are one thing and the truth is another, and in this case the latter is that both Claire and Mike would have been successful on their own, as Mike was the brains behind Pelorus, Cloudy Bay's line of sparkling wines, and Claire was the winemaker for Lawson's Dry Hills before Mike just filled her shoes. Claire's husband joined her at Lawson's, but the duo left shortly thereafter to start Huia. And they did it with practically nothing.

---

*The one Cloudy Bay party I went to certainly lived up to the reputation. A DuPont factory has fewer chemicals than I had in my bloodstream that night. I was so wasted I couldn't find my car, and once I did find it I sat in there for twenty minutes arguing with myself about whether I should drive. Once I realized I'd been arguing with myself for that long, out loud, I decided to walk home.

"We didn't have enough money to build the house and buy the place," Claire recalled of their shaky start in 1991, "so we found the few houses we could relocate, and then we found this crappy little statehouse that's on the back. Mike took three months off work from Cloudy Bay to build onto it using these huge pine trees that we'd cut down on the property. We were literally putting the concrete down at eleven at night, and the next morning we were flying off to France to do a vintage there."

Their first vintage together at Huia was 1995, one of the worst for Marlborough ever. "It was a very good vintage for us together for the first time," Mike told me as he sported his rectangular grin, which kind of makes him look like Charlton Heston. (I was wondering if I could escape Marlborough and New Zealand without asking him to scream, "You maniac!" for me, just once.) "If you could survive '95, you could survive anything."

The other thing I appreciate about Mike and Claire is that, like Hatsch at Fromm, they decided to concentrate on making sure that their wines go well with food, by adopting techniques they picked up in Europe. But they're smart enough to not try to be European winemakers. "You have to recognize that you're trying to achieve the best result here in New Zealand, not emulate someone else's," Mike explained.

Because they aim to be the best on their own turf, winemaking is much more than a nine-to-five job for Mike and Claire. "I would do something else if it were just a day job," Claire said of why she puts as much time into Huia as she does. "It's a life obsession, really. But for us it's not just a career—it's also real enjoyment."

What's more, though, Mike and Claire had the guts to go for broke and do what they felt necessary to make great wine. Though they had the experience—and not necessarily the money—when they set off to start Huia, "It was a moment we had where we could stay as career winemakers or skip out and start our own business," Claire said to me. "Looking back now you can see it quite easily, but you could say there was a moment of choice."

"Sometimes in life you just have to take the plunge," Mike interjected.

"Jump in, hold your nose, see what happens," Claire continued.

"Right from the word go, our wines didn't look like anyone else's," Mike said as he laughed. "That wasn't necessarily a positive thing."

Ask others, though, and they'll disagree.

"From the start with Huia, those first couple of Sauvignons were lean, but were as true as they could get," Brian Bicknell of Seresin told me. And he would know. Since Brian and his viticulturist, Bart Arnst, work organically, Seresin's entire goal is to produce wines that are expressive of the Marlborough land.

"A guy who was working here [for the vintage] summed it up quite well," Brian told me on a particularly nasty and cold day just as the winery was finishing its harvest. "'You get to make the wines you want to make,' he said. What I love about the wine industry is that you look for land, decide what to plant, how to plant it, and then you're dirty and covered in juice, and then get taken to the best restaurants in the world. We're on the ground all the time. You're scraping Pinot off the floor. You've been covered in [grapes], and you get to take it through to these great places of enjoyment. There's not many industries where you can be involved at all those stages."

Brian and Bart have another set of considerations to deal with because they run an organic operation. Personally, when I hear the term "organic farmer," I immediately think "granola." Dreadlocks. Piercings. BO. But Bart is the polar opposite. He's a former boxer who dresses more like a jazz musician than a farmer, much less an organic one. His head is perfectly shaved, and he's a tall, imposing figure. He looks like Marlon Brando in *Apocalypse Now,* only Bart doesn't sit in the middle of the jungle with a pile of severed heads, whispering, "The horror . . . the horror" (at least not to my knowledge). He also has a great sense of humor. Moreover, he knows everything under the moon about organic farming—which flowers to grow in the rows, what kinds of bees they attract, why those bees help protect the grapes from parasites, and so forth. So I asked Bart and Brian if they could use one chemical, what it would be.

"Does that include drug use?" Bart asked instantly—I could tell he was having a rough day. "It would be herbicide."

"In terms of above the ground, organics in Marlborough are very simple," Brian added. "On the ground it's weed control. They can affect your growth rates. You go through two years when you change from agrochemical to organic management, and it's hard then because the nitrogen doesn't assimilate as easily. And we have to build that back up into the soil with things like inter-row plantings, and using seaweed and fertilizer made from fish."

But Brian and Bart don't want to be known as guys who make organic wine—just as guys who make good wine. "People will always look at Seresin and know, 'We're going to get a good wine out of those guys.' We want people to know that if they're buying our wine, they're getting the best," Bart said.

"We make our wines very simply. We do a lot of work in the vineyard, and try to do as little as possible in the winery," Brian added.

"That's why I say I'm the winemaker nine months out of the year," Bart continued. "What we bring in is what makes the wine, basically. You're getting a true reflection of the land, which I think is really important."

"We make wine in a really honest fashion. We don't use tricks to make the wine something that it's not meant to be," Brian concluded—something I realized that Brian and Bart have in common with the Allans, Mike Just, Hatsch Kalberer, and James Healy.

Perhaps even with wine, honesty is the best policy.

Everyone says good wine is made in the vineyard, but who's actu-
ally out there? There is simply a fact that there are heavily over-
cropped vineyards in the district this year, and they will not do
justice to what Marlborough's reputation would like to be. We just
had a normal crop this year because it's what we want every year.

—Hatsch Kalberer, winemaker at the Fromm Winery

11

Much Ado About The Big One

W hen the 2004 vintage was done, ASW had harvested and crushed 1,200 tons of grapes, roughly 33 percent more than what it had ever crushed before. And if it hadn't sold off that last one hundred twenty or so tons to Montana, ASW could have hit well over 1,300 tons—far beyond its capacity. As it was, Jeremy even had to send 20,000 liters of juice to South Pacific Cellars, a contract winemaking facility, just so ASW would have enough room for all the juice still coming in. And two more stainless-steel tanks arrived in the dying days of the vintage.

Marlborough, as a whole, had a record year. Just as the harvest was getting going, New Zealand Winegrowers predicted that Marlborough would process somewhere between 80,000 and 100,000 metric tons of grapes—double 2003's frost-affected crop as well as 2002's healthy crop of just over 53,000 tons. At the end of April, Montana, trying to beat a rainstorm, processed 1,447 tons in a twenty-three-hour span. On June 29, 2004, New Zealand Winegrowers officially announced that Marlborough had crushed 92,581 tons of grapes, a 117 percent increase over 2003.

"This will be a watershed year in that there will be plenty of wine to go around," Spy Valley's Ant MacKenzie said to me as the harvest was coming to an end. The question, however, was whether the wine was any good, because the vines were carrying such heavy crop loads (the more grapes the vines grow, the harder it is for all the fruit to ripen fully to make good-tasting wine).

"There's no doubt that the crops are on the bigger side of normal," Matt Thomson told me. "I don't see that as a problem if the vines get the grapes to maturity, and you've got space in the winery."

But he was one of the few to take such a tack. The more I asked winemakers how they felt about their fruit or the ferments they already had going, the more they told me only great things, relatively few admitting to having bigger crops than they'd anticipated, botrytis scares, or late ripening struggles on this block or that. And yet it was pretty much common knowledge that everyone had faced these challenges to some extent.

"We've got some stunning flavors in the wine this year," one winemaker told me, though everyone already knew that was something that couldn't be said for certain just yet. "We're thrilled to bits to have a winery full of quite concentrated fruit," boasted another.

They were forgetting that I'd actually worked the harvest. No, I'm not a viticulturist, but I can tell when fruit doesn't look healthy (I'm not married, which means that more than a few times in my life I've left fruit sitting out on my kitchen counter). And Josh repeatedly complained to me that he thought the grapes just weren't that great. Not bad, but not brilliant by any means.

Certainly it was a better year than the frost-affected 2003 vintage, when most wineries struggled to ripen all their fruit and had to add sugar to just about everything (in 2004, ASW used only one ton of sugar for the entire winery, and some wineries claimed to have sugared nothing at all). But February was crappy and cold, and March and April had their brushes with disaster, as temperatures occasionally flirted with the freezing point and there were brief yet big bursts of rain here and there.

"There are two aspects to that question," Mike Allan at Huia told me when I asked him if 2004 was The Big One. "One is that there's been a huge expansion of planting, so the potential is there for a very big vintage anyway. And it's been a very generous year in terms of the crop loading as well. There's a nervousness around the valley about the sheer volume of wine that's going to come onto the market." In other words, everyone was worried that supply would outpace demand.

"The other point is whether the quality was actually there, and it's been a very tense vintage from that point of view. 'The Big One'—that terminology was created before harvest."

Al Soper at Highfield echoed that sentiment. "What I found a bit distressing is that people were making assessments about the quality of the vintage before they started picking fruit," he told me one rainy day toward the end of harvest. A good point, I thought. Sort of like looking at someone from across the room and declaring that person to be the greatest fuck ever—before you've even said hello to each other, much less taken off each other's pants.

The one thing that most people I spoke to agreed on, however, was that the trick to The Big One was choosing the right picking time.

"Last year was easy," one winemaker told me. "There was just a point when everything had to be picked. This year was so much harder because everything ripened at different times."

Mike Just at Lawson's realized this early in the vintage. "It certainly is a challenging season with such wide variation," he told me. "In most seasons you can take things as they come, and it all balances out in the end. Nature can sort of hand it to you on a plate. This year we have to pull all of our little tricks out of our basket, especially dealing with berry splitting, botrytis, vines that are shutting down, pH variation. It's a matter of looking very closely at everything that comes in, and never assuming it's all okay."

It was the same at Cloudy Bay, the way Kevin Judd described it. "The thing about this vintage for us was ducking and diving, and using all the winemaking we could muster. We treated things differently than what we would have done in a normal year."

"Can you give me an example of what you did differently?" I asked him.

"Not anything that I'd like to see published," he said. I asked Jeremy what this meant, and he pretty much said that it could mean anything, but his guess was the use of what's called "the black hose." The terminology simply means adding water to crushed grapes that have too high a sugar content to make sure there isn't too much alcohol in the finished wine. But who's to say? I had just met him, so I could've gotten a dirty sock to tell me the secret of life before I'd have gotten a "hello" out of Kevin.

His former colleague James Healy was a bit more sweeping, yet blunt, in his assessment of the vintage: "Anything that failed to get ripe had to be over-cropped," meaning that growers with under-ripe grapes didn't cut off excess fruit partway through the season so the grapes still hanging could ripen fully by harvest time. "There's no way it wouldn't have gotten ripe this year," he concluded.

On the other hand, John Belsham told me he felt Wairau River's vines could hold 10 to 15 percent more fruit because the leaf canopy—which captures sunlight for energy . . . remember sixth-grade biology?—was that much healthier from the February rains. "We've been able to ripen it all," he proclaimed proudly. John also told me that Wairau River and Foxes Island combined took in 1,400 tons—within thirty tons of his projections. "We've taken in exactly what we expected to take in."

Granted, John buys grapes from only a couple of contract growers (Wairau River buys none at all), a situation in which it's much easier to manage expectations. Gary Duke at Hunter's, which deals with several growers, told me that his winery processed fewer tons than it had during the previous, frost-affected year, since the winery was able to convince its growers to snip off excess fruit partway through the season. (It's worth noting that Gary also told me he's antisocial, when the very next night I saw him at the Cork & Keg with his entire vintage crew, drinking and talking up a storm. Sure, it was the winery's vintage party, but Gary seemed as social as a fraternity pledge.)

So was I just being bullshitted left and right? Just what was all this hype about The Big One if so few would admit to having a bigger year—even though the total crop was indeed bigger—yet there were so many schools of thought on just how the 2004 vintage went? Brian Bicknell at Seresin told me that his winery was right in line with estimates, and yet Digger at Mount Riley told me that he thought he didn't have enough juice. ASW processed three hundred more tons than it had the previous year, yet Hunter's processed less. Nobilo and Wither Hills claimed not to have big crops, yet they both had several new vineyards coming on-stream for the first time. In other words, while Marlborough crushed substantially more grapes than it ever had before, the vintage was different for everyone. Which I guess doesn't really make it The Big One at all. Just a different one.

What I learned—and what you should take away from this—is never to listen to what other people say in general about a region's vintage, good or bad, because every winery has different pieces of land that present different benefits or challenges. There's no sense in one person—winemaker or wine writer or wine drinker—declaring a vintage as this or that. Nineteen ninety-five was supposedly the worst year that Marlborough ever saw, with the wines turning to shit halfway through their fermentations. Yet a bottle of ASW's

Merlot from that year, which Josh and I drank a month or so after the 2004 harvest, turned out to be excellent, I thought. And Brian and Bart from Seresin claim that one of their distributors first got hooked on Marlborough wine when he tasted a bottle of their Sauvignon Blanc from that same, supposedly abysmal year.

So judge for yourself.

Do your homework by checking weather forecasts on the Internet during the peak ripening time, and read articles from the wine regions' local papers online. Find out if a winemaker is into winning gold medals or making wine that works well with food. Ask the people who work in your local wine shop what they think. Go to a wine tasting or just buy a couple of bottles and try them, as if you're taking a car out for a test drive; see how they look and feel. Just as a car salesman isn't going to tell you that he's trying to talk you into buying a crap car, a winemaker isn't likely to tell you his or her honest opinion about what's going on in the vineyard or inside the bottle.

Nevertheless, I do believe that Marlborough made good wine in 2004. Maybe even great wine, because the region's winemakers are smart enough and experienced enough to make adjustments for every little curveball Mother Nature could throw at them on each and every block. But the 2004 vintage wasn't The Big One; it was many things, among them a bigger one. It was also a trickier one. A transitional one. A nervous one. A difficult one. A tiring one. A lively one. A stressful one. An exciting one. An enjoyable one. A late one. A long one.

And for everything that it taught winemaking experts and novices alike, it was one that those who experienced it aren't likely to soon forget.

PART II

Winemaking

We'd rather be leaders than followers.

—CATHY SCOTT

12

Fresh Pork, Beer, and Sex

Pretty much the instant that the last grape is crushed, Marlborough becomes virtually silent. Equipment around the winery no longer rattles and rumbles for hours on end, fewer trucks are on the roads, and machine harvesters are locked inside their tractor sheds. The leaves begin to turn brown and fall from the vines, and the foreign vintage workers trickle out as slowly as they trickled in a few months earlier. Some of them take time off to travel around New Zealand, while others make a dash to the West Coast of the United States or Europe in search of their next harvest jobs.

Nearby Blenheim slows to a crawl, its restaurants and bars half-filled with locals. Though the city is by and large considered progressive, with some of the best food, wine, and accommodations New Zealand has to offer, it's still a farm town at heart, where civility and gruffness intermingle. The words "please" and "thank you" are uttered infrequently. The men are macho and young, single mothers hit the bars each weekend in search of guys to buy them drinks, while during the week they dream of a better life working in retail. No one batted an eye at a guy I saw in the grocery store wearing a

95

T-shirt that read, "If you think my attitude stinks, you should smell my fingers." He was a friend of Kosta's, and I think they must have gone shirt shopping together, since Kosta often wore one that read, "Blah, blah, blah . . . Show me your tits."

Just outside town, winter signals a return to normal life for Marlborough winemakers, as they finally awake from the zombielike daze of harvest work. Some go out on the road to market their wines in the United States, United Kingdom, and Australia, while others travel to developing markets. Ross and Barbara Lawson, owners of Lawson's Dry Hills, went to Russia. Allan hosted a few dinners in Vietnam and others told me of their plans to visit China and India. Some simply disappear for a month of much-needed vacation while their wines rest in barrels and tanks.

Some also change jobs. Mike Just handed in his notice at Lawson's Dry Hills to focus on his own brand, Clayridge, as well as to consult for Auntsfield, a small operation with vines planted on the oldest grape-growing site in Marlborough. John Belsham gave up the winemaking reins at Wairau River to focus on his own brand, Foxes Island, while Allan McWilliams left Cellier Le Brun to fill John's shoes at Wairau River.

At ASW, too, winter ushered in major changes. Allan and Cathy's daughter Sara went to London, as most Kiwis take a couple of years after school to work and live in another country for a while. Basically it's about earning money in a more valuable currency so you can come back to New Zealand with enough to get started on your life. Kiwis call it an OE, for "overseas experience," but from most of the stories I heard, they should probably just call it a GD: getting drunk. I'm not sure what it was for Sara, because she wouldn't return home until after I'd left New Zealand.*

On the business side of things, an opening on U.K. supermarket shelves had presented itself, so Allan quickly registered the name Kotuku (which means "white heron" in Maori), had a label designed, and purchased 10,000 liters of Sauvignon Blanc off the bulk market with the aim of using ASW fruit in the future. Meanwhile, Josh had been experimenting with a bottle-fermented beer he called Moa, which he made by a method similar to that for

---

*Aside from writing this book, New Zealand was pretty much my GD. Either that or I was just really bored, since one time I had so much to drink I wound up peeing on Cloudy Bay's big sign out in front of the winery. That's not so bad considering that one of the other guys I was with at the time puked on it.

making Champagne with the help of a professional brewer who'd fly in now and again and lend his expertise. Before Josh had the process down quite right, the beer had me hurling on his front lawn (I'd had a lot of it, though). But he eventually got it right, and Moa grew in popularity. Its rise happened to coincide with Allan's acquiring the Cairnbrae vineyard, which came with a restaurant on the property, as well as a warehouse in which ASW could build a small brewery.

With several new elements added to the business, as well as a new vineyard to manage, a twinge of trepidation emerged in Jeremy. One night as he was leaving the winery, he asked me to meet him for a beer at the Cork & Keg. It was the day after the official closing on the Cairnbrae vineyard (which Allan soon renamed Millstone because that's what he felt like he was carrying around his neck during the time he was trying to close the deal), and Jeremy had just finished an exhaustive discussion with Allan over his employment contract. Jeremy signed on the dotted line, but not before talking over several details.

For starters, just the day before, Kevin Judd (who makes a side living as a photographer) showed up at the winery to take pictures for a *Cuisine* magazine spread and accompanying story, from which Jeremy was excluded. The magazine only wanted shots of Allan and Josh.

"That really fucked me off," Jeremy admitted between sips of lager. "I told Allan, 'I don't care about photo shoots.' " What he did care about, however, was getting credit where credit's due. "I make this wine as much as anybody," he complained.

He was also concerned about Josh's budding beer business, since it was taking more of his time and attention away from the wine. It probably didn't help that only a few weeks later, Wellington newspaper the *Dominion Post*'s beer columnist gave Moa a glowing review, and referred to Josh as ASW's "head winemaker."

"He knows it'll always be about me and Dad," Josh told me when I asked him how Jeremy might have taken the article. "Jeremy's not going to be here forever, and we are. He's a big part of the business, but not that one."

"I'm fine with it," Jeremy later told me of the article and Josh's beer business, "so long as we can make it profitable, and right now it's not. It's just money in his pocket. Whose equipment is he using? Whose time is it he's using when he works on the beer or has Geoff do the labeling? Allan knows it, and wants to see Josh put the money back into the business rather than his own pocket, and that's something he said he'd talk to Josh about. He'll have to if he wants to phase out and become a director and let Josh take over the business"—something that Allan had already begun planning to do over the next three or four years. He was hoping to spend that time teaching Josh the intricacies of running the company.

There were also the little things that bothered Jeremy, like Josh's general absentmindedness and his tendency to take the easy route on small tasks. For example, he didn't give a second thought to disposing of a tub of diatomaceous earth in the vineyard as opposed to the Dumpster.

"Diatomaceous earth?" I asked Jeremy. "Isn't that stuff dangerous?"

"Shit, yeah. I said, 'What the fuck are you doing?!'" he recalled. "He's just in a hurry and not thinking. It's no big deal now, but I had to scoop it into a pile and take it away. He just creates more work. When he's in a rush, he'll just do the quickest and easiest thing possible without even thinking about it." And on the day that the auditor arrived at the winery, Josh had left empty beer kegs lying around. "That's the sort of thing that could really hurt us down the line," Jeremy grumbled.

While Jeremy tried to get his head around these changes, one week later a 2,000-case Central Otago operation called Mount Michael—an eight-hour drive south of Marlborough—came up for sale. Allan and Cathy jumped at it, seeing the small business as a good investment opportunity for Josh.

"While we could probably afford it on our own, I got a bit apprehensive," Allan told me just after the sale was completed. The investors took on 75 percent while Josh split the remaining 25 percent with his parents, with plans to buy out the other investors over time. Josh was also expected to take over the winemaking duties.

Allan's concern was more than warranted. In the early nineties he felt that the winery needed capital to expand, so through a series of business deals (some better than others), he formed a new parent company over ASW, along with his accountant and another partner, and bought several established vineyards around the valley. "I had a favorite piece of dirt that I had done some research on when I was at Corbans, and put my heart and soul into that. We needed income to support it, and I suggested we use a second label to generate income. We were carrying the debt, and we were getting a little uneasy," he said. The company was organized in such a way that each of the partners would take a percentage of the fruit.

That second label was Mount Riley, and the other two partners were guys

I'm going to call Harry and Rod. Because it wasn't long before they both decided they didn't want to be contract growers for ASW.

"The whole thing came to a head, and we had a parting of the ways," Allan said. The Harry-Rod team took the Mount Riley label with them, and built it into the well-known Marlborough brand it is today. "We lost a lot of property that we had developed, so we really had to start all over again.

"We didn't have a good amount of swing since we were the third shareholder, with only thirty-three percent. There's no joy in being a third shareholder when the other two gang up on you," Allan concluded, and insisted that I couldn't use their names due to the final settlement, which even included a clause about all involved parties not bad-mouthing each other. Even with quite a bit of prodding during the course of our conversation Allan refused to say anything bad about Harry and Rod. He didn't even tell me their real names (but I found out pretty easily, since the story has been published multiple times).

"It doesn't worry me because one day it'll bounce back at them," he said. "In fact, it probably has to a certain extent, since the two have come to blows and now parted and gone their separate ways. There are a lot of things that you can say, and history's gonna stay that way. History is history."

But the other Scotts took it a little more personally. "It still bugs Cathy a fair bit," Allan admitted. "She won't talk to or have anything to do with them."

Josh made his feelings all too clear as well. For Allan's fiftieth birthday, before the row, his business partners gave him personalized license plates reading MR WINE. Allan never attached them to his car, but when Rod later asked for them back, Josh affixed them to his Jeep, just on the off chance that he happened to pass Rod on the road.

Jeremy, familiar with the family history, saw his frustrations compound more or less overnight with the purchase of Mount Michael and the rise of Josh's beer business. They certainly had in Allan's mind as well.

"I have the greatest respect for [Jeremy], and I'm really fond of him," Allan later told me. "There's a lifetime job for him here. [Josh] will never be Jeremy's boss. I moved Jeremy's salary up, so he's getting more than Josh. It's a very difficult situation. I said, 'We're in a phase now where I want people to see that we're a family business, and short of adopting you, I can't really involve you in that.' I know he gets upset, because the press tends to focus in on Josh, head winemaker, whatever, and Jeremy gets left out of it."

Over time Jeremy began to take it all in stride, perhaps coming to a better understanding of his role or maybe just remembering that not only do he and Josh complement each other's skills, but they're also friends.

"The thing I told Allan was that there can't be any chinks in the armor," Jeremy explained to me. "These are all businesses, but they all hinge on Allan Scott being solid, making good wine," something he knew would essentially fall on him with Josh's attention divided between Moa and Mount Michael.

Even with business matters holding most of their attention during the weeks immediately following harvest, however, the arrival of winter also allowed enough time for a return to the rugby field in an attempt to resurrect Moutere's foundering season. Jeremy and Josh managed to help the team to a couple of wins, but unfortunately not enough to make it into the play-offs. In Josh's postharvest debut against nearby Renwick, it was his errors that gave the opposition the lead, which Renwick never gave back. And in true Kiwi fashion, the punishment for his on-the-field crimes came in the form of what the team calls a "court session," which is really just forced beer consumption. Shortly after Josh got home at about 4:00 A.M., he walked over to the chest-high window in his living room, opened it, pissed on the wall below it, then lay out on the couch.

"Dude, do you realize you just pissed on the wall?" I asked him.

"Yup," he said as he rolled over and went to sleep. He didn't believe me when I told him in the morning what had happened. He begged me not to tell anyone, but I couldn't help it. I told just about everyone. I think the team gave him another court session just for that.

In his next game he received a ten-stitch gash above his left eye in the first few minutes, but played out the remainder of the match after getting bandaged up on the sidelines, then went to the ER after the game.

"It doesn't hurt that bad," Josh assured me as the final suture was pulled tight, just over his eyebrow. The doctor could've hopped up onto the gurney and kneed Josh in the balls after each suture, and he still probably wouldn't have flinched.

"What'd the other guy look like?" I asked him.

"He was fine. It was just a head clash, and he got me with the top of his head, which is the hardest part of the skull." As we left the hospital, I pointed out to him that he also had blood leaking from his ear. "I've been thinking too hard," he joked.

If you think Josh is tough, in the eighties there was an All Black named Wayne Shelford, who tore, yes, tore his scrotum in the middle of a big game against France, leaving one testicle dangling free. He waddled over to the sidelines, got his sack stitched up, and went back into the game. (His ball was later surgically removed.) So with a role model like that, you can imagine that Kiwi rugby players—even at Josh's level—don't want to seem soft.

In addition to rugby (and sometimes the morning before a match), Jeremy began to hunt wild pig more regularly. Sometimes he'd go in the afternoon after work, and one day he asked if I'd like to come along. We climbed into his truck and drove into the Waihopai Valley, about a twenty-minute ride southwest of the winery that passes by countless contract-grower vineyards, as well as Seresin, Grove Mill, and Spy Valley.

Once we got farther into the valley, Jeremy drove his truck up the dirt road of a rancher's property. Since the harvest had just ended, I asked him what the hardest part of it all was.

"Managing people," he said without hesitation. "It's the worst, because when there's a problem, you're not just telling off someone who works for you. It's a friend."

Though he never said so specifically, it was clear that he was talking about Jemma, the assistant winemaker. She'd been having trouble with her fiancé, and in the first couple of weeks after harvest she'd once arrived at the winery in the morning especially hungover (and was promptly sent home). And Josh and Jeremy were concerned that her lab work was getting sloppy. In her notes she'd written down data pertaining to tank six, but had been doing all her tests on tank nine.

"Does it carry more weight if it comes from one of the Scotts, since it's a family business?" I asked Jeremy of the warning he had to give Jemma.

"Nah, they say, 'You handle it.' That way it shows it really is a professional thing, and not just a family thing," he explained.

Jeremy parked his truck near a cattle fence high up in the hills. Only a few minutes after we began hiking he spotted three black pigs digging for grubs on a distant slope. We walked quietly in their direction, but once we got closer he deemed them too small and we moved over the ridge. Within seconds the dogs had disappeared into the spiky brush and were barking furiously.

"Eel! Get down here! Quick!" Jeremy yelled at me, and I tumbled into prickly bushes at least three or four times on my way down the soggy, steep slope.

I stumbled again just as a gunshot rang out from Jeremy's general direction and began rolling through the valley like a clap of thunder.

I regained my balance and found my way to a clearing, and there was Jeremy with a smoking .357 rifle, a motionless 140-pound pig, and his three barking dogs gnawing away at it. Within a couple of minutes Jeremy's hands and arms were stained red as he cleaned the carcass—which, for some reason, involved kicking a wiggling blob of entrails down the mountain that the hawks circling above would soon began to dine upon. He slung the carcass over his shoulders—like a spring breaker in Cancún taking home a drunk sorority girl—so that he could carry it back up the steep slope. As we hiked back to the truck, I noticed that with each step Jeremy took, the lobes of the pig's liver dangled and flapped around the outside of the mostly empty stomach cavity.

Halfway back to the truck Jeremy stopped and put the pig down to take a break, probably for my benefit, since I was winded just trying to keep up with him, even though he was the one carrying the excess weight. Between labored breaths I asked Jeremy if he was bothered by his and Josh's relative winemaking obscurity, despite their track record of strong sales and even a few accolades.

"It takes time to build up a reputation—ten or twelve years, really," he said as he effortlessly slung the pig back over his shoulders and continued toward the truck. "Some younger guys who've made a name for themselves have had coattails to ride. Ben Glover [of Wither Hills] is great, but he's also working with Brent Marris"—one of New Zealand's most renowned winemakers. "Who've we had? Nobody, really."

"What about Allan?" I asked.

"He's a viticulturist, not a winemaker," Jeremy said.

The pig landed on the back of Jeremy's truck with a thud, and within seconds he and the dogs had disappeared into the brush in hot pursuit of another. A few minutes later he caught up to the pig, tackled it, stabbed it in the jugular, and quickly scooped out its internal organs.

I know, pig hunting sounds pretty grotesque. But expert hunters like Jeremy are actually pretty humane; others, though, can be downright appalling. Ra, Josh, and I once came across five baby piglets crossing the road. Ra slammed on his brakes—to avoid hitting them, I thought. Instead, he sprinted out of the truck and managed to catch four of them. Ra then built a pen behind his house and spent the next few months raising and fattening them up on scraps from the winery's restaurant. Around the time they got big enough, Josh's other housemate, Timur, decided to take a new job in Christchurch, so one of the pigs was chosen to become dinner at his going-away party. Ra heard that the best way to kill a pig is to whack it over the head with a hammer, and either because he's inconsiderate or because he's just twisted, he jumped into the pen, determined to do the job right then and there. He brought the hammer down in an adrenaline-fueled death blow . . . but missed, and instead whacked the pig in the snout, which of course began to flow with blood. Realizing at this point that the hammer was perhaps not the best instrument of death, Ra instead chose to stab the pig in the jugular, which it seemed to like even less. He put up quite a fight while the other pigs just sort of looked on insouciantly . . . and then began to lick up all the spilled blood, as if to say, "Sucks to be you, dude." (Problem number two was roasting the pig, but Kosta came to the rescue. With a quick phone call, he managed to track down a spit that we could rent for a mere thirty bucks from a local white-supremacist gang called the Lone Legion. I mean, duh, of course neo-Nazis eat pork.)

The sport that really seemed to dominate Jeremy and Josh's attention at this time of year, however, was drinking. It's one of my favorites as well, but I could never keep up with these seasoned professionals, no matter how hard I tried. One Friday night Jeremy came into Bar Navajo while I was slinging drinks. "There's someone here to see you," Kosta told me, and as I rounded the corner of the L-shaped bar I really hoped it'd be Halle Barry. Instead, there was Jeremy slumped over in the corner, barely conscious. I offered him a drink, but he slowly shook his head. He then began to reconstruct the evening's events, which involved his knocking out two guys who'd attacked him in another bar, before he came to this one.

"They juss stahted comin' at me," he told me, words blending into and crossing over each other. "I juss le'my beeah outtamah hand, 'n' dropped the cunt."

"One punch?" I asked.

"One punch. Annen his mate come amme, too . . . busted him open."

"So you got thrown out, then came here?"

"Nah, self-defense, mate. They came at *me*. So I juss wennup to the ba', an 'ey gayme another beeah."

"Did you even know who the guys were?"

He just shook his head slowly again as it drooped and his chin hit his chest, and soon thereafter the bar closed. While he waited on the sidewalk for me to give him a ride home, he took a moment to vomit on the outside wall of the establishment. You'd be wrong to take that as a sign of weakness, though. As

Jeremy stood on the sidewalk, a guy sitting in his idling car decided to antag-
onize Jeremy for whatever reason. What the guy didn't know was that day or
night, drunk or sober, if you give Jeremy shit, he'll give it right back to you.
The guy decided to raise the stakes and calmly walked around to the trunk of
his car, removed a baseball bat, and started walking toward Jeremy.

Jeremy just laughed at him.

"Ah, you're not gonna use 'at, ya fuckin' cunt!" he screamed and laughed,
and within moments, the driver got back into his car, without so much as a
swing. Jeremy called his bluff—the guy had clearly confused drunkenness
with fearlessness. On top of that, Jeremy's competitive to the point that he
won't just beat you at any game you try to play with him, he'll let you *know*
that he beat you. As the guy drove off, Jeremy tried to pull him from the moving car, through the window, before the car gained enough speed to send
Jeremy tumbling to the ground, cackling in hilarity.

What also began to shine through during that time was just how much
women slobber over Jeremy, the way men do over a free, all-you-can-eat plate
of spicy buffalo wings. They fall over him as if he's a rock star wearing
pheromone-enhanced cologne. Rugged and good-looking he is, but Jude Law
he's not. However, Jeremy has some sort of unidentifiable characteristic that
women find irresistible. Josh, unable to put his finger on what exactly it is,
calls it Jeremy's "X Factor."

Occasionally, I'd see him in bars, speaking with the women who came up
to him for only a couple of minutes before pretending to program their numbers into his cell phone (just to flatter them by feigning interest). A pretty,
petite, rail-thin South African student visiting Marlborough saw Jeremy a
total of twice (and spoke to him for only a few minutes on the second
encounter) before she was grabbing his ass in Bar Navajo one night—in the
presence of her boyfriend, it should be noted. For the next few weeks she regularly dropped by the winery acting as if she was there to see Kosta, but really
hoping to catch a glimpse of Jeremy. In a town of relatively few women, she
was the object of many a man's attention during her stay, and Jeremy did next
to nothing to attract hers. Yet she, like so many others, was drawn to him on
a near–*Fatal Attraction* level. Of course he enjoyed the attention, but he
resisted her advances. Besides, she soon found her own rugby-playing pig
hunter, who didn't live with his girlfriend in a house they owned together.

While Jeremy cruised along, however, Josh stammered and stalled. He'd
recently met someone new within a day of breaking up with his girlfriend of

the past three years. But Josh soon found out that his ex had been far less than faithful for the last several months of their relationship—a time during which he'd been supporting her financially. He pulled a canvas off the wall in his house that she had painted for him, and invited me and Timur to take turns blowing it to smithereens using Josh's twelve-gauge. He then set it on fire on the front lawn . . . I'm thinking he was bitter. The night that Josh confronted her about her indiscretions he drank an entire bottle of vodka before even hitting the town's bars, and in the span of only a few days he lost nearly ten pounds, simply from eating little and drinking much. He fell into even more of a funk as time went on because Laura, his new girlfriend, spent most of her time in Dunedin—an eight-hour drive away—at the University of Otago, studying social work.

Things went from bad to worse one night when Josh drove his car into the center of Blenheim, where he planned to leave it for the night. A police car pulled up behind him after he'd gotten out and locked the car, and subsequent breath and blood tests found him to be one-and-a-half times the legal limit. On the day of his sentencing I actually had high hopes for Josh, since he looked like a priest compared to most people in the courthouse. (The guy sitting in front of me had a tattoo of a crouching devil that looked as though it was going to spring up off his skin and devour my internal organs, which I'd normally think was pretty cool, except for the fact that this particular tattoo was on the back of his head.) Unfortunately, the judge didn't see it that way and handed down to Josh a substantial fine and a six-month suspension of his license.

Of course, this did not bode well for someone who not only produces alcoholic beverages for a living, but was also planning to move down to the tiny Central Otago town of Cromwell to take over Mount Michael. The area isn't completely desolate, but it doesn't exactly have a bustling mass transit system either. There would be no way Josh could do the job without driving.

After all the planning and strategizing over the growing business, it began to look as though one of the key people involved in all aspects of it wouldn't be able to go where he was needed. Never mind the fact that ASW, the biggest part of the business, had more than thirty tanks and hundreds of barrels full of wine that needed to get out into the marketplace.

At the end of the day it's what it tastes like in the glass that's important.

—ANT MACKENZIE, WINEMAKER AT SPY VALLEY

13

Wine 101:
From Tanks and Barrels
to Bottles

Though winter certainly isn't the most exciting time of year at a winery, each growing season and plot of land is different, so the winery is where adjustments and decisions are made so that what comes out at the end is, well, wine, and not rubbing alcohol. This is also the time and place when the differences between a region's winemakers become more evident.

Let's backtrack for a moment. Remember, grape juice becomes wine after fermentation, in which yeast converts the sugar to alcohol and sends off carbon-dioxide gas as a by-product. Now, this should raise an obvious—and very important—question: What happens to all that yeast?

Put simply, it dies. For a moment, think of a yeast culture in a tank of Sauvignon Blanc as a human civilization on a small island that eats up all the plants and animals. In doing so the people find themselves on a barren chunk of land with no shade from the sun and no resources. So everyone dies. Yeast does essentially the same thing, because single-cell organisms aren't particularly smart. The yeast gobbles up all its food (the sugar), and by turning it into alcohol, it slowly creates a hostile environment for itself. The difference between yeast in a tank of grape juice and a group of humans on a small island, however, is that the dead yeast continues to serve a purpose after its death. Grim, but true.

As the yeast begins to die and fall to the bottom of the tank, it becomes what's known as lees. (This is not the same as the lees mentioned back in Chapter 2, the mixture of solids and liquids from recently crushed fruit.) Any time you read a back label mentioning "lees contact" or "fermentation on lees," this is what it means: that the wine was left in contact with the dead yeast cells. And generally speaking, the longer the wine is on lees, the better it will taste and the greater the chance that it will develop complexity while it sits in the bottle.

Just how long the wine is left in contact with its lees depends on a number of factors. For starters, the winery might not have any more of its products on store shelves. Winemaking is a business just like Coca-Cola, which can't just say, "We're out of caffeine at the moment, so until we get some more in, we just won't make any Coke." They'll lose the shelf space in the store to a competitor. So purely due to market conditions, a wine can be left on its lees for as long as six months or as little as six days. (Or, on the flipside, there might be wine that's ready to go out, but there's still some of the previous vintage left on store shelves. To move on to the '03 Pinot Noir, ASW donated the last few cases of '02 Pinot to a local Catholic church for use in mass, which of course prompted Geoff, the bottling manager, to say, "I'm not religious, but I'm goin' to church every Sunday now!")

Of course, this means that it also comes down to style. Winemakers usually taste every tank every day while the wine inside them is fermenting, and perhaps every week or two after the wine is done fermenting and is just sitting on its lees. When it tastes the way the winemaker wants it to taste, he or she moves on to the next step in the process.

With Chardonnay, however, things are a little different. Remember, Chardonnay usually goes into the barrel to finish off its ferment (the exception, of course, being unoaked or unwooded Chardonnay, which just stays in a stainless-steel tank). Once it's in there, Jeremy and Josh go around every so often and check each barrel to make sure that the ferments are all still ticking away. The easiest way to do this is just to put your ear close to the barrel's bung hole (yes, sadly, that's what it's called), and if the wine is making a fizzing noise, like soda, it's still fermenting. Josh and Jeremy also taste for residual sugar, better known among winemakers as "RS." As they taste the contents of each barrel they mark it with chalk, writing RS_, RS–, or RS⁻ on its outside. The higher the line, the higher the sugar level, and hence the longer the ferment still has to go.

They also check to make sure the barrels haven't developed any bad characters such as VA or EA. VA stands for "volatile acidity," and simply means the wine has elevated levels of acetic acid, so it tastes and smells like nail polish or vinegar. EA stands for "ethyl acetate," which basically makes wine smell and taste like glue. EA can be caused by any number of things, but it's usually a contaminant of some sort, or maybe even a fruit fly that crawled into the barrel and died happy. Which happens a lot. If you ever visit a winery a month or two after harvest, ask if they'll let you try their Chardonnay ferments. Chances are they won't, and part of the reason for this is that the barrel hall is usually swarming with fruit flies attracted by the CO_2 bubbling out of the barrels. So needless to say, an afternoon spent in there tasting barrels is filled with swatting and cursing as much as it is with tasting. All that you can really do with an EA or VA barrel, if it isn't too foul, is blend it away. You just have to keep an eye on it and make sure it doesn't get any worse and have to be dumped.

That is, of course, unless you're French. Slight traces of EA and VA can add a bit of complexity to red wines such as Pinot Noir, but some of the most unabashedly stinky and gluey French wines—especially those from Burgundy—command some of the highest prices. As Josh and Jeremy were tasting barrels one day and came across one that was particularly revolting (it made me cough), Josh remarked, "The French would *love* this." When I asked him why, he shrugged his shoulders and said, "Hey, if a pretty woman farts, you'll still want to smell her ass."

I never really thought about it that way, but I guess he was right. Some people like pure flavors and missionary position; others like funky aromas and a phone book shoved up their ass. It's all about personal preference and style. Which is why at ASW the barrels are stirred once or twice a week to mix in the lees a little better. This not only helps the ferment go faster, but gives the end product more of a creamy texture. If you ever notice that creaminess in a Chardonnay, take a moment to appreciate it, because stirring barrels is not only time-consuming, but painful.

It involves pulling the bung on the barrel, inserting a curved, metal rod, and vigorously stirring the wine inside for about thirty seconds. But think about the fact that there are well over one hundred barrels of Chardonnay at ASW, and they're stacked three high in a room barely big enough to hold them all. So getting at each and every one of them involves climbing onto other barrels and twisting and contorting your body into positions that would make an Olympic gymnast say, "Uncle." Stirring all the barrels takes about half a day, and by the end of it, my arm developed a soreness I hadn't felt since I was fourteen years old. (I was thinking of pretty women at the time, but they weren't farting.)

Once fermentation is complete on any wine, it can then be put through its secondary fermentation, better known as malolactic fermentation. By and large, this is only performed on red varieties, but some people do try it with other varieties here and there. Before he left Lawson's Dry Hills, Mike Just put a small portion of that winery's Sauvignon Blanc blend into older barrels and through malolactic fermentation because "the barrel component always looks really smart." However, the only popular white variety that you'll see most winemakers put at least partially through "malo," as it's better known, is Chardonnay.

Malolactic fermentation simply means converting the wine's relatively coarse malic acid to softer-feeling lactic acid. This is done by adding to each barrel or tank what's known as a malo bug, which is a dried bacteria culture—just like yeast. Or you can just leave the barrels alone, and they'll go through malo naturally over the course of the next several months with the help of wild bacteria. Both techniques have their advantages and disadvantages.

"Let them run their course," Hatsch Kalberer, winemaker at the Fromm Winery, who admitted to having past problems with malo bugs, told me of his approach. "At the end, the wine just takes its time," he said. Really, though, he's a traditionalist.

The downside of leaving a barrel to its own devices is that the winemaker more or less gives up control of the wine's development. There's no guarantee that the wine will do what it's supposed to do. Then again, while using a malo bug speeds up the secondary fermentation and prevents other potentially harmful microbial activity in the wine, some say that those who do so also tend to heat up their barrel halls by a couple of degrees, and in doing so threaten the fruit flavors of the wine. It's more a point of discussion than fact, and having said that, a winery like ASW, which is highly affected by commercial realities—unlike boutique operations like Fromm and Dog Point—more or less has to use a malo bug and raise the temperature a bit to get its wine into drinkable condition by the time the distributor and the retailers start asking for it.

Now, let's say your wine is done fermenting. At ASW they try to get everything other than the sweeter varieties like Riesling, Pinot Gris, and Gewürztraminer to less than three grams of sugar per liter, but that doesn't necessarily mean that it will taste as if the acid and remaining sugar are in balance. That was especially common in 2004, when the ripening season presented winemakers with grapes that were high in sugar but also high in acid. Acid is most noticeable in a wine like Sauvignon Blanc, the lifeblood of the Marlborough wine industry. So the region's winemakers were presented with a choice: Either add a small amount of sugar to the finished wine to bring the acid into balance, or chemically deacidify the wine.

Jeremy and Josh chose to add a little bit of sugar. To some, though not many, the alternative is blasphemy. They believe that wine is a representation of the season and therefore, if the grapes are higher in acidity, the wine should be, too.

"It's a very Old World attitude," Wither Hills's Ben Glover told me when I asked him if he'd deacidified his Sauvignon Blanc—which, by the way, feels like asking a guy with a toupee what kind of shampoo he uses. "It needs to be a wine that packs a lot of natural power and fruit weight, but is also rounded. You shouldn't have two glasses and find it's stripping the enamel off your teeth. This year we did deacidify some batches. We're after balance."

Along those lines of thinking, Matt Thomson also dropped the acid in some of the wines he made.

"If you look at every wine region in the world, there's some manipulation that goes on most years," he told me shortly before he flew off to Italy to work with his clients there. "In Bordeaux you need to add sugar since you've got plenty of acidity, and in a warmer climate like Australia you have plenty of sugar but not enough acid. A winemaker must be able to respond to those conditions to make the best wine possible."

Even the winemakers who chose not to alter their wines in that way or another agree with such a philosophy.

"The wine does express the vintage, it does express the sites," I was told by John Belsham, owner and winemaker of Foxes Island. "And some years if you let it do that, you don't have a drinkable product. If the wine requires an adjustment to make it a more drinkable product, and you're not uncomfortable with the idea of manipulating it, I don't have a problem with that. That said, I do very little of it."

Setting that debate aside for the moment, let's say that your wine has finished fermenting, the sugar and acid taste as if they're in balance, and you feel confident that the wine has had enough of a rest on its lees. Unfortunately, it still has a lot to go through before it's ready to be bottled.

For one thing, the wine is still very cloudy—white wine, anyway, at this stage looks more like grapefruit juice than anything else. The wine is starting to clarify itself simply due to gravity, but it needs help. So first it's hit with a small amount of sulfur-dioxide (SO_2) gas, which kills any remaining live yeast and protects the wine from any other microbial activity as well as oxidation (even the ancient Romans added sulfur to their wine to help preserve it). This also locks in the flavors and sugar level (since the yeast cells are now all dead), so you better be happy with what you've got at the point you choose to sulfur the wine.

This is where there was a bit of a fuckup. Some of ASW's Sauvignon Blanc does get barrel time for the Prestige line, and when Jemma reported that the barrels had finished fermenting, they were promptly sulfured. What she'd done, however, was just check a couple of the barrels rather than all of them, "which is usually fine, but she just happened to get the two freak barrels that had gone dry," Josh explained to me. The rest, however, were sulfured with sugar levels much higher than he, Jeremy, or any wine drinker would like, so ASW became stuck with several barrels of what would have been good-quality wine, but had way too much sugar. "It'd have been nice to know what that could've been," Josh said to Jeremy as they tasted one of the barrels. The wine was still bottled and sold, but it wasn't their proudest effort.

Assuming that something like that doesn't happen, however, the next step is to add bentonite, which is essentially a clay substance that looks sort of like chocolate mousse or the mud they use for facials at day spas. "Bento," as it's better known, is an impure silicate, which means that it has lots of binding sites on it, so it grabs on to stray proteins floating around in the wine, and together they sink to the bottom of the tank.

The trick, however, is figuring out how much bento to add, which is determined by setting up trials, just as you would in high school chemistry. And like high school chemistry, it's time-consuming and annoying. Once you've found the right amount, you stick a submersible pump, which is about the size of a coffee pot, into the top of the tank and slowly add the bento over one hour. You then let it mix for another hour after it's all inside the tank.

Next comes fining. Bento just drops out the proteins, while fining clarifies, purifies, and stabilizes, as well as takes the astringent edge off the wine. For fining you can use skim milk or egg whites, or any collagen-based substance, such as isinglass . . . or Melanie Griffith. Trials for each fining agent are set up, and the winemaker simply goes with the one that tastes best. Whether you use milk, egg whites, or Melanie Griffith, the fining agent sinks down to the bottom of the tank over a couple of days and is later discarded.

Now the wine has to be filtered to get rid of any remaining yeast or other solid particles floating around in the wine. Unfortunately, filtering wine is a little more complicated than running it through a pasta colander. And again, there are two choices. The tried-and-true method is to use an earth filter, which is relatively cost-efficient, but very time-consuming. The other downside is that the system requires the use of diatomaceous earth powder, which not only is messy and produces a fair amount of waste, but if you accidentally inhale a whole bunch of the powder, can be carcinogenic (though you'd have to pretend you're Chris Farley and it's Colombian nose candy for it to have *that* hazardous an effect). Alternatively, you can use a cross-flow filter, which is an extremely expensive piece of equipment. There are only a few of them in Marlborough, and one of them is indeed available for rent. For a few thousand bucks, a guy missing half his teeth will show up with a cross-flow filter on a trailer attached to the back of the truck he likely lives in, and he'll filter a 20,000-liter tank of wine over about three hours (using the earth filter would take the entire day).

As for which is truly better, that's up to the winemaker. Matua Valley, a Marlborough brand produced up the road from ASW at Rapaura Vintners, did a study in June 2003 that compared earth filtering with cross-flow. What they found was that on a chemical level, cross-flow was slightly more effective—but no one could actually taste the difference between the two. The only benefit they found was speed.

For that reason alone, Josh and Jeremy brought in the for-hire cross-flow filter once a few Sauvignon Blanc tanks were ready, as ASW's U.S. importer had run out of '03 wine to sell. They were able to throw together a blend and get 2,200 cases of Allan Scott 2004 Sauvignon Blanc to the United States in significantly less time because of the advantages cross-flow technology brings. Much as they may have complained about having to churn out finished wine so soon after harvest, it did present ASW with a chance to offload some Chardonnay, which made up 10 percent of the blend of that shipment.

I know what you're thinking: "Ten percent of that Sauvignon Blanc I bought was *Chardonnay*?! Those assholes!"

Well, not really. Remember, they have to make a drinkable product. And they felt the quality of the Sauvignon Blanc they had ready at the moment wasn't up to snuff. For whatever reason, the wine didn't have the concentrated fruit flavors and aromas people typically expect in Marlborough Sauvignon Blanc. They also had enough Chardonnay to fill the pool of every summer home in Rhode Island. Granted, Josh more or less led the charge to use some Chardonnay in the blend while Jeremy resisted. "I hate adding Chardonnay to Sav," he told me. But there's nothing wrong with it so long as you stay within the legal limits.

"You have to feel comfortable with any winemaking decision that you make," John Belsham explained to me about such tactics. "If you think the wine's going to be better with 5 percent Semillon and you're still legally allowed to put 'Sauvignon Blanc' on the label, I'm quite comfortable with that. Those laws are set down on sensible, rational discussion, and they're constantly reviewed. If someone illegally labels a wine, I'm the first one to jump up and down, because that's definitely ethically transgressing what's acceptable."

What Josh and—to a lesser extent—Jeremy chose to do was in fact legal. They did what they had to do to make the wine taste better. It has to look good, too, which is why the last part of the process is achieving cold stabilization, better known as "cold stab." Cold stab is the process through which tartrate crystals are dropped out. If this step isn't taken, the wine will look as if it has tiny bits of broken glass floating inside the bottle. Some people actually like tartrate crystals in red wine, since it's just an indication that there was a "hands-off" winemaking approach (and they won't hurt you, so don't be surprised if you see the crystals floating around in your glass).

Once the tank is chilled to minus one degree centigrade, a substance called cream of tartar (basically the same thing as baking powder), known as "cot" for short, is added to the wine to help speed up the process of dropping out the crystals. The tank is then left alone for three days, and you can then check the wine for cold stability by putting a small sample of wine in the freezer. After you pull it out and the wine begins to thaw, it's stable if you don't see crystals. If they're still there, that just means the tank has to be kept cold for another day or two.

At ASW (though not at all wineries) they filter again to a new tank, this time warming up the wine along the way by passing it through a heat exchanger. This brings the wine closer to bottling temperature, which has to be around seventeen degrees centigrade or the fill heights in the bottles won't be quite right. And if the wine is too cold, condensation will form on the outside of the bottles, and the labels won't stick. At this point the wine is also hit with a bit of nitrogen gas to knock out the CO_2 so there's no spritziness in the bottle.

The final addition that's made, again through trials, is copper. Copper helps lift the aroma, so that way you can actually smell something when you stick your nose over the glass after you swirl it. Some winemakers don't add copper, but it's an absolute necessity for any winery that bottles under screw caps, otherwise the wine might smell like bad eggs or burning tires when you open the bottle. Last I checked, gagging is not the response winemakers are hoping for when you first smell their wine. But it's not like you're sucking on a dirty penny from the added copper, either. Overall, the amount of copper added is minute—we're talking maybe twelve grams total in a 15,000-liter tank.

At this point the sulfur and CO_2 levels are checked again, and if the CO_2 level is too high, it's knocked down with a quick dose of nitrogen gas. This is also when you check the sugar level and add some if the wine tastes like it needs it.

All of these procedures are different for everyone—they go with what they find works best. For example, ASW filters its Pinot, while some others let their wines sit in barrels or tanks for much longer, then go straight from there to the bottle, since the wines have had enough time to clarify and stabilize on their own. It's kind of like the raw-foods movement, only much less obnoxious and annoying, with no ditzy, uninformed celebrities calling for all wine to be made the "natural" way. Because so far as I know, neither has been proven to be better-tasting, healthier, or more helpful in preventing erectile dysfunction. They're just different means to the same end.

Speaking of which, when it comes time to bottle, you're presented with two choices. You can bottle on the premises, or send the wine to a contract bottling facility, such as Marlborough Bottling Company (known around the valley as MBC). Big operations like Montana, Nobilo, and Villa Maria are the exception to the rule, since they ship their wine in tankers up to Auckland for bottling.

Whatever you do, though, bottling is the point at which everything can go perfectly right or hideously wrong. You can make wine that does for taste buds what Viagra does for penises, but no one will ever know if you screwed up the bottling. Because unlike Viagra, a wine's quality hinges on how well it was put into the bottle and how good its seal is. That's why a wine label that says "estate produced and bottled" counts for absolutely nothing if that winery does a poor job at bottling.

In general, winemakers prefer to move wine as little as possible. They believe that the more you pump it around, the more it's harmed. And by that argument, using a contract bottler or even moving wine to Auckland is downright crazy. But there's a difference in opinion where bottling is concerned.

"We're very technically adept at moving wine around. We've had a lot of experience with it," Nobilo's Darryl Woolley explained to me. "The only harm that can come is inadvertent oxidation, and lack of attention to detail—you run a pump dry. And poor hygiene, if you don't wash your hoses. The more times you handle the product, the more chances there are of these errors creeping in. But if you manage that, I don't believe that pumping wine around is in any way detrimental. I don't consider moving wine to Auckland any different from moving wine to a bottling hall."

The big advantage is that a contract bottler like MBC will take care of everything—bottles, cases, caps, corks, foils, you name it. Moreover, if you're sending wine to MBC, they pump it into a tanker truck, and then bottle it straight from that tanker rather than pumping it into another tank before bottling, doing their best to minimize movements.

"I strongly believe that the professionals do a professional job," Mike Just told me while the bottling line was running at Lawson's Dry Hills. In other words, he thinks that wineries, such as his, often don't bottle themselves because there's greater potential for error. He looked over his shoulder to make sure that the owners, Ross and Barbara Lawson, weren't around before he continued speaking.

"I was not for this project from day one," he said as the sound of clanking bottles filled the background. "The infrastructure is not set up for it. The premises don't have a separate trade entrance. The driveway's not set up for large trucks and containers." The bottling line, he added, was plunked down in the middle of the winery. "For a job that—at the rate it's going—will take three months, squandering skilled labor. The business manager's stacking cases, the vineyard manager is putting bottles on, and all the vineyard workers are filling cases or packing bottles when they still have things to do in the vineyard."

It's worth noting that the most likely reason for such an allocation of resources is that Ross Lawson is a communist. Seriously. Ask him, and he'll show you his little red card.

"I think bottling on-site can have its merits," Mike continued. "The potential ability to bottle what you want when you want. [But] it doesn't save you anything on dry goods, because at MBC they repurchase all the bottles, so you get them at a good rate, and you only pay for the ones you use. I just think it takes the focus away from the vineyard and the winemaking, which are really what put the quality stamp on a label."

Not to say Lawson's is bad at bottling—Mike just feels there's greater potential for error. Unlike Lawson's, ASW has a building specifically constructed to house its bottling operation. Along with a well-trained staff, the winery's able to do as good a job as a professional bottling company would. The downside, though, is that bottling on-site is a lot of extra work.

If bottling starts at 7:00 A.M., that means Geoff usually has to arrive at 5:00 A.M. to begin sterilizing the line. Once it's up and running, a temp worker stacks bottles on the conveyer. The bottles are washed before passing through a device that quickly sucks the air out of each one, then gives it a spurt of CO_2. The bottles move down the line, are filled with seven hundred fifty milliliters of wine, capped, and sealed. Toward the end of the line they're labeled front and back, and another temp worker, usually a very fast and efficient sixty-something woman named Shirley—no, the other temp isn't named Laverne—at the end of the line packs twelve bottles into each case. She then slides the case down a conveyer that seals the bottom and top with tape, and another person pulls the cases off the conveyer as they arrive. They're then stacked onto pallets, each one with fifty-six cases. The pallet is then wrapped with shrink wrap, and a forklift comes and pulls away each pallet as it's completed. Essentially, four people can run the bottling line relatively smoothly, with the middle two people constantly replenishing supplies for the workers stacking and packing the bottles.

No, it doesn't sound fun. And it isn't. It's repetitive and mundane, and after an hour of stacking bottles on the conveyor, your fingers are so sore they feel like they're gonna fall off. At some point you'll get a wet bottle or your mind wanders because you think, "My God, I've been stacking bottles here for hours, and more just keep coming. This blows!" and the next thing you know,

CRASH! You've shattered several bottles all over the floor, holding up the line, when everyone else just wants to get the day's work over and done with.

A winery of ASW's size bottles about 1,300 cases or so in a day, roughly three times a week, right up until Christmas. However, opportunities to inject a little excitement do present themselves now and again. One time I found a couple of misprinted screw caps that had the ASW logo on the side, but Mount Riley's trademark "MR" on top. Geoff and I decided to let them go through, and I pulled the two sealed and labeled bottles off the line. I then went out to the winery, where I found Josh knee-deep in the messy job of cleaning tartrate crystals off the inside wall of a tank. I showed him the bottles and played dumb, as if they all had come out that way, and watched his eyes widen and the vein in his forehead pop out. "That's fuckin' Mount Riley!" he screamed as he climbed out of the tank. It wasn't until after he'd sprinted into the bottling hall—fueled as much by rage as curiosity—that he discovered it'd all been a joke. A few weeks later he tried to get his revenge when I was passed out on the sofa in his house, by putting his cock on my forehead and taking a picture using my digital camera. Fortunately, I woke up—to sounds of uncontrollable giggling—before he could figure out how to control his penis and a camera at the same time. Apparently it's harder than it sounds.

Anyway, ASW has pretty much always done its own bottling, and Josh and Sara have been working the line since they were little kids. Overall the winery is very adept at bottling, but that doesn't mean that it's immune from minor mistakes and major disasters.

Once, in a combined effort, Josh and Geoff happened to break a small part on the screw-capper that required the manufacturer to send a replacement part from Italy, delaying bottling for more than a week. Another time, several thousand bottles came with necks at a slight angle, so every time the screw-capper dropped down to seal the bottle, it would shatter. And one day, as the winery was preparing to bottle half of its small amount of rosé (which is made by pulling off juice from a Pinot tank and fermenting it separately), Geoff accidentally left the valve between the wine and water lines slightly open. The water pushed itself back through the wine line and into the tank, topping up the rosé with water. At first Jeremy and Josh thought it might help, since the wine's alcohol level was too high anyway—but not so high as to warrant about two hundred liters of water in a 1,300-liter tank.

"That's probably my worst fuckup here, ever," Geoff admitted to me after the fact. Jeremy fumed, and immediately sent Jemma to do some lab work on the watered-down wine to see if the pH had gone up dramatically. Josh, on the other hand, was surprisingly calm about it.

"I told Geoff not to worry, 'cause he works bloody hard. We'd been talking about putting a pressure lock on that ages ago," he said, "and we should've done it at the end of last harvest. We were just talking about doing that two weeks ago."

Though the pH was fine, the wine simply tasted too thin and watery. So Josh did some quick thinking and figured out that he could come up with a good alternative by adding a bit of Pinot Noir, and give the rosé its edge with some Chardonnay. Comfortable as he may have been with the decision, Josh did his best to make sure I wouldn't write that ASW's rosé was partially made with Chardonnay.

"That's how they used to make it in France, in the old days," he told me. "They used to plant four or five vines of red, then one of white, then four more of red, all down the row. That's where rosé comes from."

I didn't buy it for a second, because Josh is better known in some circles for his ability as a bullshitter than as a winemaker. But just to be safe I sent an email to wine guru Jay McInerney, whose books *Bacchus and Me: Adventures in the Wine Cellar* and *A Hedonist in the Cellar: Adventures in Wine* are loaded with facts on the history of certain wine varieties and styles. Even though most people probably associate him with his novels, such as *Bright Lights, Big City*—and imagine that he's the kind of guy who could blow a four-inch rail off a hooker's belly and tell you if the coke's from Colombia, Bolivia, or Venezuela—Jay's actually well known to be a walking wine encyclopedia. Even though the only wine from New Zealand that he mentioned in his first book was Cloudy Bay Sauvignon Blanc (hey, we all have our shortcomings), I still figured that as the ultimate wine geek, he was the perfect person to let me know if Josh was trying to pull a fast one. Here's what he wrote back:

Well, I'm no scholar, but your bullshit meter was probably operating correctly that day. The history of rosé is murky as far as I can tell not least because a lot of what we think of as red wines used to be pink, like Burgundy, because of very short macerations. Which is of course how we make rosé now. There is also a lot of evidence that red and white grapes used to coexist quite regularly in the same vineyards if you could call them vineyards—certainly they did and still do in places like Chianti, and the resulting field blend would also be lighter in color than today's Chianti or Cortons. So I guess you might say that there is some historical precedent for blending red and white. But basically it sounds like they're just fishing for a cover story. I say if it tastes good they may be on to something.

And it did taste good. Better than the unaffected batch of rosé the winery also had, I thought. Jeremy disagreed with me, saying, "I hate adding Chardonnay to rosé," shortly after he said the same thing about Sauvignon Blanc. But he couldn't help but admit that he and Josh had gotten lucky. Josh's quick thinking enabled them to mix and match so as to create something that was not only passable and met the distributor's requested volume, but was nice to drink.

Something that's especially challenging when it comes time to blend the winery's biggest seller.

It's always better to have a little more wine than you want, and sell on whenever possible. If it does mean a slight loss economically, the gain to the brand is significant.

—Matt Thomson, consultant winemaker for St. Clair, Lake Chalice, Mud House, Delta, and Cape Campbell

---

14

Blending Day

At the end of May, as the air grew colder and the sky uglier, Lake Chalice, whose range of wines is made by Matt Thomson, was the first winery to put a 2004 Marlborough Sauvignon Blanc on store shelves in New Zealand as well as in the United States. It was a run of only about five hundred cases and was labeled as "First Release," meaning that the Lake Chalice wine that arrived later in the year would be part of a bigger blend that had more time to sit in the tank and rest on its lees.

Every year, the first winery in Marlborough to release a Sauvignon Blanc proudly proclaims its feat and basks in the brief glow of media attention. But everyone in Marlborough knows that it's really just a gimmick, kind of how Beaujolais Nouveau is released on the same day every year, but the better wines from Beaujolais aren't released for another several weeks or even months. As for the Lake Chalice First Release, the wine was made of grapes from a single vineyard, supposedly one of the first in the region to ripen every year. Nevertheless, I soon heard several winemakers grumble about the harm first-release wines might do to the Marlborough image and brand. The thinking is that wine rushed to market can't possibly be good.

John Belsham, winemaker and owner of Foxes Island, told me that the first wine to be released is always "the first to fall to bits." It may taste fine at first, but a few months later it'll probably taste like a stale potato chip. Think of it as a one-night stand. Sure, it's good, but it just ain't gonna hold up for even a few months because the crucial, formative work wasn't put in early on. John was just speaking generally, though, not specifically about Lake Chalice's wine.

"I liked what Lake Chalice did," Seresin's Brian Bicknell told me. "I liked that they had First Release on their label so people understood that it was a different blend than their final one would be." However, he did go on to say that with such a practice "we run the risk of that Beaujolais kind of thing—it's made quickly, get it out quickly, drink it quickly. It takes away from being a serious wine in a way."

The only way to find out if it was a serious wine, I figured, was to do a taste test. So a few days after the Lake Chalice First Release '04 Sauvignon Blanc became available in Blenheim supermarkets, I picked up a bottle, wrapped it in brown paper, and brought it to the winery for Jeremy, Josh, and Jemma to taste. They all saw the bottle's distinctive silver screw cap, so that might have narrowed down their choices as to what the wine could possibly be. However, none of them knew that it was from '04.

"It's herbaceous, older. Maybe 2003," Josh guessed, having tasted first. "It definitely has that Chenin Blanc greenness to it. It's actually a pretty good wine. It's got a bit of fruit still there. I'd say it's a bit of a show wine. I could get pissed on that. I'd say it's not upper Wairau. Where Daniel Le Brun's place is—that sort of area."

Even if he didn't have the year right, he was on the money in terms of location. Lake Chalice's main vineyard is exactly in the area Josh described. I then showed him the label.

"That's bad news for '04," he immediately exclaimed, reversing his opinion in the blink of an eye. "That's crap. It should be a lot fresher than that. It's really green and herbaceous, like an older oxidized wine. That's unripe stuff they added sugar to, I guarantee it," he said, even though the back label claimed that the grapes were picked at 23 Brix. Then again, it also boasted passion-fruit and gooseberry flavors that it didn't seem to have.

Jeremy, who wasn't in the room for Josh's taste test, came next. "It's quite thin through the palate," he concluded. "It's Sauvignon Blanc, but there's nothing special about it." At first he thought it was '04, and then said, "I think it's '03 Lake Chalice. It's not tropical at all. It's very thin. It's quite dry, but it doesn't have that aged herbaceousness."

Then came Jemma's turn. "Sauvignon Blanc, 2002," she said. "I find it a bit flat, and there might be a bit of residual sugar there. Quite nice nose. No real fruit characters that stand out."

So both Josh and Jemma thought that it was an old Sauvignon Blanc that was on the decline but still good, whereas Jeremy pretty much had it spot on (though I still believe that he was able to make a more informed guess based on seeing the color of the screw cap). Nevertheless, what I found to be unusual about the tasting was that each person's opinion changed dramatically once he or she actually knew what the wine was.

"It's got too much aggressiveness to be '02," Jeremy proclaimed. "Look at the color. It's like weasel piss. That'll only hold up until Christmas. It just tasted thin and new—there's no lees contact or anything like that. It just seems like it was rushed."

"But I'd buy that for sixteen dollars," Jemma said, which was in fact the retail price of the wine in New Zealand dollars at the Blenheim supermarket.

"It's drinkable and would be quite nice with food. But quality-wise, I don't think it's the best. You need six to eight weeks' conditioning for Sav, just sitting on its lees, letting all the shit drop out. That's what it needs," Josh said.

Essentially, a first-release wine of only five hundred cases is a marketing ploy. It's meant to be bought and consumed quickly. Which is why I think it was easier for the three to criticize the wine once they actually knew what it was. I decided the only way to really find out what this wine was all about was to ask Matt Thomson, the guy who made it. I started by asking him if he was under pressure to get the wine out.

"Absolutely," he said without hesitation. "You can't sell wine if you haven't got any on the shelves. If you don't respond to your market, you're out of a job. That said, I did push it back a wee bit. They wanted it earlier than they got it, and there was a point at which it would've been too hard. So it came back about two weeks."

Having established that, as well as confirming that the fruit was indeed some of the first in the region to be harvested—"We harvested one component of the blend a week before we bottled the [First Release]," Matt explained—I told him about the far-from-scientific taste test I had performed, and that the tasters thought that the wine might fall apart after about six months or so.

"Absolutely not," he protested. "When it's first bottled it actually looks a bit flattened out rather than later on. They recover in the bottle. If anything, it's going to be significantly better in six months."

We may never know, since with only five hundred cases, there wouldn't be any of it left after six months. At the very least, however, I'd get to see how it performed a couple of months later, in a lineup of other '04 Sauvignon Blancs.

While Matt was getting that particular Lake Chalice wine ready, he was probably also busy figuring out what to put in his blends, like everyone else in Marlborough. Most wines that you see on the shelf don't in fact come from a single vineyard like the Lake Chalice First Release, but are instead made up of varying amounts of wine from several vineyards harvested at different times. When they're all done fermenting in separate tanks, the winemaker mixes and matches them to produce something that tastes the way he or she wants it to taste.

Blending is a time-consuming, labor-intensive process, and there are several different ways of going about it. It all depends on how many tanks of Sauvignon Blanc the winery has, as well as how many labels it has. If a winery only has one label, as say, Huia does, it's fairly easy. What Claire and Mike Allan like, they keep. What they don't like, they sell off on the bulk market. Almost every winery does this, some more than others.

"It becomes apparent as you go along which of your vineyards are going to be performing above what you expect and the ones that will be performing below," Mike told me as Huia was beginning to bottle some of its '04 wines. "We keep on our toes, and if things are not going to make the blend, they're just sold off in bulk as we go along."

At bigger wineries, however, like Wither Hills, they might have four different labels into which they can allocate their wines. Nobilo has eight different Sauvignon Blancs that it produces, and as the ferments tick away, the winemakers taste them and put them into different categories.

"We categorize them, look at the sales-volume requirements, and come back and look at the wines and select them for these individual groupings," Darryl Woolley explained to me. "We're very quality-driven at the top end. Whatever's left, we then move down to the next tier. We keep blending down."

Ben Glover at Wither Hills, however, told me that "the key is to always blend up, and don't try and blend down or fit something in," meaning that Wither Hills allocates among its labels based on style. "Our other labels aren't second labels—they can still sit on their own, and you can be quite confident in saying, 'This is a pretty smart Sauvignon.' "

That may be true, but that's more or less the marketing angle. Because by and large, Marlborough winemakers keep the tropical-flavored batches as their best wines and find some other way to make use of the greener-tasting stuff. It just has to do with preferences, in much the same way that Coca-Cola tastes different in other countries. For whatever reason, New Zealanders tend to prefer the more fruit-flavored Sauvignon Blanc, while Americans tend to like hints of grassy aromas and flavors. There are exceptions to the rule, such as Domaine Georges Michel, which intentionally makes a greener style more in line with what you'd find from Sancerre, France. But in general, Marlborough winemakers look for rich, tropical-fruit flavor, and anything with the slightest herbal or grassy flavor is put into cheaper, second labels, and much of it is exported.

A winery like Seresin, as Brian Bicknell told me, will have as many as fifty-six different tanks of wine to go through, tasting about fifteen a day for four days. "Five of us go through them," he explained, "and we come up with what is the base of the blend—the key ones. That's the base wine, then we go through the question marks" and make additions and subtractions where they think they might help.

At ASW there were twenty components that Josh, Jeremy, Jemma, Allan, Cathy, Victoria, and I all tasted and discussed over a full day. We were also joined by Liz Dew, who works the winery's tasting room, as well as Chris, a woman from Eurowine, ASW's Wellington-based distributor. The winery had already sold off some wine that it wasn't happy with, so everything left on the table, numbered one through twenty, would need to fit into one of two blends.

They already knew what volumes they would need domestically and for their export markets (total domestic volume for ASW is about three times that of export). And because this particular winery makes more money in the domestic market, it's important to satisfy that one first and foremost. That doesn't mean that the export blend is bad—anything the winery isn't happy with it sells off. But Allan, Cathy, Jeremy, Josh, and just as important, ASW's distributor, know what the domestic market wants, so they first find the wines they think will satisfy New Zealand wine drinkers.*

---

*Starting in 2005, ASW decided to no longer allocate portions to domestic and export, and instead keeps the best tanks for the regular Allan Scott label, and blends the lesser components into the Millstone and Kotuku labels. The Allan Scott Sauvignon Blanc sold here in the United States is the same blend sold everywhere else.

On blending day we all sat down around the table of the tasting room, in front of bottles of cloudy wine that looked like yellow grapefruit juice. Each bottle contained wine from a different tank.

"Every tank's been sulfured up," Josh said to open the proceedings. "We need a domestic blend, an export, and to look for any faults. Domestic is more tropical flavors, and export is more herbaceous and green. Write down any prominent characteristics from each. This was really helpful to us last year, because some we thought were shit turned out to be great."

Right about now you're probably thinking to yourself, "They sit around and taste wine all day? I want that job!" But believe me, you don't. It's a lot harder than it sounds, and it's anything other than fun. Because remember, you're tasting, not drinking. When you drink twenty wines, it's a party. When you *taste* twenty wines, it's work. Halfway through your mouth feels like tumbleweeds, and by the end your head hurts and your tongue feels like sandpaper.

Think of it this way. Sex is fun. So let's say you have to have sex twenty times in a row for analytical purposes. Before you ask where to sign up, think about the fact that it probably wouldn't be fun if you had to stop at various points throughout and write down what the sensations felt like. Not what specifically happened—"She pulled my hair, twisted my nipple, and made me scream my mother's name" doesn't count. You have to describe the sensation that resulted from having your hair pulled, your nipple twisted, and so forth, in such a way that the other people in the room can understand and relate to it. Normally, having sex twenty times is fun because you don't have to think about it. You just enjoy it in much the same way that you enjoy drinking twenty glasses of wine—you're just drinking and having a good time with your friends. But when you start to try to pull each wine apart in your brain and write down notes, you're taking all the fun out of it. That's why you should appreciate what wine-makers do for a living. By tasting twenty or thirty wines over several hours, they take all the fun out of drinking wine for themselves, so when the wine gets to you it tastes good and you have fun drinking it. You can relax and enjoy it, and think about more important things. Like sex. And how much of it you'll get if you give more wine to the person you're with at that particular moment.

If you're still not convinced that blending is not only devoid of fun but also difficult, just look at my notes from that day:

1. Grassy and fruity. A bit bitter.
2. More fruit. Really nice, smooth.
3. Very strong, but good depth. Good nose.

I already have cottonmouth.

4. Grassy nose, but nice. A bit bitter, but good.

Just noticed Victoria twist her face in disgust as she spit that one out, practically gagging on her way to the bucket. Shows how much I know.

5. Strong. Good fruit. Nice nose.
6. Fuck if I know. I like it, but I don't know why.

Mouth is now fucked.

7. A bit stinky on the nose. Good fruit. Could be very good, but I dunno.
8. A bit stinky, but in a good way. Nice range of fruit flavors.
9. Also a bit stinky. Good nose. A lot of citrus notes. Very good.
10. Mellow on the nose, but really delivers on fruit flavors. Best so far.
11. Sour on the nose, nice weight, grassy on the finish. Good.
12. Slight stink. Like it, but not sure why. A bit bitter finish.
13. Fresh smell. Again not sure why I like it, but I'd be very happy with it.
14. Slight stink. Fruity, well balanced.

Okay, now I'm just makin' shit up.

15. Not much on the nose, but nice once it gets there. Some citrus. Nice wine.
16. Weak nose, but nice. Packs a punch on the palate. Sweaty style.
17. Fruity nose; a bit better. Not bad, but not my style.

Now I just really wanna get through this. I can't take it anymore.

18. Mild nose; grassy finish—not much in the middle, but still good.
19. High RS. Blocks out the nose and everything else.
20. No nose. High sugar, I think, but I have no idea. Taste buds are shot. Good finish . . . I think.

"They actually taste a bit different the second time through," Allan remarked just as I finished for the first time, and had absolutely no intention of going through them all again. *He can actually handle that?* I thought to myself. My mouth felt as though I'd been chewing broken glass.

Fortunately it was still able to serve one of its main functions, and we began to discuss each wine. Starting with Chris and the first wine, each person had to give his or her comments. And since I was sitting in the fourth seat to Chris's right, that meant I had to be the first to give my comments on the fourth wine, as well as on the sixteenth. I wasn't looking forward to either, since, as you can tell from my tasting notes, I didn't know what the hell I was talking about.

What happened more often than one would expect, however, was that general opinion would be the opposite of what Jeremy and Josh thought. The first wine, for example, got a big thumbs-up from everyone. It turned out to be a small, 7,000-liter tank of pressings. The wine was of such low quality, they thought, that they used a carbon addition to help absorb all the unwanted particles out of the wine, or maybe even clear up what they thought was a funky smell. "We ripped the shit out of it," Josh said, amazed, referring to how much they'd had to manipulate that tank. "Always happens though, doesn't it?"

When we got to wine number four, I found that the only one who really shared my praise of it was Cathy, who, by the way, had a head cold. Throughout the discussion we often found our comments were similar, which I guess means that I, a scruffy-looking twenty-nine-year-old male, have the same palate as a middle-aged woman with three grown children, a blocked nose, and a sore throat.

There were also a couple of curveballs thrown in. Like two tanks of the same juice, but fermented with different strains of yeast. And some of the tanks that consensus agreed were among the best, turned out to be batches made entirely of or containing some juice that came from the RDV, the device that separates liquids from solids right after crushing (see Chapter 2). But by and large, a tasting such as this one takes place much as I described above: Rather than sit around and have a few drinks and laughs, the participants do their best to describe the flavors they detected and the sensations formed in their mouths. Some of the descriptions were extremely unusual, especially when it came to Allan's and Josh's comments.

"I got cooked, cold peppers," Josh said of wine twelve. "I always put things down it reminds me of." On another he tried to describe it as that smell you get when you open a can of pineapples.

"I discovered mushrooms, and that fungusy, dusty character. There's something strange about it that appealed to me," Allan said of the wine in which his son tasted cooked, cold peppers.

And on it goes like this, around the room, for each and every wine. For several hours. People detect flavors of mango, apricots, candle wax, BO, "smoking-gun flint characters," guava, pineapple, green beans, bubblegum, pears, stone fruit, you name it. It's like talking about politics with politicians—most of it is philosophical and comes down to opinion and interpretation rather than cold, hard facts and solid conclusions. Which can make it frustrating. After an hour of it you want to go home and drink beer . . . forever.

Once the discussion ended, Josh went around the room and asked each person what his or her top-five wines were. Of course, probably only two of my five were similar to other people's choices, but the same could be said for everyone else. Because at the end, even after all that discussion, it still comes down to personal preference.

During the lunch break, Josh and Jeremy began crunching the numbers and putting together the blends based on what had been designated as domestic or export, keeping the volume requirements of each in mind. So let's say a 4,000-liter tank was designated as worthy of the domestic blend. Josh therefore measured out four milliliters of it. He'd take twenty milliliters from the 20,000-liter tanks, ten milliliters for the 10,000-liter tanks, and so forth, and all these were blended together in one carafe. For the tanks that were borderline between export and domestic, either Josh split them up evenly or he and Jeremy decided where they would go based on what kind of difference they would make to each blend.

The process took about an hour and the use of a pipette and a couple of graduated cylinders. The domestic blend turned out to be varying amounts from eighteen different tanks, as well as a few thousand liters they'd fermented in oak barrels rather than stainless-steel tanks. Once it was all put together and shaken up a bit to integrate it, a couple of glasses were poured, and everyone took a taste. I thought it was very good, even though it felt as though the acid was eating away at my gums.

"It's a gorgeous wine," proclaimed Chris. "It lacks a little in the midpalate. That could be some of the RS. It could use some stiffening up with a bit more of one of the others."

"That's a two-hundred-fifty-thousand-liter blend," Josh said as he tasted it. "This is pretty bloody awesome for a blend of that size."

"It's definitely our style . . . are the aromas strong enough?" Allan wondered aloud.

"It could do with a bit more pungency," Chris agreed.

"We could take five thousand liters of this tank out," Jeremy said, pointing at the list that contained all the tanks and their volumes, "and put in five thousand liters of something else to get that drier style."

Chris quickly looked over the list in Jeremy's hand. She looked back at her tasting notes, and asked him, "Can you do the same thing, but take out tank twenty-one and put in tank thirteen?"

Josh made up the new blend over the next several minutes, and truth be told, once I tasted it I couldn't detect much of a difference. But it seemed to win over the crowd.

"It's much more grapefruity. More aromatic," Allan commented.

"This seems to be the nose you were looking for," Chris concluded. "That's really nice wine."

"I think I'd be happy with that," Allan agreed.

Josh later admitted that, like me, he didn't think there was much of a difference between the two. Nevertheless, it's what they decided to go with since everyone seemed to be in agreement that it was good, and it also helped him and Jeremy use their volumes a bit more the way they wanted to.

Josh then put together the export blend 111,000 liters (about 13,000 cases) of which would be shipped to the United States, and I actually thought it tasted better than the domestic blend. Maybe it just suited my own particular preferences. Whatever the case, it seemed as though blending is like trying to solve a Rubix Cube. You make one change to solve one problem, and in doing so you could be creating three others. In this particular case, however, the winery and its distributor were convinced that all the right moves had been made to get all the colors on the right sides of the puzzle without too much fiddling—or peeling off the stickers.

About one month to the day later, the first portion of the blend was bottled. But that doesn't mean all the components were blended together in their entirety—this would require a large blending tank. Which ASW doesn't have. Later, when Josh began to put together another portion of the blend, it was basically two-and-a-half days straight of pumping six hundred fifty liters of this and 1,200 liters of that into four different tanks that hold different vol-umes: 10,000, 15,000, 20,000, and 33,000 liters. So Josh couldn't just pump equal amounts of the blend into each tank, and instead had to do even more number-crunching. The trick of blending into multiple tanks of different sizes is that if the calculations aren't correct, the tanks may not all fill com-pletely, meaning the air in the empty space in the tank will oxidize the wine (which kills all the flavors and aromas).

The first run of 10,000 liters actually came a few days late, since no one had bothered to order labels for the bottles. But on the rescheduled day, when bottling was nearly complete, Allan asked me to set up a blind tasting with a bottle of Allan Scott 2004 Sauvignon Blanc straight off the line against six others he'd bought earlier in the day. I decanted each wine into empty bot-tles without labels and numbered them one through seven before Jeremy, Josh, Jemma, Allan, and Cathy all came into the tasting room and started swirling, sniffing, and spitting, and jotting down their notes.

We were just getting started when Josh asked me, "Five isn't ours, is it? If it is, we need to stop bottling now. I'm serious. It smells like a dirty man's toilet."

"Oh, what's that smell like?" his mother asked him with a grin.

"Maybe like Dad's socks . . . or my socks. Like you've been wearing your shoes all day, and just took them off," Josh tried to clarify.

This was a pivotal moment for me. I could play a joke, and tell him that it was indeed his wine, and watch him sprint across the winery in a raging panic. Of course, I knew by then that Josh had a good sense of humor, but I wasn't sure how good it was about his own wine. It's sort of like walking into the kitchen of a restaurant to tell the chef that you gave his food to the old lady's Pomeranian at the table next to you. You'll probably get stabbed sev-eral times before the chef hears you whimper through the blood gurgling from your mouth, "Just kidding."

"Oh, you should have said that one was ours," Cathy said, after I owned up and admitted that it wasn't. "Why didn't you?"

"I didn't want to find myself on the next plane home," I told her.

"It could be Hawke's Bay. Hope it's not from Winery X,"* Jeremy said as he swirled, then sniffed and tasted the wine.

---

*The name of the winery is disguised for a reason.

We went back to wine number one, which wasn't particularly noteworthy, but no one openly disliked it. Cathy even thought it could be their own. When I revealed it as Mount Riley, she just rolled her eyes, sighed, and said, "I can't stand that guy."

One of the more noteworthy wines turned out to be wine number three, which was Montana. Probably a million-liter blend (or more), it got mostly good comments.

Wine number five did indeed turn out to be Winery X, which sent Jeremy and Josh into hysterics. Why? Because 50 percent of that wine was juice that ASW had sold to Winery X after deeming it unsuitable.

"Half the fruit in that is ours!" Josh exclaimed as he looked at the label. "Just goes to show, if we hadn't sent that away, that would be ours. That's incredible. I can't believe that. We sent them twenty thousand liters of shit. We even sent them samples, and they liked them."*

What I found even more amazing was that Jeremy was able to connect the dots in his brain between juice he'd sent away and finished wine he tasted blind several months later. It was no surprise, then, that he was able to pick out Allan Scott '04 Sauvignon Blanc the instant he tasted sample number six. This is also a good time to point out that a few months later he was accepted to the Master of Wine program (a London-based correspondence course for the best wine tasters in the world, with only a few people passing the final exam each year), and would spend the next two years, along with his day job, studying and tasting wines from all over the world as well as writing essays and taking exams.

In the last wine in the lineup, Josh found "a lot more greenness. Marmalade, passion fruit, grapefruit." Jeremy thought it was refreshing, yet "light on the palate." Allan called it "grapefruity and herbaceous. It'll be a can of green beans in three months' time."

It was Lake Chalice First Release. The comments of the tasters suggested that it hadn't improved since the first tasting, but it certainly hadn't deteriorated, either. Maybe it wouldn't change at all—something that might have more to do with the seal on the bottle than with the wine inside it.

---

*That's why.

At least you know the wine is what it was when it was in the tank.

—Ben Glover, winemaker at Wither Hills

15

Seriously Screwed

Just as someone once said that looks don't matter, it's what's on the inside, I've long felt the same way about a bottle of wine. I never really cared whether the bottle had a cork, a screw cap, or some sort of plastic or rubber stopper jammed into its neck. To me it was always how the wine tasted that mattered. In fact, I have two words for people who believe that they need the romance of pulling a cork in order to fully enjoy a bottle of wine: Blow me.

No, seriously. I'm not trying to be insulting. With the utmost sincerity I'm asking you to kneel in front of me, undo my pants, and give me oral sex. No matter how satisfying—or horrifying—the experience is for you, I guarantee that by the time I've given you a dose of DNA you won't remember whether my jeans had a button-down or zip-up fly.

As far as I knew when I landed in New Zealand, the debate about corks and screw caps was over and done with. A couple years earlier I'd written a boring business article about the Portuguese cork industry's efforts to educate wineries on the recent improvements in cork quality, so I thought that winemakers simply went with what made them most comfortable. I had no intention of writing a single word about the differences between corks and screw caps.

However, by the time of my arrival in Marlborough in 2004 the debate was still red-hot, with wineries the world over switching to screw caps, especially in Australia and New Zealand. So much so, in fact, that today finding a cork in an Australasian-produced bottle of wine is becoming a bit of a challenge. Sure, there will always be purists and traditionalists, but the screw cap has quickly come to dominate as the closure of choice in Marlborough.

What happened? Well, there was no single event that changed everything. No lightning strike of realization and rapid conversion. It wasn't like in the eighties when soda and beer cans went from the top that you peeled off and cut your finger on before flinging it to the ground in the 7-Eleven parking lot to the flip-top you now snap forward and push back. Rather, for years winemakers had come to live with the fact that they were going to have a certain amount of undrinkable product because corks can cause two main problems: oxidation or cork taint. In layman's terms, the former simply means that the cork let in too much air, spoiling the wine, and the latter means that the wine smells and tastes like your grandmother's basement on a rainy Sunday morning.

But accepting a certain failure rate is not really a very smart line of thinking if you're trying to run a business. It's a bit like Ford saying that it's perfectly comfortable with the wheels falling off a small percentage of its cars the moment they drive off the lot.

Putting this back in wine terms, though, let's say that ASW made 60,000 cases in a particular year. That comes out to exactly 720,000 bottles of wine, and the amount of wine that's generally believed to suffer some sort of cork-related fault is about 5 percent (though many, especially APCOR, the association of Portuguese cork producers, would say that it's significantly less). So that means that ASW would have 36,000 bottles of wine that are corked, are oxidized, or have some other cork-related fault that makes the wine undrinkable. And if the wine retails for twenty dollars a bottle, that calculates to exactly one hell of a lot of pissed-off customers who vow never to buy the wine again.

By 2000, Ross Lawson of Lawson's Dry Hills had had enough. Communist though he may be, he had a business to run, and he was sick of the inconsistency corks were providing. It didn't help that New Zealand, thousands of miles from Portugal, had access only to the bottom-of-the-barrel corks on the market. So Ross and some other Marlborough winemakers started to look at screw caps as a viable alternative.

"Ross was the first person who sent out an email to the other winemakers in the country, saying, 'Is anyone interested in talking about it?' " Mike Just recalled. "And I thought, 'Oh . . . my . . . God.' " In other words, "What has this nut job done?"

He probably felt that way because, let's face it, a screw cap simply doesn't look as sleek as a cork. And the romance of twisting in the corkscrew and making that popping sound as the cork is yanked out? Replaced by the teeth-grinding crackle of the screw cap.

And don't get any silly ideas in your head about a screw cap being cheaper. On the contrary. While yes, the cap itself is cheaper than a cork by a long shot, the technology required to apply the cap to the bottle is significantly more advanced.

"Technically, it's not a simple closure to apply," Nobilo's Darryl Woolley admitted to me. "People think it's a simple answer to a complex problem. But it's quite a complex operation to get it one hundred percent correct."

It's also very expensive. We're talking an initial investment of about US$300,000 for the proper equipment, never mind the cost of educating and training staff, as well as routine maintenance.

So what Ross was asking of his fellow winery owners was probably something that they didn't want to deal with. They wanted a solution, sure, but they didn't want to spend the money. And at that point, no one really knew how wine would develop under a screw cap as opposed to a cork, or if it would at all. Nevertheless, over time more and more wineries in Marlborough started to make the switch. But why?

"It's not that I love screw caps," Matt Thomson told me one day as he and I drove to his new vineyard, Delta, which spans an entire rolling, north-facing slope at the southwestern end of the valley. "It's that I fuckin' hate corks."

A couple of months later, when I met him again, he explained his position in greater detail. "Under cork, three bottles out of the case are good, six are all over the place, and three are cork damaged," he complained. "How do you tell someone when to drink it when there's so much variability in the case? And that's just due to the amount of oxygen they let in, not to mention the tainting aspect. It's how well we actually seal that bottle."

"So, last time we spoke," I reminded him, "you said you didn't love screw caps, but that you hated corks. Are you saying that now, two months later, you love screw caps?"

"Screw caps are pretty fuckin' good," he said.

Matt had the change of heart because he'd finally seen that some of his red wines bottled under screw cap had developed the way he'd hoped they would. So the question was never really how wines like Sauvignon Blanc and Pinot Gris would perform under screw cap. In New Zealand and much of the wider world, these wines are made to drink young. And I don't mean you buy it, then drink it a few months later when the mood strikes you. I mean young as in bottled one day, on the store shelf within a month, purchased and consumed an hour later. So it wouldn't matter if you sealed the bottle with Saran Wrap, just so long as it's airtight.

No, the real question was how red wines, which often do need time to develop, would age under screw cap. Someone like Ant MacKenzie at Spy Valley, at the time of writing, wasn't yet ready to find out.

"I think there's a place for both," he told me. "I'm very happy to have corks in my red wines. But aromatics that are designed for early drinking, no question, screw caps are the best closure. For our reds, because we do wild ferments, and the wine's spent twelve months in barrel, the evolution of the wine has been in conjunction with oak and air. Corks are oak, and they leak through air. To continue that same development, putting the bottle of wine under cork is fine. The wine can handle oxygen, and can handle the flavor of oak or wood. So, no worries. The white wine that's never seen a barrel or oxygen, you want to bottle with a closure that emulates exactly that same evolution. Those wines can't have oxygen. The aromatics disappear very quickly."

Reading into Ant's opinion a bit, you could go a step further and say that air actually helps red wines develop. That the best wines in the world bottled under cork taste the way they do because the corks have let through a consistent amount of air over time. And many people do believe that. Like Hatsch Kalberer at Fromm, who will probably never make the switch to screw caps.

"Some people now put their top lines under screw cap, and I have great doubts that they will develop the same as under a good cork," he predicted. "To me, the nature of the screw cap does almost inhibit a graceful development. If you take a bottle of wine and put it into a nice underground cellar, and it has a screw cap that's totally sealed, there's no point in putting it in a nice cellar. It's isolated. There is no lifeline to the outside world. If you're into drinking wines young, open them earlier." In other words, he's saying that a screw cap will keep the wine from aging the way that it would under a cork.

"Clearly, there's never an excuse for a bad cork," he continued, and went on to explain that he gets his corks from a producer in Sardinia, which also supplies the Bordeaux wine industry. "We'll go out of our way to get a good cork. A little more respect for a good cork would go a long way."

On the contrary, Matt Thomson has absolutely no respect for a good cork, but not for the reason you'd think. It's because he believes that screw caps do indeed let in a small amount of air, helping the wine develop the way that it's supposed to.

"There's a lot of confusion about this, but I've done a lot of reading recently, and some people are saying otherwise," he started to explain as he ran into his kitchen, poked around here and there, eventually returned with a screw cap in his hand, and stuck his index finger inside it. "What does the sealing is that little disc there, which does actually let through a very small amount of oxygen. It's a consistent amount for every screw cap, because [they're all] the same."

Confused? Well, so was I, because Matt's hands are huge—remember, he's a competitive kayaker. His fingers are big enough that he could have been pointing at the inside of a truck tire, and I still wouldn't be able to see what he was talking about. So he started to explain it in a more conceptual way: that it's like a bike tire. Tires slowly leak air over time, otherwise you'd never have to pump them up. Screw caps, he believes, do essentially the same thing, just on a smaller scale.

"On a screw cap there's a very small area, and a very small amount of air getting in. If you look at how much that is, and compare it to corks, corks have an enormous range of permeability," he said. "Some are just about like sieves, and some are tight. The best corks let in pretty much nothing, but very few corks are like that. A screw cap fits into that range—it's just at the very tighter end of corks. And we all know that Pinot Noir hates oxygen. So if we put a dirty piece of bark in the bottle that's letting a lot of air in, we're stuffing it at the last hurdle."

To prove his point, Matt went down into the cellar underneath his garage and came out with a 2002 St. Clair Pinot Noir that had been bottled and aged under screw cap. And sure enough, it was a great wine. All the fruit flavors were still there, so far as my untrained tongue could tell. I thought I'd tasted the proof that screw caps do let in a small amount—yet the right amount—of air.

So let's recap for a moment. In theory, a screw cap is supposed to be a perfect seal that doesn't let in any air—that's why wineries use screw caps on drink-young wines. However, Ant MacKenzie, Hatsch Kalberer, and to a lesser extent, Matt Thomson believe that red wines age the way they do because they actually require a little bit of exposure to oxygen. Matt takes it a step further by saying that screw caps serve exactly that purpose, and do it consistently from bottle to bottle since every screw cap is the same, whereas every cork isn't.

Head spinning yet? Well, mine was, too. And it started going around even faster after I visited John Belsham, who had just switched Foxes Island from cork to screw cap specifically because he believes screw caps don't let in any air at all.

"If you actually distill it right down, the most compelling statement was the one made at the University of Bordeaux, which has since been reemphasized," he said. "Bottle development happens in an anaerobic condition, not an aerobic condition. A good cork is a perfect seal that does not let air through. Therefore a good cork and a good screw cap are doing exactly the same thing."

After this conversation I could really only conclude that the Marlborough winemakers who were switching to screw caps were all doing it for completely different reasons. Villa Maria was the only major player to take the it's-screw-caps-or-it's-nothing approach with its distributors around the world, while some wineries, like Wairau River, Cloudy Bay, and Seresin, were still bottling under cork just for their shipments to the U.S. market because the distributors felt that consumers there weren't ready to accept screw caps. Hell, Claire and Mike Allan to this point had refused to make the switch simply because they felt that screw caps are too ugly-looking.

"When you set the bottle on the table and you have that ugly screw mark, that's not okay when you're in a nice restaurant," Claire insisted, even after admitting to me that in all of Huia's trials on screw caps versus two-plus-twos (corks that are basically reconstituted and treated—kind of like a Chicken McNugget), screw caps came out on top every time. Yet she still stood by her two-plus-two corks. "It has to look attractive and make the people who bought it feel good that they bought it, and not some slightly lesser wine. In no way can we look lesser."

This was a bit disappointing to hear from a winemaker I have so much respect for, especially considering the first line of this chapter. She seemed to care more that the bottle looks good than about having the 100 percent assurance the wine inside it tastes good. I passed along Claire's opinion to another winemaker, who responded, "That is grossly underestimating their con- sumers, especially at the end that New Zealand wine operates. I think you've got to have some respect for the consumer in terms of them wanting a better product."*

So who was right and who was wrong? It became clear to me that the answer simply wasn't to be found in Marlborough, so I stopped asking the questions even though the trend was certainly in full swing, worldwide. Within a couple weeks of each other, Hogue Cellars in Washington and leg- endary Château Margaux in France had announced that they were both turn- ing away from corks, though to different degrees. Hogue was switching over about 70 percent of its production, while Château Margaux was testing screw caps on its second label. (And that's probably only the very beginning. Pechiney, the biggest supplier of Stelvin screw caps in the world, is a French company.)

About the time that I gave up on asking Marlborough winemakers about corks and screw caps, ASW purchased Mount Michael in Central Otago, and a few weeks later Jeremy, Josh, and I made the eight-hour drive to the tiny town of Cromwell to check it out. Along the way we stopped overnight in Christchurch for a night out on the town, which of course included Jeremy happily and fearlessly taking on four guys outside a bar. It never escalated into a brawl or anything, and didn't even develop into anything interesting, since the cops broke things up before they got beyond a little shoving and grabbing. The following afternoon, when we arrived at our destination, the only wounds we'd suffered were self-inflicted—to our livers.

Despite a recent wave of new plantings in Central Otago, the terrain and climate are much more like those of western Colorado than Marlborough, and in terms of production, in 2004 the whole of Central Otago produced only slightly more wine than ASW did. Nevertheless, the region is fast becom- ing a Mecca for Pinotphiles, and is beginning to creep in on Marlborough's majority share of the New Zealand wine spotlight.

Up to this point I'd been pestered repeatedly by a PR firm in New Jersey to visit its client Amisfield Wines, a Central Otago operation that is partly

---

*In the summer of 2005 I bumped into Mike Allan in New York, and he confessed to me that he and Claire finally bowed to pressure from their distributors and agreed to bottle their entire range under screw caps from then on.

owned by an American, the former COO of Levi Strauss. Though I told them time and again that I wasn't writing about Otago, they still insisted that I stop in and see winemaker Jeff Sinnott should I ever happen to be in the area, and I eventually agreed.

Jeff's a pudgy, shaggy-haired guy who looks as though in his younger years he was the life of the fraternity party. In fact, he probably would have been if he had the interest and ability in botany back then that he has today. He's also legendary for his ability to talk your ear off, and sure enough, I wound up spending about two hours with him, most of it talking and tasting barrels from the '04 vintage.

Jeff eventually pulled out the '03 Pinot Noir, which had been bottled, but was about two months away from release. He twisted off the cap, and then and there I tasted one of the best Pinot Noirs I'd ever come across . . . okay, so I was drunk by this point. But I suddenly recalled that somebody, somewhere once called wine "bottled poetry." I never took the expression seriously because it managed to sound elitist *and* idiotic all at once. I mean, I've never opened a Snapple and compared it to art, music, literature, or even late-night Cinemax. However, then and there, as I was tasting that particular wine, the saying struck a chord with me.

"I like to think of it as a trout in a stream," Jeff explained. "Constantly shifting back and forth between oak and fruit." Hokey, yes. But he was right. For the first time I could taste the flavors both of the wood and of the fruit, and they were constantly duking it out for my mouth's attention. Almost like when you chew two different flavors of Bubble Yum at the same time, but in a *much* better way.

"So what do you think about screw caps?" he finally asked me.

"Nothing, really," I said. "I guess the only thing it tells me is that the wine is probably in the condition that the winemaker intended it to be in, so it's therefore up to me to decide if it's good or not."

Jeff nodded in approval and started to talk about how screw caps can actually make his job more difficult, what with finding the right level of copper to add and all the technical requirements. And without really thinking about it, probably because I'd been swallowing much more of his wine than I'd been spitting into the receptacle he'd provided, I asked him what he thought about this theory that screw caps actually do let in a little bit of air to assist wine in its development.

"Let me show you something," he said, and he then disappeared behind a stack of barrels. I could hear him tearing and rummaging through boxes and other pieces of junk, like someone in search of an old Beatles LP in his attic. When he reemerged a few seconds later, he had another bottle of wine in his hand, this one sealed with a red screw cap instead of Amisfield's trademark gold. The bottle had no label on it.

He poured us each a glass, and said, "Taste this."

It was horrible. The fruit flavors were all gone. I couldn't even describe what it was I was drinking. There was just something wrong with it. It even smelled funny, and I scrunched my face as I spat out the wine.

"This is a screw-cap trial," Jeff informed me. "What you just tasted is exactly the same wine, bottled the same day, just under a different cap. This cap is designed to let in a little bit of air over time, and that one isn't," he said, indicating the Pinot about to be released. "This other wine is now much lower on free sulfur, and within a few months will be totally oxidized."

So there it was, right in front of me. Wine that hadn't touched air, good. Wine that had touched even a little bit of air, bad.

Wines with corks? From now on I think I'll proceed with caution.*

---

*If you're wondering where plastic corks play into all this, I really couldn't tell you since nobody in New Zealand uses them. Mostly I just find them really fuckin' annoying, since they sometimes won't come out of the bottle (particularly if you use one of those Rabbit corkscrews). While they're at it, they should start selling cars with the doors welded shut.

. . . A beautiful woman—the best thing to be kept awake by.

—MICHAEL SERESIN,
OWNER OF SERESIN ESTATE

16

Trade Secrets

If during the vintage, winemaking is mostly cleaning, then after that time winemaking is mostly marketing and sales. I mentioned at the beginning of this part of the book that winter is the time when winemakers hit the road, but toward the end of August they all head to Auckland for the wine section of the New Zealand Hospitality Show. For three straight days the wineries schmooze: They talk to each other, their distributors, their vendors, and bar and restaurant owners, and taste as much of one another's wine as they can.

It's a stretch to say that every winery in New Zealand is represented, but most do have some sort of presence. All of the wineries attending the show are able to fit into one large room; some have booths the size of a Fiat, and others have just a little round table as part of a larger booth set up by their distributors. The first day of the show is open to the general public. Anyone who shows up and pays twenty-five dollars is given a ticket and a glass and then spends the next several hours getting absolutely smashed. By the end of the day I noticed that people were coming up to the ASW booth only to lean on the table for balance, rather than to try more wine.

The following two days, however, are specifically for trade. From 10:00 A.M. to 6:00 P.M., buyers, retailers, restaurateurs, journalists, and just about anyone else who can justify attending goes from booth to booth, swirling, sniffing, tasting, and spitting wine poured by the people who made it. When you look around the room, however, you realize that there really aren't *that* many wineries, and the room's not all that big. This isn't E3 or the Consumer Electronics Show. Hell, it's even smaller than the Chocolate Show held in New York every year. There really weren't that many wineries present that I hadn't heard of, and at this point I'd been in the country for less than six months.

So what was the point?

I'm not really sure. And neither was anyone else I spoke to. What's always interested me about trade shows, no matter what industry they're devoted to, is that everyone in attendance really sees them only as an opportunity to escape their usual environments and get stinking drunk. I don't have a problem with that, since I like to do that sort of thing, too; I just wish they'd admit that other than this, they really don't know what exactly it is that they're there to accomplish.

"It's just to get out there," Bart Arnst from Seresin told me. "We go to London, and everyone knows who we are—we're ninety-five percent export. But here people say, 'Who are you?' And we have a new vineyard coming on stream, so soon we're going to have a lot more wine to sell."

Sounds reasonable, I thought, but he was really the only one who seemed to have a compelling reason to attend. He probably would have elaborated more, but on this first day he was extremely frustrated, standing behind an empty table since none of Seresin's wine had arrived on time. I then bumped into Georges Michel, who probably enjoys less brand recognition in New Zealand than Seresin, and I asked him if people know who he is or about his wine.

"Of course," he said. "[But] there are something like fifty new labels every year."

"So what do you do to stand out at something like this?" I asked him.

"Just make sure we have wines that are different," he said.

His winemaker Peter Saunders, however, admitted to me a minute later that "these things get pretty boring, especially when you consider that you have to do them three times a year."

The person I least expected to see at the show was Hatsch Kalberer from the Fromm Winery, and his attitude about such an event pretty much confirmed my surprise at seeing him in attendance.

"It's more just to catch up with people, really," he said. "I have too little time or enthusiasm to really go around and see what other people are doing. But it's good for restaurants and retailers to see us and be reminded of what we're doing."

When I dropped by Framingham's booth, the lack of enthusiasm was more than evident. Winemaker Andrew Hedley wanted to talk about English soccer more than he did about the wines sitting on the table in front of him. His boss, the winery's CEO, yawned.

I wandered back to the ASW booth and asked Josh if he'd been busy.

"Not really," he said. "I've sold some beer, but like Dad says, you just have to be here."

I next dropped by a booth set up by the distributor for Spy Valley, Foxes Island, Amisfield, and several other wineries.

"It's just sort of nice to see where you fit in, and what you're doing differently from everyone else," Ant MacKenzie told me. I wandered a few tables down the line, and John Belsham agreed, adding, "What's interesting in this environment is that around 1:00 P.M. there's a wine that everyone's been talking about, and everyone's huddled by their table. You just hope you're one of them."

But I didn't notice that happening to anyone. The crowds just seemed to move around evenly and equally, and more and more slowly as their collective blood alcohol content increased and the day dragged on. The only people moving through the room quickly were the so-called Power Tasters, a group of black-clad guys tasting and jotting down notes as quickly as they could.

"Who *are* those guys?" I asked Josh.

"I don't know, mate," he said as they scurried from booth to booth, oohing and aahing. "But they're here every year. They're fuckin' dorks."

Clearly, they were all still virgins.

Even if no one really knew why they were at the show, paying God-knows-how-much for booth space or day passes, at least Jeremy and Josh knew why they were there.

Pussy.

Okay, so they were there for the same unclear business reasons as everyone else, but while most people were trying to taste as much wine as possible, Jeremy and Josh were trying to get as many phone numbers as possible. Not that they were going to use them or anything—it was just for pride. Man who gets the most numbers has the biggest cock. That sort of thing. Jeremy didn't even have to leave the booth, though, his so-called X Factor doing all the work for him. On the first day, when the general public was allowed to attend, a woman with a staggering gait mentioned to Josh—with a complete lack of subtlety—how much she wanted to fuck Jeremy, who, by the way, hadn't spoken a word to her.

That night, once the trade show had closed for the day, Josh ditched me, Jeremy, and Allan to go see an old girlfriend from his teenage years. After dinner, I needed to recharge my batteries, so I went straight to bed. Jeremy, however, headed straight for the Globe Bar, a popular hangout for backpackers that even has a hostel directly upstairs from it.

Josh came back to the hotel room shortly after midnight, and before he even said hello, he grumbled, "I couldn't do it. Just couldn't, man. She wanted me to, but I couldn't do it."

"Laura?" I asked him. (That was the name of the new girl he'd met shortly after breaking up with the ex who'd cheated on him.)

"Yeah," he said, in such a way that I could tell his stomach knotted whenever he thought of her.

"That was big of you," I complimented him.

"I'm just so in love," he said. "I couldn't do it."

A few hours later, Josh and I were both awakened by the sound of an entire bag of McDonald's French fries and a supersized drink spilling onto the floor of our hotel room, and a drunken cackle as Jeremy stumbled over his own feet and the furniture in the room.

It was just after 3:00 A.M., and Josh immediately confessed to Jeremy.

"You didn't root 'er?" Jeremy asked as he stuffed French fries into his mouth.

"Nah . . . I love Laura," he said as he rolled over to make space in the bed he had to share with Jeremy.

"Ahhhhhh ha! You pussy! Ya gotta do that!" Jeremy said as he took off his clothes. He flopped onto the bed and passed out.

Just because Jeremy suggested that he'd have acted differently, that's not to say that he doesn't have a conscience. He does have a very clear and good-natured one, but it's just one voice in a crowd of many. It's like that screeching you hear when you watch old footage of the Beatles or Elvis on the *Ed Sullivan Show*. One voice of dissent in a crowd of thousands of women with pure estrogen streaming down their cheeks is just impossible to hear. Never mind the fact that keeping track of the number of women throwing them-selves at Jeremy is like trying to keep score of a hockey game with no goalies.

Think that's an exaggeration? As I wandered around the trade floor on the second day of the show, a woman in her late thirties stopped me as I passed by her booth.

"Excuse me?" she asked. "Do you know the guys at Allan Scott?"

"Yeah," I said, knowing exactly what was coming next.

"Who is that unbelievably gorgeous one pouring wine?" she asked. I'd been pouring wine the day before. That left me out, and I was relatively sure she wasn't talking about Allan, either. "I'm a married woman," she sighed, "so it's not for me. It's for my friend."

"Well, are you talking about the taller one or the shorter one?" I asked her.

"The shorter one," she said, cooing again.

"That's Jeremy," I told her.

"Is he single?" she asked.

"This is for your friend, right?" I asked again, and she nodded. "Tell your friend she has to do her own dirty work."

Another fan of both Jeremy as well as Josh, though strictly in a business sense, was a woman named Rachael Carter, who works for a company that sells chemicals and supplies to wineries. She's pretty famous in New Zealand, partly because her brother played for the All Blacks, but also because she's hot. I don't know that she'd turn heads in New York or Los Angeles, but she sure as hell does in an island nation of four million people. Rachael is in her mid-thirties, wears the latest fashions, and has a hairstyle straight out of *Vogue*. She's sexy, smart, friendly, and funny. Her family is one of the wealth-iest in all of New Zealand, as the company her parents founded was eventu-ally acquired by a European entity for several million bucks.

That night, Rachael and the rest of her family threw a dinner party at an upscale Italian restaurant in Ponsonby for all their winery clients—there were about forty people packed into a small room at the back of the restaurant. I wasn't invited, but neither Rachael nor her father seemed to mind my crash-ing their party when Allan introduced me to them because, well, showing up uninvited to a wine dinner in New Zealand with Allan Scott is like showing up at Yankee Stadium with Don Mattingly. When I arrived at the restaurant, Jeremy and Josh were already at the far end of one of the long tables, close to the most attractive women in the room, of course. I sat in the only seat avail-able, at the opposite end of the table, with Allan, John Belsham, and Kerry

Hitchcock, one of the godfathers of Marlborough Sauvignon Blanc. A couple of decades ago Kerry brought a bottle of wine he'd made to an Australian surfer dude named David Hohnen, who also owned a winery called Cape Mentelle. I'm guessing Hohnen was impressed with what he tasted, since he subsequently founded a winery in Marlborough called Cloudy Bay. I hear that went well for him, kinda like how that TV thing worked out for Oprah.

"You totally lucked out," Josh told me once the party moved from the dining room to the bar. "You were sitting with three living legends of this business."

Perhaps, but I wasn't thinking about it at the time. Only after he pointed this out did I realize that having an expensive meal with winemakers of such stature is fun for reasons you wouldn't expect—mostly because they talk about everything other than wine. Sure, they get into the intricacies, joys, and perils of owning property and farming it. After all, it's what they do. But these guys spend their careers focused on—obsessed with, really—making sure that your dinner at a nice restaurant is enjoyable in part due to their efforts. They're not like chefs, who are only a few feet from the enjoyment they provide. They're physically miles away in a small farming town in the South Pacific. So a dinner like this is not only rare for them, but a chance to relax and have fun like normal people do—even if it is ultimately a business dinner.

Somewhere between dinner and dessert Josh disappeared, only to be found at the bar with the ex-girlfriend he'd met up with the night before. After an hour or so in the cramped bar area, about a dozen people moved up the street to Whiskey Bar, a swank after-hours joint, and rang up a NZ$700 tab in a matter of minutes, opting for Cognac, Manhattans, Laphroaig, and Cuban cigars. Allan and a few others left at about 2:00 A.M., and the last remaining stragglers piled into cabs and headed for Rachael's house.

From the street the place didn't look special in any way, but we passed through a garage that was home to her Porsche SUV and Vespa scooter, and into a kitchen that looked like something out of a TV cooking show. Almost the entire house was constructed of glass and steel, making it look like a spread in *Architectural Digest*. The outdoor pool was softly lit, gently bathing the living room in blue light.

The seven or eight in attendance, some of whom the host didn't even know (myself included), mostly stuck to single-malt Scotch and beer. It was an escape everyone seemed to need: no business talk, no pretension, and absolutely no wine (well, okay, maybe a little). As night became morning, people started to make their exit—some in pairs, seemingly with the unspoken rule that whatever happens in Auckland stays in Auckland. Others just disappeared. I'd long since lost track of Josh (never mind my motor skills, balance, and speech), so I decided to call it a night, but Jeremy was still going strong.

The hotel room was empty when I arrived in it shortly before 6:00 A.M. A disheveled Josh rolled in an hour later, and a beat-up-looking Jeremy returned at about 8:30 A.M. All of us smelled like booze, but Jeremy stank so much of whiskey that he'd have burst into flames if someone had lit a cigarette ten feet away from him. His face wore an expression conveying the torture inflicted by a monster hangover. Neither he nor Josh had slept a wink, but somehow they were making a quick, nearly flawless transition from party mode to business mode, like flipping a light switch.

Allan arrived at the hotel a few minutes later, and we all met him in the lobby. We had coffee before the three of them went back to the trade show, and I headed off to the airport to return to Marlborough.

"You know, I have to tell you guys, you're doing a great job," Allan said to his winemakers as they sipped their coffees and stealthily rubbed their aching foreheads. "The wines are bloody good. I just want to say that you guys are representing the brand to our customers and suppliers very well."

Though probably none of them realized it at that particular moment, Allan was correct in his compliments. Sure, it's ironic that party animals are able to make some of the best wine. But that also makes them the best salesmen of it. Jeremy and Josh make great-tasting wine because they seem to know better than anyone that ultimately, wine is about fun—about living and enjoying your life.

Something that many others—whether they write about wine, make it, or just drink it—seem to have forgotten.

It sometimes seems to me that it's about how much you conform versus what you actually like.

—ALISTAIR SOPER, WINEMAKER AT HIGHFIELD ESTATE

17

And the Winner Is . . .
No One

When you develop an interest in wine, or do something so dumb as to try to make your living writing about it, you inevitably get asked one question on a regular basis: What's the best wine you've ever tasted?

Happens to me all the time, and admittedly, I've asked the question of many wine geeks, every one of them more knowledgeable about the subject than I am. And if there's one thing that pisses me off to no end about each and every one of the people I've asked the question, it's that they always give the name of a wine that's completely inaccessible. Meaning, it's obnoxiously expensive and a normal peon like me could never afford a bottle in a million years.

"Why, it was a Château Latour '61, decanted at an embassy dinner, from the ambassador's private cellar! This was back before the monarchy fell and the ambassador was sent home and beheaded."

Shut the hell up, I usually think when someone answers the question in such a way. *They should have sent you back instead.*

But there is something important to note about a response such as this, and you'll see what I mean when I tell you about the best wine I ever had.

Shortly after I graduated college, I backpacked around Europe. Well, barhopped, really, but that's beside the point. For a couple of nights I stayed at a convent in Florence, where I met two other Americans who'd just finished the Peace Corps in the small African country of Malawi (whose primary export is babies for Madonna), and the three of us went out to dinner one night.

The restaurant was the first one listed in the chapter on Florence in the *Let's Go* guide. Which of course means that this establishment was not only in the sketchiest part of town, but also where greasy locals sit on their scooters just outside, gnawing on toothpicks and watching for tourists they can potentially mug, fuck, or both.

The restaurant had no printed menu, and no chair had all four legs the same length. There were probably only a dozen tables in the whole place (each covered with cheap, easy-to-wipe plastic), so diners were just seated wherever there happened to be space. We were joined by two Italian guys who looked like they'd just been released from prison.

A massive jug of Chianti was plunked in the middle of the table to commence what turned out to be one of the greatest dinners I've ever eaten. The wine was silky smooth, its flavors blending perfectly with each course of the US$10 meal. Like it was yesterday, I remember all of the threads of conversation we had with the Italian guys about our lives, our families, our hopes, our ambitions, and our dreams.

"I love this wine," the Italian guy sitting to my right said as he finished off the last little bit in his glass. "You can just knock it back."

Now, I should note that the Italian guys didn't speak a word of English, nor did any of us speak Italian. Yet somehow this Chianti—this cheap-shit cockroach blood in a giant bottle—had forged a bond between everyone at the table. Cultural differences, languages, religions—they all disappeared in this tiny rathole of a restaurant on a sweaty July evening in 1997.

I haven't had an experience like it since. And the next morning I had perhaps my worst hangover ever. We're talking an H bomb of a headache. I couldn't walk a city block that day without hurling my internal organs into a garbage can. I eventually passed out on the lawn of a monastery.

My point is that whenever you ask people about the best wine they ever tasted, they usually talk about the setting in which they drank it rather than the wine itself. Even the best wine critics, consultants, and writers will agree that the circumstances in which you drink a wine play the dominant role in your evaluation of it.

This is why, as you've probably guessed by now, to this point I'd never been a particularly big fan of the idea of a wine competition or even a scoring system that awards wines stars, points, the number of Advils you'll need the next morning, or whatever. Because all of this stuff often scares people into believing that a wine has to have a minimum score of 92 and a gold medal in this competition or that one for it to be enjoyable.

Sounds silly, I know. But just as I was writing this chapter, a friend of mine in Denver called me up and told me that he'd seen four Central Otago Pinot Noirs on the shelf in his local wine shop. He'd bought the one with the sticker on it proclaiming that the wine had won a silver medal at the Air New Zealand Wine Awards. "None of the others had awards, so I wasn't about to buy one of them," he said of his choice—and this is a guy who knows a hell of a lot more about wine than I do. What he didn't think about, of course, is that perhaps the other three wines might be better, but the winemakers opted not to enter the competition.

And that's just the tip of the iceberg. I once met a sommelier from a ridiculously expensive restaurant in San Francisco who told me that she often sees diners tapping at the screens of their Palm Pilots or eyeballing pages printed from *Wine Spectator*'s website before they order. Not that there's anything wrong with having a *little* info, but sheesh, God help these people if they do the same sort of thing before they have sex.

So far as New Zealand is concerned, the influence of competition is undeniable, a critical and measurable factor in a wine's commercial success or failure. However, if you ask fifty different people what they think of wine competitions, you'll probably get fifty different answers.

Even with the best tasters, there is bias toward their favorite styles, Matt Thomson told me. "People try to grade according to how good the wine is rather than how much they like it. There certainly is influence on what you like. If you're outside the range of the palate of the preference of that taster, your wine isn't going to do very well. The losers are the consumers, who don't have the blueprint of the palate of the taster who's scoring it."

In other words, the system isn't perfect. And there are ways to manipulate it, too. Though it's more an issue of finger-pointing than outright admission, there have always been rumors that many wineries bottle the best components of their blends first and make sure those cases are entered into competition. That way if the wine wins a gold medal, the accolade will assure that the rest of the blend—even if it doesn't really taste the same—gets sold.* Villa Maria, on the other hand, sets aside small batches that the winemakers think stand up well on their own, bottles and labels them separately, and enters all of them into competition essentially to stack the odds in their own favor. And it works. In the 2004 Air New Zealand Wine Awards, Villa Maria had fifty-three total entries—twenty of them in the Chardonnay classes alone. Of all fifty-three entries, only nine were made in quantities of more than one thousand cases, and thirty-seven of the forty-four wines of limited quantity won medals (84 percent). Villa Maria took home nine of nineteen trophies, including the Champion Wine trophy for its 2003 reserve Pinot Noir of, you guessed it, limited quantity. (To Villa Maria's credit, though, eight of its nine entries produced in quantities of more than one thousand cases also won medals, including gold for their regular Sauvignon Blanc that you, I, and just about anyone else can indeed afford and buy in just about any wine shop for about US$12.)

But getting back to Matt's earlier point about the wines needing to be in the range of the judges' personal preferences, there's another factor that weighs heavily on all of this: Even the best tasters in the world fail to pick up on certain characteristics as their mouths numb and the day drags on. Again, it comes down to environment, and what the judges tend to home in on are show-friendly wines that stand out in a lineup for one reason or another—unlike, say, Huia's wines, which are designed to go well with food, and which picked up nothing higher than a bronze medal in this particular competition.

Brian Bicknell from Seresin told me that he and his staff set up a blind Chardonnay tasting, "And the one that scored the lowest was the gold-medal winner. It was a fruit-bomb Chardonnay, and then a lot of oak, but neither of them together." The reason they were likely able to pick it apart, of course, is that Seresin's tasting involved perhaps ten, or at the most a dozen, Chardon-

---

*In late 2006, Wither Hills was found to have submitted a smaller, separate batch of its Sauvignon Blanc to several wine competitions. The winery was cleared of intentional wrongdoing, but the ensuing hullabaloo resulted in head winemaker, Brent Marris, resigning as head judge of the Air New Zealand Wine Awards. It was kind of like when George Michael was caught exposing himself in a public restroom: 90 percent funny and 10 percent sad for about a week, then pretty much forgotten. Brent left Wither Hills in early 2007 to focus on his own brand.

nays from other New Zealand producers—not the more than 250 that were entered in the 2004 Air New Zealand Wine Awards.

The other problem is sugar, he explained. "Anything with a little bit of sugar in it gives that perception of fruit weight, which in a lineup you can't really pick as sugar because you're desensitized to the fruit characters.

"I think there are some really good people who judge, and probably some who judge who you don't respect that much," Brian told me. He added that Seresin doesn't enter competitions anymore. "I thought that as the wine-buying populace became more knowledgeable, [competitions] would diminish in importance, and maybe they'd fall away."

Of course, that didn't happen. They only got more important. So I figured the best person to ask about wine competitions is perhaps one of their biggest advocates, John Belsham, owner and winemaker of Foxes Island. John has been judging wine competitions for more than twenty years, and was the chairman of the judges of the Air New Zealand Wine Awards from 1999 to 2003. Needless to say, he takes wine competitions very seriously, so if you want a bit of a giggle, dig through your old copies of *Food & Wine* magazine for a story Lettie Teague wrote about her experience as a guest judge at the Air New Zealand Wine Awards. Some of her shots at John are a bit harsh, probably because he thought she wasn't qualified to be a judge. So I took that as the first indication that John sees himself as some sort of valiant knight, protecting the integrity of the system. I was expecting a Pinot bottle to the jaw when I asked him in an oh-come-on tone, "What do you think of awards shows and competitions? What's your take?"

"How long have you got?" he asked right back, cracking a smile. John's a tall, well-dressed, serious-faced guy with salt-and-pepper hair that I never once saw out of place. He's personable one-on-one as well as in front of an audience, his mannerisms suggesting that he could talk intelligently and passionately about anything, wine-related or not. With his immediate response to my question I suddenly knew I was in for a better answer than a spirited defense of the faith.

"In my view, it is an exercise that is more reproducible and more precise in a group than with an individual because it's a very subjective exercise," he began to explain. "The issue is how much value and credibility the competition has. That's where it becomes quite complicated. I liken them to one-day cricket games, or a baseball game. It's exciting, and let's say it's not an ordinary baseball game, and there's got to be a winner."

I decided not to break his train of thought and tell him that baseball, unlike cricket, cannot end in a tie—unless Bud Selig's a bit moody and wants to go home and get some sleep.

"Everyone puts in one hundred percent, and everyone enjoys it," he went on. "And basically, it's forgotten by the time the next one comes along. Because in any one competition there are wines that deserve to do well, some that might have been unfairly judged, and others that might have been lucky on that particular day.

"The issue, and this is the difficult part, is what the consumers do with that information. It's frightening when consumers, and you see it more in the U.S.—and dangerously in the U.S.—where consumers are constantly bombarded with this one-hundred-point scale that they believe in implicitly. And unless you've got ninety-one points you might as well not pack a lunch with you when you go out on the road. To me, that's dangerous. It's not empowering the consumer to make decisions. They feel that they're not smart enough—they don't have enough trust in their judgment."

John was referring to the popularity of the ratings system employed by the likes of Robert Parker and *Wine Spectator*. Regarding the trust people have in *Spectator*, he's not kidding. Around the time that ASW was putting together its '04 Sauvignon Blanc blend, the '02 Chardonnay got a 90 rating and Wine of the Week status on the *Spectator* website. Almost instantaneously, several hundred cases had to be labeled and sent to the United States. (Due to an ordering mistake, the labels had to be pasted on by hand, so if you got one that was a bit crooked, that was probably my fault.)

"Then you get this other side that is equally unhealthy," John went on, "which is thinking they're all show wines that have no integrity, and the judges wouldn't know a decent wine if it struck them on the back of the head.

"There is another factor that overrides all of this. When you look at a range of wines in a lineup, the reality is that wines with more obvious flavors do show. Because what we look for is texture, concentration, and power. We also think of balance, elegance, and structure. But what first attracts us is an element of concentration. Maybe if you had that wine with dinner, it might be a bit overpowering. By the same token it may be fantastic. There are no guarantees. I think people expect more of a competition or magazine tasting than the very nature of that environment is able to deliver."

So how about that? The guy who takes wine competitions very seriously is essentially telling you, the consumer, "Don't take them too seriously." And I can certainly see where he's coming from. The system has to be serious in its structure and its procedures for anyone to be able to decide in the first place whether the results should be, well, taken seriously.

What you should be wondering by now, though, is just who are these people judging the wines? Good question. They're winery owners, winemakers, wine writers, and maybe sometimes a sommelier or two. More interestingly, though, for the better part of two decades in New Zealand, this clique has been a tough nut to crack. Becoming a judge seems to be more about who you know than about what you know. Case in point: Who would you rather have as a wine judge? Someone like, say, Matt Thomson, who makes wine for five different companies in New Zealand and a couple more in Italy, or Rod, one of the owners of Mount Riley, who's essentially an accountant? Which one do you think knows wine a bit better? Now guess which guy is actually a judge.

In fairness, Matt told me that he really didn't want to be a judge, but I sensed that part of it simply had to do with the fact that he didn't know how he could be considered other than by working his way through the system. In New Zealand there isn't a wine-judging course or official, recognized measure of who's qualified to be a wine judge and who isn't. The route in seems to be through volunteering your time as a steward, pouring wines for the judges at the various competitions. Maybe after a few years of that someone will let you be an associate judge, and up the ladder you go over several years.

But in late August 2004, it looked like things were finally about to change.

It came time for the Bragato Wine Conference (named for Romeo Bragato, the country's first viticulturist), which is basically a few days of seminars, trade booths, and information-sharing, primarily for grape growers. As part of the conference there's also a wine competition and awards dinner, and this year the whole bash was held in Marlborough. The only difference was that this year there was a tasting evaluation where anyone could show up and be assessed for his or her potential as a wine judge.

Just under ninety people—a combination of winemakers, wine dorks, and at least one hungover American writer—had signed up and paid roughly NZ$70 to be assessed. In the morning session I attended I was joined by Chris Seifried from Seifried Estate in Nelson, Ant MacKenzie from Spy Valley, and Al Soper from Highfield, along with about thirty-five others.

"I don't go for the whole judging thing," Ant told me just before we walked into a small banquet room set up with long tables and twenty glasses of white wine at each seat. "But I thought you can't complain about it unless you know it."

I plopped myself down at the back of the room, with twenty glasses of Chardonnay arranged in an arc in front of me. The proceedings were then opened by John Belsham, who was running the evaluation alongside Brent Marris, head winemaker and managing director of Wither Hills, and the 2004 chairman of the judges for the Air New Zealand Wine Awards.

"We're evaluating your judgment of the wines versus our judgment of the wines," John explained to the room, which, if I recall correctly, was immediately followed by the sound of everyone's heart sinking half an inch or so. Everyone would be assessed in terms of their ability to taste and score as compared to John and Brent—two of the most esteemed and experienced wine judges in Australasia. It was a bit like saying, "We're testing your ability to play for the Chicago Bears by having this four-hundred-pound noseguard run straight into you. Good luck!"

The way the judging works is that you give each wine a score on a 20-point scale. Basically, the first 10 points are free, so the worst wines usually get a score of 13 or 14. If you give a wine 15.5 to 16.9 points it gets a bronze medal; 17 to 18.4 a silver; and 18.5 to 20 a gold. You also have to write a few comments about the wine's color, balance, structure, mouth feel, or whatever else you can ad lib on the spot.

"Where we're right or wrong is irrelevant," John continued. "We're looking for consistency, and your ability to support your remarks."

So basically, you can't give a wine 19 points and write a negative comment, like how there's so much oak flavor you feel like you just tried to eat out Kim Cattrall in the movie *Mannequin.*

"You have one hour to taste twenty wines," John instructed, before Brent chimed in with some advice.

"We're judging for quality, not style," Brent explained. "So if you see one full of fruit but overoaked, it's out of balance. Look for balance and drinkability. Try to score positively. If you think it's outstanding, give it a 19. But be aware of overt flavors. If you think it's too tannic, it probably is. If you think it's too oaked, it is. You often pick up the best characters straight away."

I felt like I was taking the SATs all over again, when they tell you to go with your first instinct. Now that I think about it, my SATs might've turned out much better if I had twenty glasses of wine when I took them.

The clock began ticking and everyone began tasting, until someone ig Crush

quickly discovered that wine number twenty in the Chardonnay lineup was corked.

"If anyone's unhappy with their wine twenty please raise your hand," John asked the room. He might as well have asked, "Who'd like sex twice a day for the rest of your life?" because everyone's hand shot up. At first I hesitated because I've never been particularly good at telling if a wine is corked. Around the time I first arrived in Marlborough I was at a tasting with several people when a sommelier in the group swirled a glass of wine under her nose and declared it corked. "You could tell that just by smelling?" I asked, and she nodded quickly, almost embarrassed by the question. I could see out of the corner of my eye a few heads turn, as if they all said in unison, "'Can you tell by smelling?' Sheesh, a Mormon with a sinus infection could've picked up the TCA taint. Who invited this loser?"

But this time the wet-basement smell reached out of the glass and socked me in the nose. Actually, that's being generous. Wine twenty exhibited the aroma of an old man's feet. So it was discarded, lucky for me, because when the ten-minute call came, I was only halfway through scoring all of my wines. I managed to speed through the rest before time expired, which of course spoiled my plan of stopping after wine number ten and shouting out, "Dude! I'm soooo wasted! Where we goin' next?"

We took an hour's break, which was enough time to give our mouths a rest and let the organizers begin pouring the next lineup of wines, nineteen Pinot Noirs.

"That it's light in color doesn't mean it's not good. Be conscious of balance," Brent instructed us. "If it's in balance, great. If not, penalize it."

John also reminded us of the rules of the game. "We'll benchmark your results and your comments against ours."

As they did with the first Chardonnay, John and Brent each scored the first Pinot aloud and gave us their comments to show us what they were looking for. I was way off. They both scored it a silver and I gave it bronze, two points lower. It didn't matter, I thought to myself, since my mouth was sandpaper by wine six, and the rest became a guessing game.

And my scores showed it. A week or so later, John invited me to his office to go over my results. "We're not going to ask you to be a judge," he said as he smirked, and I suddenly felt like I was back in high school, with my math teacher explaining how I'd screwed up each and every problem on the test.

But actually, it wasn't as bad as I thought. Or maybe it was just John's way of letting me down easy. He opened an Excel spreadsheet on his computer that displayed a series of statistics and bar graphs that had been developed based on my scores. I don't think my doctor extrapolated as much information the last time he gave me a physical. At least John didn't shove his finger up my ass.

On the Chardonnay class I'd scored the same as Brent and John only four times out of nineteen. And on the other fifteen, where we disagreed, well, I was off by a huge margin pretty much every time. It was more or less the same situation on the Pinot Noirs, only there I'd scored the same as Brent and John eight out of nineteen times. Which I took some comfort in, since I'm much more of a Pinot drinker than a Chardonnay drinker.

"You have a conceptual understanding of difference," John said soothingly. The fact that my scores were all over the place "shows that you have courage. Some people hug the center line. Those sort of people can fool you."

Of my low scores for wines that he and Brent had scored highly, he said, "Sometimes even with experienced judges you get something like that. The right answer is not an average. That's a cop-out. It means that we can either convince you that you're wrong, or you can point out something that we overlooked. And I've seen it happen."

So essentially, he didn't tell me that I'm hopeless. Even though I hadn't broken my way into the judging ranks, I didn't feel so bad considering that none of the other winemakers and viticulturists I knew to have taken the evaluation got the call up to the majors, either. The only one who did was a woman who turned out to be unable to judge at the Air New Zealand Wine Awards anyway because she'd become pregnant.

Before I could slam the system, though, I needed to see up close and personal how it all works. So I asked Brent to let me come and observe the first of three full days of judging at the Air New Zealand Wine Awards. I flew up to Auckland the night before, and when I arrived at the city's main rugby stadium early on the morning of November 1, the banquet room overlooking the field had been converted into the venue for a wine-tasting marathon. Most of the room was sectioned off with black tarps, behind which the stewards would spend all day pouring wine after wine from thousands of bottles lined up on rows and rows of tables. The rest of the room was set up with tables for the tastings. Before I had much time to consider the contrast of a prestigious wine tasting occurring in an arena normally used for a sport that involves big guys knocking out each other's teeth and stomping on each other's testicles, Brent called the proceedings to order.

I didn't recognize many of the judges, other than Ben Glover from Wither Hills and Simon Waghorn from Whitehaven (he also makes Astrolabe and Tohu). But as everyone went around and introduced themselves and the wineries they worked for, I gained that sinking feeling that says, "Dude, you are so in the wrong place. Didn't you hear? The drunken idiots are meeting across town."

Brent started by giving everyone general instructions. "There are 1,406 entries this year. If you want to finish at a reasonable hour, don't shag around. There are seventy more Sauvignon Blancs this year, so that's an indication of the vintage." There were also increases in rosé, sparkling, and Merlot. There were even categories such as Cabernet, Cabernet Dominant, Merlot, and Merlot Dominant, just to make things extra-special complicated to someone like me.

After introductions were made and instructions given, Brent came straight over to me and said, "One of the associate judges couldn't make it this morning, so you can just fill in for him." I pleaded to have my scores not count for anything, and even suggested that there were plenty of people there who'd put in their time stewarding who were much more qualified than I was or ever would be.

"Nah, you'll be fine," he assured me, and assigned me to a panel headed by Kate Radburnd, winemaker at CJ Pask in Hawke's Bay, and with senior judges Jeff Clarke of Montana and Terry Copeland, a wine buyer for Foodstuffs, which supplies New Zealand's supermarket chains. My fellow associate judge would be James Rowan from West Brook, a winery near Auckland. "You need help at all, just ask Kate," Brent told me. "She'll tell you everything you need to know."

Now, not only was my inclusion as ridiculous as it was offensive to all those who entered, but when you think about it, it probably wasn't that bad considering who I was replacing: Rod, who, if you recall from the first chapter in this section, walked away from ASW with what eventually became Mount Riley, but also knew relatively little about wine before he got the job at ASW. "It's bullshit that he's a judge," Josh told me on more than one occasion. So essentially, one useless judge was replaced with another, perhaps the only difference being that I'd be the first to admit that I didn't know what the hell I was doing. I didn't even know what table to go to, and the way things were situated I was wondering if each of the five judges had to take a sip out of the same glass.

Out of place as I felt, I made it clear to Kate that I didn't want my scores counted. Knowing how seriously Kiwis take wine competitions, I felt as though having me judge at the Air New Zealand Wine Awards was a bit like having a monkey on the switch of a nuclear missile. I figured I'd at least try to have a little respect for something these people hold sacred, much the way that an atheist doesn't believe in God, but also doesn't exactly go around pissing inside churches, either.

Kate agreed and showed me to my table, where I began slurping and spitting. But as we began to go through the tastings and the ensuing discussions, it became clear that Kate was not only keeping track of my scores, but also asking for my comments. Which I thought couldn't be good, just considering the first group of seventeen wines we tasted. The first wine of the day was Verdelho, a variety I'd never even heard of. The third wine was a Viognier (in the "other specified white varieties" class), which is a variety I like, but know very little about. It's typically grown in the northern Rhône River Valley in France as well as in several parts of California, but in the three decades or so that winemaking has been a serious business in New Zealand, relatively few have bothered with Viognier. As with Verdelho, most people would probably assume Viognier was an obscure, sixteenth-century composer rather than a wine variety if they'd never heard the name before. (Two weeks later, at the awards dinner itself, the sponsor who presented the trophy for the champion Viognier pronounced it "Vee-og-ner." In case you didn't know, it's "Vee-awn-yay.")

Then it was on to forty-three dry Pinot Gris. Jeff, a longtime maker of Pinot Gris at Montana, gave us the judging advice: "The style, mostly it's been about Alsatian, so ripe, poached-pear aromas." *Oh, great,* I thought. I think I've probably eaten a dozen pears in my life, none of them poached. Maybe one, for a dessert on New Year's at a friend's house four years ago. How the hell am I supposed to remember what that smelled or tasted like?

I just decided to go with my gut, which was probably the best approach, although I wasn't really liking any of the wines. I was struggling by number thirteen because thirteen of anything, no matter how good—sodas, beers, porno mags, slices of pizza, whatever—is tough to get through. At twenty-four I wrote in my notebook, "I'm so grossed out now."

I was the second to finish behind Kate, and as I sat down across from her at the table where we'd share our scores and comments after each group of wines, I could tell she was as unenthusiastic as I was. *Maybe I'm not so dumb,*

I thought. While we were going through our scores, Brent came over and said, "To be honest, the class is really disappointing, but go through and pick some that stand out."

The three that stood out were nine, sixteen, and twenty-three. Wine nine I gave my highest score to, 17.5, and that got silver—which the other judges agreed with. Sixteen I didn't really like as much, but gave it a bronze. The senior judges gave it gold, so that's what it got. Wine twenty-three I gave a silver, and that, too, was raised to gold.

Now I was finally seeing how this was working. My scores never really counted at all, since I was an associate judge. Basically, the three senior judges' scores were what counted, and the two associates, James and I, were there as a sort of second opinion. So if all three senior judges scored high and James and I scored low, they'd go back and look at it again. Same if it was the other way around. But ultimately the decision rested with the senior judges, and if they liked it, it got gold. If they thought it was shit, it got nothing. On a wine that I scored low and everyone else scored high, I caught Kate shooting me a dirty look as she said, "That one gets gold."

Over the course of the day I also began to notice a couple of trends. About one in every ten wines, I was way off from everyone else—either I liked it and they all hated it, or they hated it and I liked it. When I told Kate that I was a bit concerned about this, she told me not to worry—that the same thing happens to the senior judges. And the more I watched for it, the more I realized she was right. It happens all the time. Unless a wine is exceptionally good or exceptionally bad, the scores tend to vary quite a bit. So everyone goes back, tastes it again, and talks it out. Essentially, wine judging is very democratic and diplomatic—and about coming to a consensus everyone can live with.

Next we went through twenty-seven medium Pinot Gris. (I actually never knew that "medium" meant "sweet" until I worked at Bar Navajo, and a girl came in asking for a medium wine. I told her we only had one size glass, and she looked at me like I'd gone insane. When I found the wine, in a cask tucked in the back of the fridge, and saw that it said "medium" in big letters on the box, I felt like such a moron.) And then came the Sauvignon Blancs. Seventy of them, broken into two groups of thirty-five. Some of the judges wanted to power through all seventy at once, but I was glad that Kate opted to break them up, because by wine seven I couldn't smell anything anymore. My gums were on fire. By wine twenty my teeth were starting to hurt. At the end I felt as though someone could punch me in the jaw and I wouldn't notice.

Out of that first group we awarded seven silvers, and brought them all back to see if any could be elevated to gold. Wine ninety-seven, which I originally gave a silver, was given a gold. It turned out to be Astrolabe, which eventually went on to win trophies in two white-wine categories. Before you get in a tizzy and scream, "Hey, Simon Waghorn was a senior judge in the competition! That's not fair!" know that he didn't judge this wine, and probably none of the others that he made, such as Whitehaven and Tohu. The stewards look to see who's judging what, and can swap wines in and out easily, so it isn't likely that a judge will score his or her own stuff. (John Belsham takes a harder line, refusing to enter his own wines in a competition at which he's judging.)

After that we had two more wines in "alternative" classes, but I could tell that no one would give them high scores, so I lauded them just for fun. For one of them I wrote, "I can see people liking it for some strange reason . . . like they've just tasted seventy Sauvignon Blancs."

By the end of the day I'd tasted and scored one hundred fifty-seven wines over eight hours (with a short lunch break in the middle), and reevaluated perhaps twenty of those at some point or another. I wasn't tipsy, since I'd been spitting, but I had a headache, my gums were sore, and my tongue felt like I'd spent all day sucking on sandpaper. Apparently I hadn't made too much of an ass of myself, since Brent asked me to come back the next day. Sure, it was a matter of convenience, since there was an empty slot, but if I'd done a truly terrible job, I guess he wouldn't have asked me to come back at all. Having had enough, I had to pass, and thanked him for the opportunity.

"I hope I didn't corrupt the system too much," I said as I stepped out of Brent's souped-up Mercedes in the middle of Auckland after a hair-raising, speed-demon ride along the motorway and city streets.

"You couldn't corrupt it if you tried, since you were only an associate," he told me, and the image of a wild pack of winemakers with rage in their eyes and empty bottles in hand, chasing me to the airport, quickly evaporated from my head.

I've since come to realize that wine competitions aren't the problem. *Spectator* or Robert Parker scoring systems aren't, either. Even though the tasters doing the assessing are not only trying their best to be good consumer advocates and are usually very knowledgeable and experienced, often tasting dozens of wines each and every day over several years, the problem is that people who are new to wine—myself included, until I experienced the judging environment—often don't understand what medals and scores actually mean. A gold medal in the Air New Zealand Wine Awards or a 95 from *Spectator* simply means that wine tasted good in that environment on that day. Period.

For the Air New Zealand Awards, it means that the wine stood out from the others for whatever reason. That doesn't mean that the wine will go nicely with your chicken cacciatore or, if she drinks enough of it, make it possible for you to convince your girlfriend to try a new position. And the same goes for rating systems. If a wine scored 96 points when the taster was fresh in the morning or just had a rough meeting with his boss, you might rate it as highly under similar conditions or whatever other time and place you happen to drink it. Or you might not.

Furthermore, you have no idea what might have been going through the judge's mind at the time. He or she could be in a great mood and give a gold medal or 91 points to a wine that tastes like skunk piss to you. Or, if the taster has just been to a funeral the day before and found out that rich uncle Benny, whom he loved so dearly, left the Ferrari and the house in Tahiti to that whore-bag of a distant cousin he'd been banging since she was seventeen, well, the best wine in the world is going to taste pretty bitter.

So long as you understand that no competition or ratings system is perfect, and simply use them as a guide in the long-term—lifetime—process of discovering what you personally like and dislike, you can't go wrong (I, for example, tend to like New Zealand Sauvignon Blancs that get silver medals but not gold, and ones that score around 85 to 89 points, but not 90 or higher). The instant that you accept either system whole and follow it without question is the one at which you will, indeed, go very wrong, and will probably stop drinking wine altogether. Because it won't be fun anymore.

The very least I could do, I figured, was try to make it fun.

Food and wine matching is not a sport, it is a fact of life. And it's one that far too many poseurs are ruining for the rest of us.

—Keith Stewart, wine critic for
The New Zealand Listener

18

Juice Guys and Meat Pies

The Air New Zealand Wine Awards dinner was held a couple weeks after the judging, and it turned out to be a party to remember. Just under one thousand people attended, and each of the five courses was accompanied by the wines that had just won trophies.

The hangover, however, lasted a couple of weeks. The results of the Air New Zealand Awards were, in some cases, relatively inconsistent with the country's two other major wine competitions, both held a couple months earlier. Inconsistency is one of those things about wine competitions that those who enter and follow them reluctantly accept as part of the package, much the way that a new CD always comes with that annoying plastic seal along the top edge of the case. So really, inconsistency was just the headache component of the hangover. What caused the retching was an email written by Keith Stewart, wine critic for the *Listener*. In the message that he sent just after the Air New Zealand Wine Awards to other wine writers around the country, he not only labeled the competition a "Mickey Mouse festival of self-delusion," but also attacked the system itself and the ability and qualifications of the judges. His argument was that the way the competition is run doesn't hold New Zealand wines to a global standard. Just a New Zealand standard.

To be fair, I didn't read the email in its entirety (I read most of it over someone's shoulder), but Keith did tell TVNZ—the country's publicly funded TV station—that he'd gotten a "massive response from the industry." That's a bit vague, since "massive response" could mean hundreds of emails telling him he's brilliant, or an equal number of replies telling him to go fuck a cheese grater.

I have no problem with Keith Stewart or anyone else attacking an institution, whether it's a wine competition, the tax code, or anything in between. But to me, the way to do such a thing is by explaining how that system works, pointing out its faults as you do so. In what I saw of his email, Keith didn't do either in his attack on the Air New Zealand Wine Awards. As for the judges themselves, they certainly looked like a who's who of New Zealand wine to me, but Keith didn't mention one of them by name or even offer up some alternatives.

A couple of weeks after his infamous email, Keith wrote in his December 18, 2004, *Listener* column that the number of wines to be tasted in a competition is so great "that the judges do not taste all the wines. They smell them all first, then decide which to taste." I'm not sure which competition he was referring to, but at the Air New Zealand Wine Awards judging—for the first day of which, I should again point out, I was actually present—all judges smelled *and* tasted every wine placed in front of them, as did I. So rather than laying out facts and making a coherent argument, Keith opted to whine.

What the hell is happening here? I wondered. Isn't wine supposed to be fun? Isn't it something we're just supposed to drink and enjoy? People don't argue this way about beer, whiskey, vodka, or tequila, and that's probably why consumers drink a hell of a lot more of those things than they do wine. It was then that I realized that discourse and debate such as this among those supposedly "in the know" is pretty intimidating to those who aren't, when really, all we're talking about here is a *drink*.

The thought had occurred to me that one of the things that scares people about wine is that it's meant to go with food. People are afraid of mismatching, as if they eat white fish and drink red wine, a crack will open in the ground beneath their feet, swallowing them into a dark, stony abyss. Because typically, when the so-called experts talk about matching food and wine, they either talk about restaurants that regular people can't afford or, if it's home cooking, the need to source ingredients from alleyway Asian shops* in the bowels of Lower Manhattan that one can only enter by saying the secret pass-word.

While I pondered this I happened to meet an American couple from Port-land, Oregon. The two were traveling around the South Island, and when they asked me about good places to eat in New Zealand I really didn't have much to tell them. Sure, there are great restaurants even in semicivilized parts of the world, but variety is not really the spice of everyday New Zealand cuisine. Fish and chips is pretty standard, which I humbly admit, I do like. But stop at any gas station, convenience store, bakery, or even grocery store, and you'll see the New Zealand food item of choice available at all three: meat pies.

Kiwis love meat pies, whether it's for breakfast, lunch, or just a snack. There are even songs about certain towns' pies. They can be a fairly decent hangover remedy, and they're pretty much the only thing available when you get the late-night munchies after the bars close, even though they make KFC look like haute cuisine. There are several different varieties: steak and cheese, steak and kidney, kidney, steak and oyster, mince, pork, chicken, rabbit, mus-sel, bacon and egg (which for some reason has peas and carrots in it), and countless more. It just depends on where you go. The grocery stores even sell them frozen in packs of six or more, ready to be heated and served. Some places, at the time of writing, were even experimenting with possum pies. The true favorite throughout New Zealand seems to be the sausage roll, which is basically a chunk of mystery meat wrapped in pastry dough and baked to greasy perfection.

This American couple seemed pretty sickened by the gastronomic cata-strophe I was describing,† but a lightbulb went on over the guy's head. "Hey, you should do a story where you pair wines with meat pies," he said to me.

He meant it as a joke, but I remember thinking that it was a pretty good idea. After all, look at the situation in which New Zealand wine found itself at the moment: inconsistent judging from one wine competition to the next; one winery sweeping the Air New Zealand Awards with wines that relatively

---

*Sixteen-year-old sex slave and imitation Fendi bag free with purchases of seventy-five dol-lars or more.

†A Kiwi opened a meat-pie bakery in Brooklyn about two years ago, called DUB (Down Under Bakery) Pies. They're every bit as greasy and sloppy as the real thing, and, I humbly admit, I go get one now and again out of nostalgia.

few regular consumers would be able to locate much less buy; a wine writer ejaculating vitriol. It was time, I felt, for an act of extreme stupidity, and I was just the man to carry it out.

So to show that pairing food and wine is something that's been blown out of proportion, it made sense to pair wine with the kinds of foods that regular New Zealanders eat every day. It just so happens, too, that Renwick, the town closest to Marlborough's wineries and vineyards, is home to what's considered one of the best pie bakeries in the country. I realized that nothing says "Marlborough" more than great wine and a greasy, heart-attack-inducing Renwick pie.

However, since I'm not the kind of guy who could match a tequila shot with a lemon wedge, there was no sense in my telling people what to drink with their pies. I needed the experts to do that. So I rounded up some of the region's best winemakers and asked them to do my dirty work by sitting in the classy setting of ASW's restaurant and spending all morning downing good wine and greasy food as if they were eating dirty-water hotdogs at the Union Square Café in New York. I should point out, too, that asking Marlborough winemakers to do this is a bit like a movie reporter from your local paper asking Meryl Streep, George Clooney, and Anthony Hopkins to come over and watch *Weekend at Bernie's, Weekend at Bernie's II,* and each of the *Leprechaun* installments that went straight to video. But through careful selection and a little bit of pestering, a few of Marlborough's most respected winemakers turned out to have a really good sense of humor and paid me the compliment of not telling me that I'd totally lost my mind. And they all happened to be fans of Renwick pies to boot.

Along with Josh and Jeremy, the other winemakers I talked into this were James Healy from Dog Point, who, as you may recall, was at Cloudy Bay for a little more than a decade; Al Soper from Highfield, who prides himself on making food-friendly wines; and Simon Waghorn, who not only makes the Whitehaven, Astrolabe, and Tohu wines, but was a senior judge at the Air New Zealand Wine Awards. I also invited the local paper, the *Marlborough Express,* since they always have more than enough space to fill, and I figured something as silly as this might actually raise a few eyebrows as well as make the locals think again about the wines made right next door to them.

I have no idea if that actually happened, but there was a page-two story the following week with the headline, "Matching Wine with Food Isn't Exactly Rocket Science," complete with a color photo of Al Soper digging into a sausage roll. I can only assume that it was at least a step in the right direction, because I later heard that a wine importer in Japan heard about what I'd done and tried the same thing there, only with everyday Japanese food. The important thing to note, however, which I told the local paper then and I'll repeat to you now, is that not only is wine and food matching not rocket science, it's not an exact science, either, so it's not something you should stress over. Just throw caution to the wind and try this with that. Maybe it'll be great, and maybe it'll be gross, but you never know until you try—much the way you discovered as you grew up that you liked green beans but not Brussels sprouts.

As they all tucked into their sausage rolls, "What I'm finding is that the Sauvignon is very Sauvignony, and the sausage very sausagey," Al told the group. I hope he felt that way, since he'd made the Sauvignon—it was Highfield '04. In fact, with the exception of James, each of the tasters had a wine in the lineup, unbeknownst to them. The Chardonnay was Allan Scott '03, made by Josh and Jeremy; the Riesling was Spy Valley '03; the Pinot Noir was Tohu '03, made by Simon; the Merlot was Drylands '03; and the rosé was Hunter's '03—all well-known and, in some cases, highly decorated wines in competition.

"The highlight would be the Pinot with the sausage roll, for sure. Absolutely," James told the other tasters. The Sauvignon Blanc, however, was "like having a mouthful of barbed wire," he said. I was impressed that James was willing to find that out for himself so you don't have to.

"I'd have to agree. The Pinot actually—you can actually taste the meaty flavors when you have it with the Pinot," Al said, and the rest of the group came to a consensus—just as if they were in a normal wine-judging environment—that Pinot Noir does indeed go well with a sausage roll.

Next up was a steak-and-cheese pie, which, the judges agreed, was a great match with Riesling.

"It's the citrus flavors, I reckon," James said as he dug in for more and more. "It makes the citrus look really ripe."

"Well, the cheese is no blue-vein," Jeremy commented, and he was certainly right about that. The pale-yellow slime oozing from the pie as he cut into it barely resembled cheese, much less any other substance produced beyond the borders of New Jersey. "But it's all the same."

Right again. Think about it: If some of the best winemakers in this part of the world found Riesling to be the perfect match for a steak-and-cheese pie, no matter what the quality of what was presented to them as steak or as cheese, just think how Riesling might go with your next cheeseburger or even one of those famous cheese-steak sandwiches (made with Cheez Whiz, I should note) you get in Philadelphia. Or maybe even if you're at an expensive steak house in Chicago, and you have a filet mignon with Roquefort melted on top.

"I think the Riesling and the pie were great," James said as he finished tasting this round. "The last thing I'd run to the cellar and grab when I'm sitting down to a steak-and-cheese pie. I'd be hitting the reds: soft Merlot, Pinot, Syrah . . . something like that."

"Steak-and-cheese is number three or four [for me]," Simon, the most experienced wine judge at the table, noted. "It's steak and kidney, steak and mushroom, then it might go down to steak and cheese."

"Steak and kidney is next," I promised him.

"All right!"

Appropriately enough, the chatter around the table moved on to the subject of obesity (a study supposedly performed at some point in New Zealand concluded that there's a golf-ball-sized amount of fat in each pie). I noticed that the tasters were all getting into their pies a bit more slowly than they had at the start of the session. I admitted to the group that I'd never actually eaten a steak-and-kidney pie before, and they all gave me the same look I gave someone from a farm town on the North Island who told me that she'd never been in a taxi until she was eighteen years old.

"This is the king of pies," Simon said as he started cutting it apart and scooping it into his mouth. I realized I was doing the same, as the pie was actually pretty good.

"There are two types of steak-and-kidney pie, too," James informed me. "There's this one, and then the sort of sanitized one, where they play the kidney flavor down. These are fully matured kidneys," he said, shaking his head as he stuck in his fork again.

"The Sauvignon with that," Simon commented, "it's sort of lamb's pee on a gooseberry bush," he said, mocking the expression that describes Marlborough Sauvignon Blanc as cat's pee on a gooseberry bush.

"Maybe they should use cats' kidneys," Al noted, and the rest of us probably wondered if the bakery had, in fact, done just that. But before I could contemplate what a cat's kidney might actually taste like, James started to share his thoughts with the group.

"My initial thought was that both the reds stood out, but for different reasons," he said. "The Pinot, it was sort of the meatiness and the red fruit—the fruit showed in the Pinot. And the Merlot, it was a dark, ripe, spicy, fruity character. The rosé, actually, this was the first food where it kind of looked okay as an accompaniment, sort of like Pinot Grigio would be as a wine, rather than a flavor. I wouldn't have a pick between the Pinot and Merlot."

But majority opinion ruled that Pinot Noir was the best match for a steak-and-kidney pie.

"The earthiness of the kidneys really fleshed out the fruit of the Pinot," Al explained. "It took the Pinot toward the fruity spectrum."

Simon agreed. "The Pinot Noir was a really good combination—that earthy, gamey character that gives you that sort of appeal that you want your Pinots to have."

"That slightly visceral character," Al noted.

"And kidneys *are* visceral," James said.

"Not being a huge kidney fan, myself—I rip them out when I'm hunting—the Pinot combined well with the gamey, savory characters," Jeremy added. With a wave of nausea I suddenly remembered him doing just that and pointing out the kidneys to me as I watched him clean the pig he'd shot on the day I joined him for a hunt.

"More of a texture thing as well," Josh added. "The way the kidneys feel on your palate seemed to go better with the Pinot."

"I thought the Pinot was really fantastic," Simon said to close this round, and I breathed a sigh of relief yet again since, as I mentioned before, he'd made that particular wine.

It was at this point that I realized the tasters were not only taking this seriously, but having fun with it. I could only conclude that what I'd asked these guys to do was a bit like inviting a bunch of probability mathematicians to play strip poker. Yes, the whole exercise is silly and juvenile, but when presented with the raw materials that define their life's work they can't help but use their talents.

Damn good thing, really, because next up was a Mexican pie, which is filled with ground beef, cheese, beans, and various spices. It's kind of like an enchilada in a pie shell, and is, surprisingly, not as bad as it sounds. But "it's a bit of a liberty to be calling this Mexican, isn't it?" Al asked, which I had to agree with, considering how much I love Mexican food. That said, after several months in Marlborough I hadn't seen so much as a taco, so this would have to do.

"This really brings out the passion fruit in the Sauvignon," James said, surprised. "What is that, the spice?"

"I see what you're saying," Simon said. "I just realized there are a lot of onions in here, which changes things a bit as well."

But James ultimately gave his vote to the Merlot, and more or less bestowed an honorable mention upon the Sauvignon Blanc. It was at this moment that a couple of tourists walked into the ASW restaurant, looking horrified and confused, almost as if they'd just walked in on, well, a bunch of mathematicians playing strip poker. They turned around and walked back out, probably never to return. This was also the point at which opinion began to divide.

Simon preferred the Riesling with the Mexican pie for the "sweet, spicy combination." Jeremy chose the Merlot and also gave a nod to the Riesling, while Josh chose the Sauvignon Blanc. "I was surprised how the spices made the fruit more prominent and gave the wine a bit of a lift," he said. "I thought the spice and fruit of the Sav complemented each other."

So a Mexican pie—or Mexican food in general, one could conclude, since I don't think I've ever seen Mexican food that *wasn't* meat, cheese, beans, and spices in some form or another—seemed to be pretty wine-friendly across the spectrum. Everybody liked at least one of the wine varieties to some degree, with the exception of the rosé. So it became time to bring the tasters back down to earth, I thought, and introduced steak-and-oyster pies, which were met by a collective groan followed by chuckles in a tone that conveyed, "Eric, you are one sick bastard . . . when does your visa expire again?"

"I'm gonna eat the whole pie, then think about the wine," Simon said sarcastically.

"What's next, lamb's fry and bacon?" Al asked me.

In my defense, James told the group, "Every so often down at the Woodbourne Tavern"—a pub directly next door to the Renwick pie shop—"there's a tripe night. And then a couple of days later they have tripe pies."

Everyone at the table shuddered in disgust, and I noticed that Josh wasn't eating much of his steak-and-oyster pie.

"Doin' okay there?" I asked him.

"I hate steak and oyster," he said, as I detected a touch of greenness in his face. "I think this is the worst combination."

"It's surf and turf in a pie," I said.

"I'm with Josh on the pie—not my favorite," Al said. "Oysters by themselves, raw, great—but there's something slightly dirty and corrupt when they're cooked like that. The Sav was disappointing, since I possibly might have expected that to work okay. Chardonnay was disappointing. Riesling was the pick for me. The pie still looked a bit dirty and corrupt, but it brought out the nice, fresh characters of the Riesling. The Pinot was disjointed, and the Merlot was dominated. And the rosé was just . . . wrong."

Really, though, the pie itself was just wrong. But people do eat them, so the tasters pressed forward.

"It's not a pristine oyster in this," James remarked, and I couldn't help but agree, having spent almost as much money on oysters as alcohol on each of several past visits to New Orleans.

Indicating one of the local area's dodgier fishing spots, Josh said, "They're kind of like rock oysters from White's Bay."

"Picked up at low tide," Al agreed, shaking his head.

"The pie didn't do justice to any of the wines," Josh said, pushing away his plate.

Jeremy liked the Riesling and Simon gave his nod to the Pinot, but really the only conclusion that could be drawn here was that a steak-and-oyster pie is disgusting. But if you dare eat one, take Josh's advice and drink Merlot with it, since it'll cover up how bad the pie is.

Last but not least was the curry pie, which Al noted was curry "in the same way that the Mexican one is Mexican."

"At first sniff, I think the Mexican pie was more Mexican than this is curry," James said as the smell of cheap curry powder filled the air.

"It's no vindaloo, is it?" Simon asked, shaking his head. I looked around the table and saw that the tasters were no longer eating the pastry portion of the pies, instead opting to scoop out the contents, as their bellies were, by this point, full of golf balls of fat. Early on Al noted that he was trying to eat only half of each pie, but that would still total three in one sitting. Even at Josh's drunkest, I only saw him eat two.*

"The Riesling seems to be the wine for all seasonings," Simon said as he tasted. "It seems to come through more regularly than the other ones."

Jeremy also found that the foods were bringing out different flavors in the wine.

---

*Actually one and a half. Whenever I was driving him home after my shift at Bar Navajo, he'd pass out in the backseat of the car, sitting upright, with a half-eaten pie in his hand, oozing steak and cheese all over the seat.

"Riesling was the best match," Josh said of the curry pie, and the rest of the group agreed.

"The spice in the Mexican killed the fruit in the Pinot, but here it looks really ripe," James explained. "It's got great balance with the Riesling, which is delicious. This is the best match for a Riesling out of the whole bloody lot, surprisingly enough. I don't know what it is, but the Riesling's got this floral, honey note, which if you see it in the right way, gives the wine a real beauty."

"I'm a big fan of the Riesling as well," Jeremy said. "The ripe, sensory characters have been brought out."

"The Riesling was the best match out of all of them, because I actually felt my palate was refreshed," Al said, which I suppose is a pretty critical factor when you're eating curry—whether it's made properly by someone from India or completely besmirched by a pasty New Zealander and baked inside a single-serve-sized pie shell.

As the tasting concluded everyone leaned back in his chair. Fortunately, no one unbuckled his pants.

"That was quite an interesting concept for a tasting," James said, seeming surprised that there turned out to be some very good pairings. Even the knuckle-dragging food items on the chart of culinary evolution could be enhanced by wine—and these particular foods could even affect the wines. "It's amazing how one or two subtle differences with the pies—well, not so subtle, maybe—did change some of the bits and pieces in the aromas," he concluded.

But perhaps most important was James, along with all the others, admitting that he'd had fun eating the pies and drinking the wines, learning as much from the combinations that turned out great as the ones that the most mad of scientists wouldn't dare attempt. Because if people who deal in flavors to make their living can have fun with them, that certainly means that you, I, and everyone else can, too. And that's whether we're eating pies, pâté, or anything in between.

I'll drink to that.

PART III

The Vineyard

*[Our] team is very experienced. You don't get those who turn up on
Sunday morning with such a hangover they can hardly see the plant.*

—CLAIRE ALLAN, OWNER/WINEMAKER OF HUIA VINEYARDS

19

Hard to Find Good Help
These Days

Please don't think that I've spent all this time trying to destroy the enchanting mystique that wine held for you before you started reading this book. If
that's the case I haven't been doing a very good job. But after eighteen chapters I hope that by now your attraction to and enthusiasm for it comes at least
partly from an appreciation of the fact that wine is indeed very much a product of planet Earth, as are the people who play a role in the production of it.
It shouldn't come from some rabbits-out-of-hats or walk-on-the-beach
notion, because in wine regions, just like everywhere else in the world, the
days last twenty-four hours, the skies are blue, and the grass is the same shade
of green. And people come and go.

Marlborough, and ASW in particular, is no exception. Kosta disappeared
from the restaurant kitchen a few months after the harvest, though I never
found out exactly when, why, or where he went. Shortly before he left town
he was chasing the skirt of an eighteen-year-old bartender at Bar Navajo who

I never really thought was all that good-looking. Since she was only eighteen—and especially dense—I tried to convince Kosta that if and when he did finally get her into bed she'd probably whine, "I didn't know you were supposed to move it." Sure enough, one day he came screeching up to the winery, leaped out from his car and asked me, "How did you know?!" I'm not gonna answer that, but either way I don't think that experience had anything to do with why he left.

Not long after the ferments finished and the Sauvignon Blanc was being bottled Jemma and her fiancé decided to move to Australia so they could settle down far from the party-all-the-time lifestyle her better half had enjoyed for several years as an employee of Cloudy Bay. How or why she felt Australia—well known to be a continental fraternity party—was a clean-and-sober alternative to Marlborough I'm not certain, but for whatever reason Jemma felt it was time for her to move on personally and professionally. She was replaced in ASW's lab by Susan van der Pol, an enthusiastic, chatty go-getter who used to work with young vines in the Cloudy Bay nursery and, for a time, owned a small vineyard near Nelson with her husband. More important, she proved to be a pretty reliable worker, much like the two new cellar hands, Linus Maxwell and Danny Pauw, who were hired shortly after Susan's arrival.

Linus, a tall, muscular, late-forties Maori surfer dude with dreadlocks, is one of the hardest-working guys I've ever met, but also one of the most easy-going and young at heart. I never once saw him get stressed out during even the longest, toughest days, nor did I hear him complain about whatever task he'd been assigned, no matter how menial or dirty. Maybe it's because he spent eighteen years employed at a freezer works and no longer has to look at dead animals every day, but more likely it's because he knows that whatever difficulties he faces Monday through Friday will be completely washed away come the weekend, when he slips into his wet suit and rides the waves just north of Kaikoura from dawn to dusk.

While Linus's weekends were set aside for tranquility, Danny's spare time involved brutality—given as well as received—since he was one of two South Africans brought to town to play for the Marlborough rugby team. Nice a guy as he may be off the field, however, Danny didn't exactly get off to a fly-ing start in New Zealand. Within his first couple of weeks he and his room-mate accidentally burned down the house they were renting from Jeremy after they disposed of embers from the fireplace in a cardboard box. So they probably weren't exactly rocket scientists back home in South Africa. But "everyone deserves second chances," Jeremy told me, and he offered Danny a job. Though slightly aloof and never showing much interest in his work or the wine industry as a whole, Danny's a massive guy, and proved to be the answer for several winery tasks that require brute strength. Josh and Jeremy quickly began referring to him as Dan the Donk. It was probably a term of endearment as well, since Danny's usually smiling and has a friendly disposition. Sure, after a night on the town he'd wake up in someone's flowerbed, but he's really just a gentle giant.

In the vineyard, Uncle B hired a jolly forty-something tractor driver named Allan Miller, who seemed to fit in with the other guys pretty quickly, as well as a lanky seventeen-year-old named Phillip Heather. Phillip seemed to perfectly complement Ra's big-brother antics, considering the amount of abuse he proved willing to accept, but as time went on he proved able to dole it out as well as take it. One really needn't look further than any of the new staff—and the employees who'd been at ASW all along—to see that wineries are lean, tough businesses that involve a hell of a lot of extraordinarily grueling work performed by regular, everyday people. If you're still not convinced, though, the place to look is the vineyards during the winter months. I'm sorry to say that this is not the part of the book where I tell you that the winemaking was all done and the weather all of a sudden beautiful, warm, and sunny again, and everyone in New Zealand began to frolic in majestic, green vineyards like hobbits on magic mushrooms.

I discovered, much to my chagrin, that it just doesn't work that way.

While certain parts of the winemaking process are indeed linear, overall it's a cycle. But it's not a perfect circle by any means, since there aren't enough hours in the day, or days in the year, for the winemaking to finish before the focus is shifted back to the vineyards. For all the work to get done, several stages in the year-long process have to overlap. And one of the most crucial of them all begins while the wine is still fermenting, right after the harvest.

The vineyards are buzzing with activity the very instant the last brown leaf falls from the vines. Daylight hours are in short supply, so work begins at around 7:00 A.M., long before the sun even thinks of spreading its yellow rays on the brown, defoliated valley. The ground crunches beneath your feet from the hard frost. Even though it's usually sunny in Marlborough during the winter, when it does cloud over each raindrop that hits your face seems to sting a bit more than the last as the air gets colder and colder. Perhaps worst of all, just like the harvest, there's no such thing as a weekend. In other words, you'd have to have a screw loose to want to work in such conditions. So who does?

The pruning gangs.

I like to think of the pruning gangs as what America would be like if it really did welcome absolutely everyone to its shores. Tired, hungry, or poor, it doesn't matter what country you're from, whether you left of your own free will or were chased out by an extremist government, or if you were released from prison just this past Tuesday. It doesn't matter if you came to New Zealand via airplane or paddled there in a canoe. It doesn't matter if you've never even heard of wine. There's work for you as a pruner. And from the looks of them, I think some of the gangs have a seven-tattoo minimum and a three-tooth maximum in order to get the job.

Don't get me wrong, though, pruning isn't reserved solely for the dregs of society. Some pruners are backpackers making their way in and around the world over the next couple of years, needing to finance their travels. Some are perfectly well-adjusted locals who make pruning a three- or four-month part of their annual income. And some people take an immense amount of pride in their pruning ability. In August, around the time of the Bragato conference, Marlborough held its annual pruning championships, with the winner going on to the national championships a month or so later. If you're good at it, there's some serious money to be made. The best pruners get unleashed on some of the blocks with the oldest and most vigorous vines, which are so twisted and tangled they look like the botanical equivalent of a Rorschach blot. Those brave enough are compensated as much as two dollars for pruning each one of these vines. The best pruners can cruise through them, and take home about NZ$1,000 each week.

Before you buy your ticket to New Zealand and pack your bags, though, I should tell you that many pruners, especially those just starting out, don't make out nearly as well. One pruner, a Canadian named Brad, whom I met early on in the season, complained to me that he was making only fifty cents per vine on an old block in the Awatere Valley. Never mind the fact that it took him half an hour to drive there every day (gas is very expensive in New Zealand). Before he really had a handle on how to do the work quickly and efficiently, it took Brad an hour to prune one bay of four vines. You don't need a calculator to figure out that it was a while before Brad honed his pruning skills and managed to make some decent money.

This is why many wineries and growers prefer to pay their pruners hourly, especially the ones lacking experience.

"I only pay by the hour, because I don't want them rushing through my vineyard," Mike Just told me of his own block, Clayridge. "It means I'm completely within my right to say, 'Slow down, do it this way.' "

So what exactly is pruning and why is it so important?

Essentially, pruning is trimming. As John Belsham of Foxes Island put it to me, "The wood you're trimming this year is directly related to the wood you grew last year." So you have to be careful. The trick is trimming off the right branches (better known as "canes") in the right places so as to position the vine to grow the best possible leaf canopy and grapes the following year. That's why pruning can't commence until all the leaves have fallen off—the pruner needs to be able to see what the hell he's doing before he starts snipping away. To get the process moving along, some wineries buy sheep and pen them into the vineyards to eat the last little bits of leaves off, as well as any weeds that might still be growing on the ground. The downside, of course, is that the pruners need to watch where they step.

"The cut decisions are what map that vine's future for the next season," Mike Just told me around the time he left Lawson's Dry Hills. "You can see it so accurately once the leaves are gone—what it's done, whether it was a little stressed, and what it needs. I'm not just looking at how to improve it for next season, but how to improve it long-term, so I've got a vine that's going to last me for twenty, thirty years, giving me good-quality fruit."

And because the pruning season arrived while he was still employed full-time at Lawson's, Mike did much of the work on Clayridge at night, with a headlamp. He actually prefers it that way, since it has him focused only on one vine at a time. "At night, the light's only got enough glow to focus on the one vine in front of you," so he can concentrate on that single vine and its needs without getting distracted by the ones lined up behind it.

Whether you do it during the day like most people or at night as Mike does, there are several different types of pruning that depend on soil, climate, or other conditions. Most wineries and growers in Marlborough use a technique called vertical shoot positioning, or VSP for short. What this means is keeping one cane (or branch, whatever you want to call it) on either side of the vine and hacking off everything else—save for a couple of short spurs that might grow into full-length canes the following year.

As the pruners hack, lop, and snip off canes they don't want, they toss all the debris into the middle of the row so a tractor can come through later and mulch it all. When a vine is fully pruned, it should look like the letter *Y,* until someone comes through later and twists and ties the two canes to the bottom wire, also called the fruiting wire (since along this wire is where most of the grapes will grow later in the year), so the vine looks like the letter *T.* So a whole row of vines looks like this:

The vertical part (|) is the trunk, and the top horizontal parts on either side (⁻) are the canes. Come spring, the canes will grow shoots straight up out of their buds, hence vertical shoot positioning.

Since each cane has a bud every inch or two, how long the canes are on each side of the plant dictates how many shoots will grow out of them come spring, which gives you a rough idea of how many bunches of grapes the vine will grow. This can be tricky if some parts of a vineyard are more fertile than others, as Ant MacKenzie found in some areas of Spy Valley's property.

"Within our blocks, there's no point having one row with some vines carrying seven kilograms [of fruit], and some carrying two kilograms, and then harvesting that row of grapes and saying that there's four tons per acre," Ant explained to me. "The fact is, half of them are overcropped, and half are undercropped. So to make better wine, if we can get the balance right, we try to get the ones that were at two kilograms up to four kilograms, and the ones that were seven kilograms down to four."

The way you do this is by snipping the cane to the appropriate length (if a vine's growing too much fruit, you snip the canes shorter; if it's not growing enough, you leave the canes longer). In addition, the VSP method also sets up the plant in such a way that you'll actually be able to get at the grapes when it comes time to harvest them. In other words, if you don't prune the vine it'll just grow all over the place like it's George Clinton's hair, sending shoots every which way, and growing way too much fruit in places that can't even be reached, much less get enough sunlight to ripen fully.

Some varieties, like Pinot Noir, Gewürztraminer, and Chardonnay, are usually pruned to two canes because they require low crop loading for the grapes to develop good, concentrated flavors. On ASW's main Riesling block, the Moorland vineyard, the vines can be pruned to four canes—two on each side of the plant—since the vines are old and can handle the extra crop load.

Sauvignon Blanc can also handle a much heavier crop load, so most every-one in Marlborough prunes it to four canes as well.

In theory, pruning sounds simple. But in practice pruning is not only extremely boring, it's tough, grueling work. Grapevines are durable, stub-born plants, and can withstand all sorts of environmental and physical stress. And because they're vines, they rely on their surroundings for support and strength, growing tendrils that spiral around the wires and even around other shoots from the neighboring vines to hold themselves in place. So even with precise snips and cuts, getting the canes ripped out and onto the ground can require patience, stamina, and even a touch of brute strength. Pruning can be extremely frustrating, and the harder it gets, the more you can hear the vine laughing at you as you try to trim it and rip out the unwanted canes.

The ones who laughed exceptionally hard, however, were ASW's full-time vineyard guys—Ra, Terry, Gerald, and a guy I'll call Robert—as I helped them prune the Sauvignon Blanc block next to Allan's house. Even with hands-on instruction it took me about forty-five minutes to prune one bay of four vines, and in that amount of time the other guys did four or five bays each. I was a pretty constant source of amusement for Ra, and though Robert joined in on the ridicule I didn't let it bother me since he wasn't a particu-larly well-liked member of the full-time ASW vineyard crew anyway, and he left the company a few weeks later. (Though he was skilled and experienced, Robert's personality didn't quite mesh with the rest of the group—I'm not sure if those complications arose before or after he told his vineyard cowork-ers the story of how his cat bit the tip of his penis, but I'm guessing after.)

When we finished the block after about a week, there were two main things I had learned about pruning with pros. The first one is to pace your-self rather than try to keep up with them. Because once you get the hang of pruning you tend to go too fast, and not only do you make mistakes, the next morning your hands and arms are so sore it'll hurt to do something as sim-ple as pouring your coffee or unzipping your fly. The second thing is to respect the vine and its strength. You may have the shears and the highly evolved central nervous system, but the vine is tougher, stronger, and meaner than you are, and it doesn't like being mistreated. At least two or three times a day I'd tug a cane a bit too hard this way or that, and it or another one it was tangled with would smack me right in the face—sometimes even draw-ing blood. The best way to approach pruning is to think of it this way: If the vine is Bobby Brown, you are Whitney Houston. There's only so much of your shit that the vine will take from you before it gives you a good, old-fashioned bitch slap.

With that analogy, this is as good a time as any to point out that pruning also happens to be very sexist work. Female pruners are few and far between, and the ones you do find don't really look feminine at all (think Rosie O'Donnell with tattoos, BO, and far fewer teeth). Men do the pruning, since they're generally stronger than women. And women, with their gentler touch, follow the men through the vineyards, tying down the canes to the fruiting wire without breaking them, as the men likely would. The women who wrap and tie down canes make anywhere from ten to twenty cents per vine, bringing home about NZ$100 to NZ$120 per day.

On this particular block, however, Gerald, Robert, and I did all the wrapping and tying—no contract workers, male or female, followed us through the rows. The reason is, simply, that there are certain blocks on which a winery can trust contract workers to do a good job and others where it can't. Terry and Ra pruned the entire block of young Riesling vines outside Josh's house in the Omaka vineyard to position the plants correctly for the following year: Having inexperienced contract workers in there would be a bit like having a blind guy perform your bypass surgery. One wrong snip, and it's over, Charlie. On the older or more difficult blocks, like the one next to Allan's house or the new Millstone vineyard, it came down to an issue of cost—which Uncle B, the vineyard manager, calculates down to the single vine. "On that block it'll cost ninety cents a vine if we use our own guys, but NZ$1.10 if we use the contractor," he told me. And with literally thousands of vines at Millstone, that twenty-cent difference adds up.

In general, the bigger the vineyard, the lower the level of hands-on care, and since Marlborough has vineyards of all shapes and sizes, the region can't survive without the misfits who crawl out from under rocks to join the pruning gangs of the region's labor contractors—there's simply too much work to be done. "We're struggling to get people even with offering a good weekly wage," Wither Hills's Ben Glover told me once pruning was well under way. "It's just the nature of the beast."

An operation the size of Nobilo has no choice but to rely entirely on contract crews. "We've got that core of very experienced managers who we use as policemen—call them whatever you like," said Darryl Woolley of his company's setup. "We put them in charge of the contract gang, so they go through and monitor the pruning jobs all the way through. Each gang will have an experienced person who will do nothing more than ride around on his horse and say, 'Good enough,' or, 'Not good enough.' Obviously, we can't get sixty or seventy experienced contract pruners year in and year out," since there just aren't enough people who can or even want to do the work.

So the trick for any winery that needs workers is to make sure that it finds a contractor it can trust and work with over a long period, as ASW has with Fred Russell, owner and operator of Russell Viticultural Services. A gray-haired guy with a year-round tan and a big smile backed by a deep, dry laugh from a lifetime of smoking, Fred has worked with ASW for more than a decade, so I took several opportunities to work in the vineyards with his crew. On the morning I cruised around with Fred's right hand, his stepdaughter Michelle, I quickly gained an appreciation for how difficult a contractor's work can be.

Michelle picked me up bright and early on a Friday morning that I happened to be especially hungover. She drove me to the southern-valley plains, to the vineyard of long-term client Blue Slape, a crotchety old guy with a dry sense of humor and a few acres of vines that produce a crop that Blue sells to Matua every year.

"This year we have all new pruners," Michelle told me as we bounced along in her truck and my head and stomach swirled. Fred is a hands-on guy, however, so he takes the new pruners under his wing and shows them what to do. He even does much of the work himself on the older, tougher vines, and in the middle of pruning season he returned to the vineyards less than two weeks after a long-overdue back surgery.

Fred has a core of a few experienced full-time workers, all of whom seem to be women in their sixties named Shirley. He gets the rest of his workers from a Blenheim hostel, the owner of which arranges for work permits through New Zealand Immigration. They come and go all year long, and on this particular morning I met pruners from Holland, Hungary, South Korea, South Africa, and England. Deep inside the vineyard, somewhere, were a Czech, a Chilean, and a Brazilian. The only person missing seemed to be Kofi Annan.

"If they make a complete stuff-up, what a nightmare it is the next year. And there's no one to blame because they're gone," Michelle lamented to me as she shook her head and my stomach turned over from having mixed beer, wine, and God only knows how many cheap spirits in Bar Navajo the night before (I'm not sure why, but I think I even drank Chartreuse).

To make sure the right canes are selected for keeping rather than snipping, Fred does his best to teach all the pruners the importance of what they're doing. "When Fred teaches them," Michelle went on, "he explains why—where it's going to grow and how."

He'd obviously done a good job with Richard, the pruner from Holland. "For me it's about getting comfortable with the vines you're on," he told me during his smoke break. "And that's a good feeling."

Around this point, however, my head and stomach were so out of synch that I walked over to the end of the vineyard and knelt by the road. As I was hurling the pale-green contents of my stomach onto the ground, I could hear been-there-done-that cackles from within the rows because pruners are notorious for showing up on the job drunk, hungover, or not at all because they're still at a bar. Only moments after I was finally able to stand again and regain my composure, I overheard Michelle arguing with Blue about the pruners leaving long canes and overlapping them on the wires once they were tied down.

"Do you want them to overlap?" Michelle asked him.

"No!" Blue yelled at her.

"Fred said to overlap," responded a voice from within the rows.

"Well, you can if they reach, but they should just be touching," Blue tried to explain. But really, all that was happening was that the lines of communication between the grower, the contractor, and the pruners were becoming more tangled than the vines themselves. Michelle then had to go back through the vineyard and repeat Blue's order to leave the canes long, and then let the wrappers snip them to the appropriate length once they were tied down. And of course, the pruners were just as confused by the conflicting instructions as Michelle was.

"I see where they're coming from," she told me of how upset some of the more experienced pruners get, especially considering how seriously they take their work. And the rest of them just get confused. Shaking her head in frustration, Michelle added, "Blue will come out a few hours later and tell them something different."

Miscommunication is the source of most vineyard-related headaches. But if a winery or its contractor can retain staff over the long term, the headaches become fewer and further between.

"We've circumvented the whole problem by building a stable team of people we encourage and look after, and hopefully they stay around forever," Whitehaven's Simon Waghorn told me. His core vineyard team actually consists mostly of one family, starting with a seventy-six-year-old grandmother and extending to "two of her daughters, her son, one of her daughters' lesbian partner, her son-in-law, and granddaughter." It sounds like the makings of an extraordinarily bad reality show, but "it's important to build up a relationship with a team of people," Simon explained. "The more they've worked in the same vineyards, the more they can get a bit of ownership of what they're doing. If you do the right thing pruning, the vine is easier to manage in subsequent years. The longer you can keep the same gang in the vineyards, the better. That requires your being reasonable about what you're paying them, otherwise they'll go do something else."

They often do. With the massive expansion of planting in Marlborough and no major rises in the population or vineyard pay rates, the region suffers from a labor shortage in which most growers or wineries are lucky if they ever see a single worker who stays from one year to the next. It doesn't take a genius to see how Marlborough got into this mess, but it may very well take one to get the region out of it as the demand for workers continues to outpace the supply—similar to a race between Michael Schumacher's F1 Ferrari and a defective Pinto. It doesn't help that hundreds of the workers hired by contractors are known to be illegal immigrants or overstayers. The less-than-reputable contractors and subcontractors who hire them also tend to favor such practices as overworking and underpaying, and not providing adequate training (something I'd investigate later in the season). But any grower or winery with a shred of business or common sense will only work with honest contractors who they know only employ willing, hardworking people and treat them well—whether they're from the next town over or half a world away.

And there's an easy way to tell the difference: Drink the wine. If it tastes good, that means there were people in the vineyard who took pride in their hard work through the cold and bitter winter months because they were paid well, treated well, or both. In much the way that a space-shuttle mission won't be successful unless the launch is set up perfectly, it's impossible to grow good grapes—and, in turn, make good wine—if the pruning wasn't done with a little blood, a lot of sweat, and even more TLC.

The only job in the vineyard that doesn't hurt your back is consuming the final product.

—MIKE JUST, OWNER/WINEMAKER OF CLAYRIDGE

20

Wine 101: The Vineyard

Whether you drink wine with dinner every night, need to suck down a few glasses just to get out of bed in the morning, or have never even touched the stuff, it's relatively easy to pick up how things work if you spend a couple of months in a winery. I'm not saying that working one harvest will turn you into a winemaker, just as watching the Discovery Channel for a week straight won't get you a million-dollar grant to study the mating habits of rhesus macaques (but you will get the gist of monkey sex and feces-throwing). Learning how things work in the vineyard, however, is a completely different story.

I've often heard people say that it takes about three full seasons to really get your head around the ins and outs of a vineyard, and I believe them after just the one season that I spent in Marlborough. I suppose it doesn't help that my knowledge of botany is pretty much limited to what's grown in dank basements and eventually sold by New York City bike messengers, but I found vineyard management and grape-growing to be not only complicated, but also difficult to get enthusiastic about. And there's a very simple reason for this.

Vineyard work sucks.

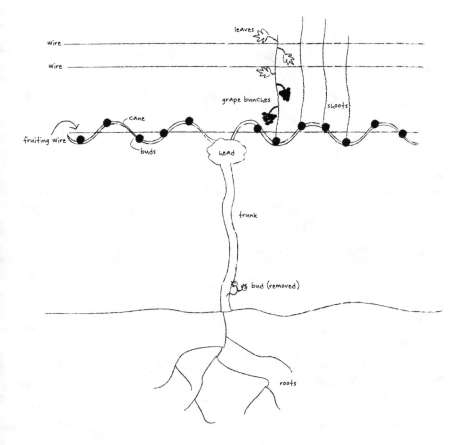

not-too-overly simple grapevine diagram

Not only do you have to get up at the crack of dawn to do it, vineyard work is, for the most part, mind-numbingly repetitive and physically exhausting. I've never had a job that's more difficult or less satisfying. I feel comfortable saying this because I've had some really awful jobs in the course of my career. I've painted houses. I've had to wear a tuxedo and hand out flyers to tourists to promote unheard-of acts performing in a Boston comedy club. I've even worked for PBS. And the pay, should you choose to become a full-time vineyard worker, is pretty awful. As Allan told me in not so many words, on NZ$12 or NZ$13 per hour you can't live a Rolls-Royce sort of lifestyle.

That said, however, there are some people who genuinely love working outside each and every day. They love getting dirty and they love being a part of a process that helps grapevines reach their full potential. Some of them couldn't give a rat's ass about vineyards, grapes, or wine, but with each vineyard job I did alongside them, I gained an ever-increasing amount of respect for the people who do this work day in and day out.

If you're talking established vineyards (young ones are a different pain in the ass altogether, so I'll get to them later), it all starts with pruning and tying down canes, of course, and this work lasts pretty much all through the four winter months (it felt like eight). The vineyards remain browner than a pair of old Hush Puppies that stepped in shit until one day, in spring, the buds on the canes wrapped to the fruiting wire begin to burst. The varieties that do this first are the early-ripening ones like Chardonnay and Pinot Noir, and slowly but surely the buds begin to grow little green shoots and leaves. The Riesling kicks in a couple of weeks later, and two or three weeks after that the Sauvignon Blanc and Pinot Gris join in as well, bringing lush, green life back to the vineyards.

Much as this brings a sense of excitement, sheer panic is never out of sight or mind since this is the time of year when the vines will suffer the most damage if there happens to be a frost. A spring frost can essentially do to the little baby leaves what a fire hose would do to a house of cards. If that happens, the shoots won't grow, and therefore no grapes can grow off the shoots, which means no wine.

There are a couple of ways to fight frost, depending on where the vineyards are and how susceptible those particular spots of land are to it. When I asked Josh how the ASW crew protects against frosts, he just clasped his hands together and looked at the sky, essentially asking the Big Guy Upstairs, "Please don't fuck us this year."

But there's a little more to it than that, as I learned when Josh and I drove down to Central Otago to spend a few weeks tending to the newly acquired Mount Michael vineyard. (Actually, I drove, since Josh's license was still suspended from the time he parked his car outside Bar Navajo, and the police breathalyzed him.) Mount Michael is a very good example of how frosts can be managed and predicted, because the vineyard is on a hill. Frosts slide right down the hill and settle at the bottom, turning the vines planted in these low-lying areas into Popsicle sticks.

So what Josh had to do was wake up every hour in the middle of the night and go out and take temperature readings throughout the vineyard. The difference in temperature between the top of the hill and the bottom, a change in elevation of about thirty or forty feet, was often pretty dramatic—as much as three or four degrees Celsius. Fortunately, Mount Michael has a simple and fairly reliable preventative measure on that bottom block: sprinklers.

I know it sounds like the exact opposite of what you should do, but spraying the vines with a bit of water forms a protective coating on the leaves, since it takes longer for the water to freeze than the air, which, in the case of frosts, is already frozen. Hence the name. The sprinklers are mounted on top of each post throughout the block, and when turned on they spit water back and forth, splattering the tops of the plants and their vulnerable baby shoots and leaves. When the threat subsides and the temperature rises, the sprinklers can be turned off.

In Marlborough, however, standard practice for handling this sort of thing is either to hire helicopters to hover over the vineyards and blow warm air down onto the vines, or to install giant windmills. The latter has become so popular a frost-fighting method, in fact, that after the 2004 vintage one hundred new wind machines were put up in the region's vineyards. Some people complain that they're too noisy and wake them up in the middle of the night, but somehow I think helicopters are a bit worse. One particular night that Marlborough had a spring frost scare, helicopters took to the sky at midnight and didn't land until after 7:00 A.M. "It sounded like *Apocalypse Now* out there," Josh, an avid fan of war books and movies, remarked the next morning.

But really the best way to prevent frosts is to think about where you plant vines, which means doing your homework and researching that piece of land's weather history. On one night in mid-October, when the western end of the valley was rumored to have suffered crop damage in every vineyard that didn't have a helicopter or wind machine, Josh just shrugged and said, "No one would be making such a big deal about frosts if no one had ever planted past Renwick." But they had, and then some, as the demand for Marlborough wine increased around the world, and this particular year the owners of those vineyards paid the price.

Around the time that the potential for frost rattles nerves and causes a few sleepless nights, during the day the vineyard crews have the job of going through the rows and dropping all the wires to the ground. At Mount Michael, Josh and I were able to do the entire vineyard over a couple days, and probably could have done the whole thing in even less time if there weren't other odd jobs that he and the on-site vineyard manager needed to do.

It isn't long before the wires have to be brought back up again. The wires are what keep the rows of vines looking the way they do, like soldiers standing at attention. A grapevine doesn't really care about much other than growing, and it'll send shoots every which way until it becomes more of a grape bush than a grapevine. In other words, the leaf canopy doesn't grow in perfect rows because vines do this sort of thing naturally. Quite the contrary. As the shoots grow this way and that the vineyard workers have to go back through the rows and lift the wires back up again, pushing the shoots into place as they do so and training them upward.

Think of it this way: The shoots on grapevines, just like the hairs on your head, naturally flop all over the place as they get longer. So think back to the last time you got a haircut. In the same way that the stylist or barber pulled up patches of hair between their fingers to make your hair easier to cut, the wires serve exactly the same purpose—just on a slower, much larger scale. The wires pull up and squeeze the leaf canopy into neat, organized rows, and the workers have to go through and raise the wires two or three times over the course of the spring as the shoots grow longer and longer.

And they waste no time doing it. On a warm, windy day in early December when Fred's gang was lifting the wires on a small block of Sauvignon Blanc behind Allan's house, he remarked, "We lifted these just last week. They've grown more than a foot." That's well more than an inch per day, so a constant and watchful eye has to be kept on the vineyards, since if the wires aren't lifted when they need to be, the spring winds will just knock the plants right over. Special attention is also required when the wires are lifted because the land isn't always perfectly flat, so if a worker goes into a gulley and doesn't put the wires on the right clips on the posts, the wires can get crisscrossed. If that happens, when Terry or Ra comes through with the tractor to trim the tops and sides of the canopy, the wires can snap.

The reason that the vines are trimmed isn't just to make them look pretty, much as they may right after the tractors have passed through. "A grapevine basically wants to ripen its seed," one viticulturist explained to me. "It doesn't give a shit about sugar, acid, or pH. It wants to ripen its seed because it wants to proliferate. Our job as viticulturists is to manipulate and control the plant so we don't allow it to become overvegetative . . . manipulate those vines to slow down and ripen that fruit." Trimming the tops of the vines brings them under control so there's the right ratio of sunlight-capturing leaves to grapes that need to be ripened. Too big a leaf canopy and the fruit ripens too quickly. Too small a canopy and the fruit doesn't ripen enough.

In other words, the vineyard is all about finding balance for each variety and maintaining it throughout the season and making sure no energy or nutrients are wasted. Since the vines don't care about which way they grow shoots and from where, they pop out of just about every part of the vine—including the trunk. Since this isn't a particularly lush or fruitful part of any plant, all those little shoots and other buds on the trunk need to be removed—there's no point in letting the vine push energy or nutrients into anything other than the grapes. Pulling off all this growth on the trunk is a job called bud-rubbing, and is certainly a top contender for worst vineyard job of all time.

To do bud-rubbing all you need is a pair of special gloves that are covered with rubber nodes on the palms. A pair of these gloves will only cost you about NZ$1.99 in any grocery or hardware store, though I imagine someone, someday, will get the bright idea of selling the left or right glove in the Adam & Eve catalog for US$34.95. Appropriately enough, bud-rubbing requires you to grab on to the trunk of the vine with one of your gloved hands and rub it up and down until all the little buds and shoots come off, almost like you're rubbing sand ticks off a camel's dick. Honestly, that sounds like a much better task. Because bud-rubbing is so hard on your back and knees that after you've been bud-rubbing for about an hour you can barely stand up straight, let alone jack off yourself or anybody/anything else. In fact, I don't even know why they pay vineyard workers to do this—the contractors should just give the money directly to the chiropractors, which is where all the workers eventually wind up going for treatment.

They should also work out a deal with the psychiatrists, because after all the work that's gone into growing good shoots and lifting them into perfect rows, the vineyard workers have to go back through and rip many of them out. This masochistic act is known as "shoot-thinning," and the reason for it goes right back to balance and having vines that can actually ripen the fruit load they're carrying. Each shoot will grow two bunches of grapes toward its base, and leaves and tendrils above them. But as I've mentioned throughout, the point isn't to just grow as many grapes as you can on each vine, because the fruit won't ripen. And certain varieties can carry heavier crop loads than others, so the trick is to rip out the right amount of shoots on each vine, depending on the variety.

Some of it's a no-brainer. For example, there's no point in keeping a double shoot since it's just going to divide up nutrients between the two. Or if a shoot doesn't have any bunches on it, well, what's the point of keeping it? None, so you rip it out. Varieties like Pinot Noir and Pinot Gris, for example, can't carry particularly heavy crop loads, so the shoot-thinning on these varieties has to be pretty extensive, as Josh and Jeremy discovered through trial and error. They had the vineyard workers shoot-thin the young Pinot Gris plants in the Omaka vineyard, but not the older ones in the Millstone vineyard. Toward the end of the season, when Josh and I tasted the Pinot Gris at Omaka, it was sweet, delicious, ripe fruit. "Now let's go try the worst Pinot Gris in the world," Josh said as he sped out of the row and along the roads over to Millstone, where the vines were all carrying more bunches. "It has no flavor," Josh said as we both picked and tasted grapes. "It's just watery and the skins are really rose-petally." I asked him if it had something to do with the crop loading, and Josh just shook his head. "I don't know," he said. "The vines are older, so we thought they could handle it," but he guessed that they'd have to go ahead and shoot-thin the Millstone Pinot Gris the following year.

Other varieties can be just as tricky. With Riesling and Chardonnay, it depends on the quality and flavor concentration you're looking for, and Sauvignon Blanc, which can carry the heaviest crop load, may not need any shoot-thinning at all.

The way to tell if a shoot will be fruitful is simply to look at its base just before Christmastime (the middle of the summer in the southern hemisphere) and see if it's already grown miniature bunches. These actually aren't little grapes—they're flowers. And if you ever happen to be in a wine region during this time of year, especially a windy one like Marlborough, bring your Claritin. Each one of those little flowers pops open and sends pollen into the air, making Marlborough a giant sneeze-fest for about two months. If the flower is fertilized, it will eventually become a grape. If not, it won't become anything. So the weather needs to be dry, warm, and windy at this time of year for the pollen to carry through the air and settle on other flowers and get the whole show on the road. Once the wind dies down you start to see the formation of little berries, a process called "the set." This is the time at which wineries find out for sure how good the flowering really was. If they see berries forming everywhere, the flowering was good. If they don't see any, well, they take any leftover tissues they bought during flowering and cry into them instead of sneeze.

Again, this is where balance comes back into the equation, because around this time the trimmers are making another pass through the vineyards. If they trim too early, particularly on a variety like Pinot Noir, the vines will produce what's called a second set—more flowers. "You're forcing it out after trimming," Gary Duke at Hunter's told me. Second set not only means more sneezing and eye-rubbing, but more grapes that the vine divvies up energy and nutrients among, even though these later-forming ones won't have a chance in hell of ripening by the end of the season. ASW found out the hard way when it trimmed the Pinot in the Omaka vineyard, behind Josh's house, and second set started growing all over the place—even way high up in the leaf canopy. It took Fred's crew nearly seven hundred man hours to remove all the little flowers by hand, which was a substantial—and certainly unintended—extra cost that snuck up on ASW.

As the desirable berries and bunches start to grow and the leaf canopy gets bigger and greener, it comes time to do an especially important job called leaf-plucking. This is yanking off the leaves around the fruit zone, and the whole process can be done either with an attachment on a tractor or by hand. Certainly, having people do it by hand is more expensive and far more precise and thorough, but there are several reasons why a winery might do one or the other, or even why it's done in the first place (ASW chooses based on the age, health, and variety of the vines on each of its blocks, but is able to do mechanical leaf-plucking in most places).

The main reason is for disease control. Now, there's a really easy way to think about this: In what regions of the world do you most often hear of all those nasty diseases, viruses, and infections like dysentery, cholera, and diarrhea? No, not the restrooms in Penn Station. I'm talking warm, humid places like India, Bangladesh, or Malaysia. Don't blame the curry; it's the climate, because diseases flourish in hot and humid conditions, whether you're a human or a grape. So think of a grapevine's fruit zone in the same way: If you rip out all the leaves on the part of the plant where the fruit grows, air can better pass through so heat and humidity aren't trapped on and around the fruit, and the grapes are not as likely to get infected with something nasty.

The other reason leaves are plucked off is to get more sunlight hitting the grapes directly, which helps the skins ripen and, in Sauvignon Blanc especially, develop those signature Marlborough tropical-fruit flavors people rave about. But there are different leaf-plucking strategies for different varieties, and two people who are dependent on meticulous leaf-plucking are Marlborough's boutique winemakers—Hatsch at the Fromm Winery and Hans Herzog, owner and winemaker of Herzog Estate.

I was a bit reluctant to go see Hans, mostly because I wanted to make sure that any wine I mentioned in these pages was reasonably priced and available for you to try. While Herzog wines can be found around the world, they're in pretty short supply since only about 3,000 cases are produced each year—and that should give you some indication of what the prices are like. However, growing high-quality grapes is in Hans's blood. His family has owned vineyards in Switzerland since 1630, and he was only a teenager when he began studying at the Swiss Wine University of Wadenswil (which is somewhere near the Swiss family of Robinson, I'm guessing). It was four years after Hans and his wife, Therese, bought the thirty acres they have today that they produced their first vintage, and the wines weren't even released until a couple of years later. In other words, Hans takes his time in the winery and is a perfectionist in the vineyard.

"For the first vintage in 1999, I did too much leaf-plucking, shoot-thinning, and bunch-thinning," Hans told me when I visited his tiny, specialized winery—in which he employs only one assistant—as the ripening season was in its final stages. At least I think that's what he said, since he's only been in New Zealand full-time since 2000, so his accent is still pretty thick. "There were six or seven bunches per vine, and it was overripe. So I needed more leaves around the bunches."

Similarly, Hatsch found that he had to treat his Riesling a bit differently. "We try to pluck all the inside leaves," he explained, "but not the outside ones so you get a good airflow inside, but you're not cooking the fruit . . . and probably about five or six weeks before harvest we'll take off the outside leaves as well. No machine can selectively take the inside leaves and leave a filter on the outside," which should give you a hint about why his and Hans's wines cost more than the average for Marlborough: It all adds up to higher costs in the vineyard due to extra labor requirements, better concentration, and significantly lower volume.

Both these guys have to rip off basically all the leaves around their Merlot and, in Hatsch's case, the Syrah. The reason is that these are both warm-climate varieties that grow best in places like France, California, and Australia. So to simulate the hot, dry weather that the vines need, the fruit has to be totally exposed and drenched in sunlight for as long as possible. But where some people like to expose Chardonnay grapes to a fair amount of light, Dog Point's James Healy found that didn't quite work for him since "it gives a real, up-front tropical flavor. The wines don't age very well."

The final stage the grapes go through before they ripen fully is called veraison. It's easy to see when red varieties are going through veraison because the berries change color, from green to purple. The grapes swell with water and sugar, and the skins begin to soften. In other words, they're starting to look and taste the way grapes should—plump, sweet, and juicy. If the grapes don't taste that way or don't look as if they ever will, they're snipped off, since, again, there's no point in the vine wasting energy or nutrients on grapes that won't fully ripen.

However, some people contend that this is really too late a time to drop fruit. "The last removal, seventy percent through veraison, is when we can tell whether the berries and therefore the bunches are sizing up," John Belsham explained to me after he'd left Wairau River and was working exclusively on Foxes Island. "Any later than this, I would be concerned that we wouldn't get the benefit, because the nutrients have already been distributed into the berries. If you remove them much later, you're probably not going to change the flavor of what you have left . . . theoretically."

Definitely theoretically. Because some wineries still yank off fruit only a few weeks before harvest, and by John's way of thinking, if the shoot-thinning is done properly, not much fruit will have to be snipped off later on. Shoot-thinning, he added, is "a much more cost-efficient way of removing fruit, because every time you flick a shoot out, you're removing two bunches."

Dog Point winemaker James Healy, on the other hand, believes that it's best to bunch-thin at the end of veraison. "If you go through and do it early, later on when you look at the vineyard you'll find variable ripeness. You've got the low crop, but you've got uneven ripeness."

And ripeness, from here on out, simply becomes a waiting game with one eye on the sky, the primary reason being the weather, which one hopes will stay sunny and dry so the vine will push all the water and nutrients it has into the grapes for the remainder of the season (which is why the irrigation is usually turned off at this point). However, while one eye is on the weather, the other is on the birds.

In Marlborough's own version of a Hitchcock nightmare, little birds love to nest in vines and peck at grapes, wreaking havoc on the vineyards. Not only do they eat the grapes, but the ones that they just peck at ooze out moisture and become a perfect home for any one of several diseases that need a warm, wet place to set up camp and start spreading from grape to grape and bunch to bunch. Much like people, birds are also fairly picky about what they eat. They especially love Chardonnay and Pinot Noir, but they don't seem to be as fond of late-ripening varieties like Riesling, Merlot, and Sauvignon Blanc. So on the early-ripening stuff it's crucial that the wineries and growers put bird nets up and down the rows, which is expensive and time-consuming, but absolutely essential.

The other way to fight off the little bastards is with sound. Some vineyards, like one across the street from Josh's house, have devices that set off a high-pitched squeal that's supposed to be displeasing to birds. But really I think it's just displeasing to humans, since I always saw more birds in that vineyard than in any other. Some people just drive through the vineyards on ATVs and blast air horns to scare away the birds, making Marlborough sound like Midtown at rush hour. But the overall preferred method is warfare, pure and simple.

When I first arrived in Marlborough before the 2004 harvest I thought the region was under attack. The dawn silence was broken by shotgun blasts, and as I leaped out of bed I said, far too loudly, "What the fuck!" The birds are hungriest in the late morning and early afternoon, so that's when gas guns, set up around the vineyards, are timed to go off and scare the birds away. The local paper is also loaded with job ads seeking guys with firearm licenses to cruise through the vineyards all day with shotguns—they each fire off about 150 to 200 shells a day, right up to and through the harvest.

If the recruits see rabbits they'll go ahead and shoot them, too. (Not as good a shot as I was in my skeet-shooting days in the northern hemisphere, it took me seven shells to get just one rabbit that was pretty much sitting still.) Bunnies may be cute, but they dig burrows, which are no good for grapevines. Shooting rabbits also sets in motion the great food chain, since dead bunnies attract hawks, which also like to snack on little birdies. Unfortunately, while the hawks do help, they're seriously outnumbered. A couple times I saw a flock of hundreds of birds chasing a hawk from a vineyard. It looked like that scene in *Top Gun* when Iceman is outnumbered six to one, waiting for Tom Cruise to leap off Oprah's couch and save the day. It was a classic dogfight, nearly as entertaining as the movie (which, in case you don't recall, was about gay volleyball players flying F-14s).

When all these things are done successfully and according to plan, the grapes will ripen easily and evenly, providing the one and only necessary ingredient for good wine—if the weather stays warm and sunny and dry.

But that's a big if.

You don't want people buying it just because it's organic. If it's crappy, you shouldn't drink it at all.

—GLEN THOMAS, WINEMAKER AT VAVASOUR

21

Clean and Green or Down and Dirty?

Toward the end of July, when the weather was still cold and crappy in Marlborough (but scorching hot in the northern hemisphere), it came time to rip out a block of Chardonnay in the newly acquired Millstone vineyard, since, as you may recall, if there was one thing ASW didn't need, it was more Chardonnay.

It's a pretty simple process, really. A digger hired from a local construction company slowly worked its way up and down the rows, ripping the vines out of the ground one at a time. Ra would then roll through on a bulldozer with a flatbed trailer attached to the back, while Terry and I walked behind and piled on any vines that the front of the bulldozer had missed.

It was dirty, backbreaking work, but at least it went relatively quickly, since all the posts and wires had been ripped out beforehand. This, too, requires heavy equipment and lots of time, and it's also dangerous, which Terry discovered the hard way. I noticed a scar healing on his forehead, the result of a wire that Ra accidentally snapped as Terry cruised by on the ATV. Six inches lower, and the wire would have slashed Terry's throat as it unleashed a few hundred meters' worth of tension.

As Terry and I walked along and picked up the vines, I came across several that hadn't been completely uprooted by the digger. They put up a mighty struggle as I gave them tug after tug to break their grip on the soil, the decade-old vines hanging on for dear life in a last-ditch effort to prove their potential and promise. Alas, they were piled at the end of the block and set ablaze, which left me a little sad at first, but felt great only minutes later, since I'm not much of a Chardonnay drinker in the first place, and because it was an exceptionally cold day. I only wish I'd brought a bag of marshmallows.

All in all it took a couple weeks to rip out the block and have a contractor install the underground irrigation system (irrigation is pretty standard in modern vineyards). Once the weather warmed it would come time to repost and replant, half with Gewürztraminer and half with Pinot Gris. What kind of life those vines would enjoy and the quality of fruit they'd produce would remain to be seen a couple years down the track—something that has as much to do with the land's natural properties as how it's treated by those who own and farm it.

"We put our first spray on fourteen days after the buds burst along the canes," Uncle B began when I asked him what chemical sprays he uses in ASW's vineyards, when, and why. "In the first two rounds we put on copper and sulfur. The sulfur is a powdery mildew preventative, and the copper is a downy mildew preventative." Both diseases look like spider webs and attack the grapes as well as the leaves of the vines, just sort of eating away at them until they can no longer capture light and pass energy along to the rest of the plant. "It also improves our frost resistance by two to three degrees. Our normal spray program is every fortnight. It's copper for a start, then sulfur."

Now, don't freak out just yet about what chemicals are or aren't in the wine you drink. This is a bit more complicated than black versus white, nature versus nurture, or Red Sox versus Yankees. And everyone has different opinions about what works well in the vineyard and why.

First of all, remember that winegrowing in New Zealand has only been a big business for about thirty years (and something the rest of the world's been excited about only for the past ten). So when the industry first got going there, grapevines were treated like any other agricultural product. Kiwi grape growers had access only to the same fertilizers and compounds that were widely used in New Zealand (and around the world) on a variety of other crops, so they just went with what they had. As time went on, however, they figured out that good-tasting wine involved a hell of a lot less work in the winery if you had good-tasting grapes from healthy, disease-free plants. So it wasn't as simple as spraying or not spraying—it was about finding the right balance with nature.

As a result, today in Marlborough there are basically four types of vineyard management: unaffiliated, sustainable, organic, and biodynamic.

Put simply, unaffiliated companies like ASW pretty much do what they find works to get the best-quality grapes they can. So in addition to copper and sulfur, they have at their disposal chemicals like weed herbicides, flowering sprays, botryticides, insecticides, bunch-tightening sprays, and mildew preventatives. Uncle B might have the vineyard guys make one or two passes through the vineyards with each spray over the course of the season in the biweekly program he's designed, while bigger companies like Montana and Villa Maria have so many massive vineyards that they'll have sprayers driving up and down the rows even in the middle of the night to make sure every piece of ground is covered.

Sustainable Winegrowing, on the other hand, is a program that started about twelve years ago, and most wineries in New Zealand, not just Marlborough, are members of the initiative—even the big ones. What it basically does is set guidelines to minimize the impact that sprays have on the vineyards and the environment at large. "Most people would be on it now, wouldn't they?" Gary Duke, winemaker at Hunter's, asked me in an all-the-cool-kids-are-with-it tone when I posed the question to him about what his winery does in its vineyards.

The answer to his question is, "Yes, but not everyone," and with relatively good reason. ASW, for example, does the best it can to adhere to the same principles as members of the Sustainable program. "We only spray when we have to," Josh told me, "so it doesn't make sense to pay extra money to be part of Sustainable when we're basically doing the same thing."

In other words, don't think for a second that wineries not affiliated with Sustainable Winegrowing are just spraying whatever the hell they want, whenever they want, as if they're hosing down a Slip 'n' Slide—not only would it be expensive, it'd do a lot more harm to the grapes than good. Furthermore, a member of Sustainable Winegrowing can spray the vineyard with pretty much any chemical when and if it needs to.

"You can hit the whole vineyard with Roundup if you want to, and it's minus twenty points or whatever," said Gary Duke at Hunter's, explaining the points system the Sustainable program works on. But what Sustainable also does is help winegrowers forecast infections based on weather or other conditions. They put on a botrytis spray, for example, only when they know it's going to stay warm and rainy for a while, since the mold thrives in such spells. "We try to use less sprays if we can—less everything. But to be sustainable, you have to make a reasonable tonnage without rot or disease. We're still putting sulfur sprays on early, and all that sort of stuff," Gary added.

So there's no reason whatsoever to think, "Sustainable good, unaffiliated bad." Really, the only difference between the two is that with Sustainable the information is available to you if you want to learn about what's used and when, "because 'sustainable' could mean anything," said Glen Thomas, winemaker for Vavasour, a winery about the size of ASW in the Awatere Valley that produces the well-known Dashwood label. "You can go on the website and have a look at what it means. Consumers are entitled to that information," he explained. But rest assured that wineries that aren't members do their best to minimize sprays as well.

Okay, so if all these guys are allowed to spray pretty much whatever they want, this means that organic producers don't spray at all, right?

Wrong. Big time.

I hate to tell you this, but organic grape-growing doesn't mean hairy armpits, granola, and bra-burning, or tuning in and dropping out. The difference is just that organic producers like Seresin are simply limited as to what they can and can't spray (none that I know of spray absolutely nothing at all). It's perfectly well within the principles of organic agriculture to use, say, copper and sulfur. And they do. What they don't use, however, are manufactured chemicals like insecticides or botryticides. And that may or may not be a good thing.

"In all honesty, some of the chemicals you use in organic farming are a lot harsher than the ones you use in traditional farming," I was told by Dominic Pecchenino, viticulturist for Matador Estate, a massive vineyard that sells all of its fruit to Nobilo, right next door. Dominic is outspoken about this and other issues because he heads up the research and technical seminars for the Marlborough Winegrowers Association, and was one of the first five members of Sustainable Winegrowing in New Zealand. He's also just blunt and opinionated by nature because he's American, a proud product of the California wine industry. "Organic farming doesn't mean that you don't spray," Dominic went on. "Organics means that you can use a hell of a lot of coppers and a hell of a lot of stuff that's harsh on the environment."

In other words, that a chemical is natural doesn't mean that it isn't more harmful than a synthetic one. The example Dominic points to is the fact that most agricultural products aren't made by big chemical companies anymore—they're made by pharmaceutical companies, and are designed to suit a single, specific purpose. A spray called Mimic, for instance, "is a product that actually only works on the light-brown apple moth"—also known as the leaf-roller caterpillar, which just from the name should tell you that it can cause a significant amount of damage in the vineyard. "Mimic causes it not to go through one of its stages when it's pupating. It's very light, and very soft on the vines," Dominic explained.

That's not to say that a producer like Seresin uses products that are environmentally unfriendly, as Dominic claims that some organic operations do. But as a fully certified organic operation, Seresin is perfectly within its right to use a natural chemical that could potentially throw the balance of nature out of whack without a single dirty hippie knowing the difference, much less holding a candlelight vigil or protest. Seresin does in fact use copper and sulfur, but Bart Arnst, Seresin's viticulturist, uses a variety of other tools as well.

"We do maintenance sprays of seaweed and fish oils," Bart told me of his spray program. "Seaweed's always been known as good for any plant. It has some nutritional value and stimulates a lot of reactions in the plant. Fish oil seems to scare off powdery mildew pretty well."

He's also trying to cut down on his use of sulfur. "In other parts of the world they're talking about not using it—that's why fish oil is good, so we're starting to look at that," he said. "Milk and whey have been used in Australia," but Bart hasn't had a chance to give this a try, much as he'd hoped to. When the spring winds kicked in, Seresin's tractor shed accidentally caught fire, and that's where Bart happened to be storing his sacks of milk powder at the time. "Powder burns as well, I found out." So perhaps he'll try next year.

Overall, here's organic grape-growing in a nutshell, as Bart explained it to me: "All the things we're doing are to bring up the nutrition in the soil, which passes on to the vine to make the vine healthy. A healthy vine has less pressure from disease."

The better question, though, is how and why Seresin chose to become an organic winery, since it wasn't when it first started. I found out when I met with owner Michael Seresin in a little café in nearby Picton, a small coastal town close to his home in Waterfall Bay. It's actually pretty rare that Michael's in New Zealand, since his primary job is as a cinematographer, so he's usually in London or Los Angeles. His spiky gray hair and Malcolm McDowell crazy-man stare make him look inescapably Hollywood, much as he may try to hide it with scruffy clothes and a five-o'clock shadow. Though he's best known for working on one of the *Harry Potter* films, check out imdb.com just for a laugh, since there are some real stinkers with Michael's name on them. But hey, we all have skeletons in our closets, and one thing you can't fault Michael for is how and why he decided to make his winery and vineyards organic—gut feeling.

As he tells it, he was driving through Tuscany with a friend of his, "and I said, 'It's amazing, all that grows around here are the vines.' [My friend] looks at me, and just keeps driving. By the third time I mentioned it he said, 'Seresin, what kind of idiot are you? It's because they put on so much fuckin' weed killer.' We only spray once or twice a year, and I said, 'Is there residue in the grapes?' And he says, 'Well, generally, no, but who knows?' So I thought fuck it, and this is typical me—I didn't even research it."

Instead, what he did was call up his winemaker, Brian Bicknell, and said, "Brian, we're going to become organic," Michael recalled. "I said, 'It's not up for discussion, that's what we're doing.' He said, 'It's not going to be easy,' and I said, 'I don't give a fuck. That's not a reason not to do something. It's just the right thing to do, and we're going to make it work.' "

And they did. Granted, Michael admitted to me that he'd love to take it a bit further and use horses instead of tractors, but with a few hundred acres of vineyards that's where Brian and Bart step in and tell Michael he's nuts.* But considering the generally high quality of the wine, "What's strange is we're still the only organic vineyard in Marlborough, and if we can do it, anyone can do it—they just choose not to," Michael proclaimed over his peppermint tea as we sat in the café. "I don't do it as marketing. It's an ethical consideration. If you treat the soil as a living part of what you do as opposed to a medium for water and chemicals, you'll ultimately be repaid. If you treat

---

*Bart took it a step further—in 2005 he quit to become a private viticultural consultant. Brian quit in the middle of 2006 to focus on his own label, called Mahi.

the land well, it treats you well. If you treat the land like shit, it treats you like shit."

I opted not to comment on the fact that he'd pulled up to the café in a spanking-new SUV, and left it at that. A couple of months later, Bart summed up organics for me this way: "If you want to make a wine that reflects the site on which the grapes are grown, you can't do it if you have high chemical input because you're changing everything in that system, in that area of land. There are some who argue in France, 'Can you call yourself a *Grand Cru* vineyard since when you were given that status, everyone was organic? Do you still warrant that title?' It's probably a fair argument."

He makes a good point. Chris Seifried, winemaker for Seifried Estate in Nelson (Marlborough's little-brother winemaking region, about an hour's drive northwest), has worked throughout Europe, and one of the things that surprised him most in France was seeing tractor drivers who didn't know what they were spraying or how to apply it. Instead of putting the tractor in gear outside the rows and turning on the sprayers as they drove in, they'd park the tractor just inside the row, turn on the sprayer, and then put the tractor in gear, literally dousing the ends of the rows with copper rather than applying the spray evenly along the vines. "The ends of the rows were just blue . . . solid fuckin' blue," he recalled.

That's not to say that all the great vineyards of France are the chemical-waste equivalent of New Jersey, nor is it safe to conclude that nonorganic or unaffiliated vineyards don't do a good job of making clean, good-tasting wine. What is or isn't sprayed, how much, and what effect it all has on the vineyard is only one in a series of variables. Especially when you get into biodynamics.

Biodynamics is basically organics taken to a whole new level of, well, some say weirdness. You judge for yourself, though. There are no strictly biodynamic vineyards in Marlborough, but James Millton, owner and winemaker of Millton Vineyards in Gisborne on the North Island, is essentially the godfather of biodynamics in New Zealand. A good, step-by-step explanation of exactly what biodynamic farming is or how it works is hard to find, and I didn't unearth many specifics after a pretty thorough web search, nor after I had lunch with James months later, when he happened to be visiting New York. But I did find a reasonably good summation on his website. Here's part of it:

The difference that biodynamics presents from "organic" farming practices is that it does recognize that there is a growth force or energy force, which is related to the cosmic rhythms. This means that the movements of the moon and other planets have a profound influence on the soil, plant, and animal life.

Uh . . . okay. Some people have even suggested to me that biodynamic farmers also drive the tractor naked at certain times of year and bury strange objects in the vineyard at midnight under a full moon. I think they might be confusing biodynamic farmers with those Goth chicks who lived down the hall from them in college, but I can sort of see where they're coming from. Biodynamic farming, so far as I can tell, is pretty odd.

However, there are bits and pieces that some people believe in and take advantage of. Like composting with herbal preparations, manures, and egg shells, which Seresin does a fair amount of. And then there's all that stuff with the moon and cosmic rhythms, which Hatsch at Fromm and Hans Herzog both dabble in.

Hans just does it because he likes it. "I don't know much about it," he admitted to me, but, "I worked the last few years with the moon phase with pruning and trimming or spraying. I don't think about it for the marketing, but for myself. I have a good feeling being in the vineyard and making a clean, healthy product for the customers."

It should be noted, too, that Hans lives on the same property as his vineyard, winery, and high-end restaurant, and drinks his own groundwater. Since he lives, breathes, eats, drinks, and sleeps there, he wants to make sure that it's as clean as possible. I asked him if all this makes a difference in the taste of the wine, and he just shrugged his shoulders and said, "Probably not." But most important, "It makes me happy," he said.

"One thing I like about it is that it's not so abstract," Hatsch told me after he'd started to research biodynamics a bit more with the help of James Millton. "It's obviously working with nature's forces and energies, and while it looks a bit witchy for some people, I always like when something works and the explanation is not forthcoming. It just takes it away from being an industrial product that's recipe-made.

"Some people just grow better vegetables than others. They know there are certain times to do the trimming. They trim only on the descending moon because you get far less growth—it's the same as mowing your lawn and cutting your hair," he explained, but I'm not sure where he got this from, since I don't think Hatsch has had a haircut since the seventies. "These are things they know—they don't need to be explained. The moon is obvious, and it has an effect on the tides—everyone can see that."

When he put it that way, I could certainly see the attraction of biodynamics. Essentially, if you know that you'll get that extra little boost in quality at the end of the day if you try to work along with the forces of nature, whatever they are, as opposed to trying to circumvent them, then go for it. But Hatsch is still just sort of dipping his toe in the biodynamic waters. He sees it as a decade-long plan, since it's not something you just jump into, much like grape-growing in general. More than anything, though, he just wants to have a clean, healthy, good-tasting product for you to drink.

But having said that, he knows there's never an excuse for a wine that doesn't taste good. "They should buy our wines because they're really, really good," he said. "If it happens to be healthy at the same time, that should be the bonus." In other words, there's no point in making an organic wine if it ultimately tastes like a dirty hippie's Birkenstock.

The nice thing about organics and biodynamics, overall, is that they really don't have any negative connotations if they're practiced with a reasonable level of science-based environmental concern. The problem they do have, however, is weeds, which suck the same nutrients from the ground that the vines depend upon so heavily to grow good-tasting, healthy grapes. If you take a look around any wine region, and especially Marlborough, it's often the case that the cleaner and greener the vineyards on paper, the messier they are on the actual ground, since the weeds are so difficult to control.

Al Soper at Highfield, which is a member of the Sustainable scheme, told me that "we've identified that we need to be seen as clean and green—that it's not an empty catchphrase." But that's about as far as he's willing to push it. Where organics are concerned, "There are some people doing it and it works for them, and they market themselves that way, and they sell their wines because of it, but I'm not convinced that those wines are better. And it comes with all the connotations of howling at the moon . . . which is a bit strange. I like vineyards to look tidy and clean. In my experience, organic vineyards often don't."

What you should take from this is that all of these guys work in the manner that they feel is best for them. Nobody wants to force a glass of chemicals down your throat, just as organic or biodynamic producers don't want to make crap wine and have you drink it just because it's supposedly "healthier." (I once tried organic wine in Australia that was also sulfur-free—it tasted like kerosene from a rusty old can that had been sitting in someone's garage for six years . . . don't ask me how I was able to draw the connection.) Try the wine, and if you just go with what tastes best and makes you feel the best, you won't be disappointed.

As the weather began to warm toward the beginning of December, the Millstone block was finally replanted. Beforehand, Ra and Phillip spent the better part of two weeks driving in new posts—840 of them, perfectly spaced along forty-two rows. They also strung up wires and laid out new irrigation lines.

A crew Fred had assembled of about twenty workers, myself included, planted two rows at a time on a hot, sun-drenched morning. A couple of guys dug holes ahead of the planters, and in between them a couple other workers would drop cuttings into each hole. Working as a planter, I found that my lower back got more and more sore with each time I knelt or bent to cover the base of a cutting with dirt.

"You'll start to feel it in the tops of your legs," I was warned by Shirley, one of Fred's longtime workers. "Every time we change jobs we have a different set of muscles that gets sore."

The planting was finished by about 2:00 P.M., and the workers were dispatched to other jobs that would require—and stress—different muscle groups for the remainder of the day, just as Shirley promised. I looked up and down the rows once the workers had all left, and I wondered what would happen to these vines, which, for the moment, just looked like little pieces of dead wood protruding from the ground.

It was then that I realized that growing grapes, no matter how you do it, is a gamble. Sure, grapevines are resilient plants that can grow in just about any conditions, but the quality of the fruit they eventually bear depends on countless factors—some chemical, some physical, some completely unexplainable.

But there's one that has more influence than any of the others combined: Mother Nature.

It's hard to be farming sheep one year and growing grapes the next.

—Dominic Pecchenino, viticulturist at
Matador Estate

22

Grower Pains

If you live in the northern hemisphere it's difficult not to associate Christmas with seeing your breath crystallize as you throw another log on the fire. Though it's supposed to be just the opposite south of the equator, as 2004 rolled over into 2005, New Zealand was pretty much the same.

For three weeks the weather was wet, cold, and overcast when everyone was supposed to be at the beach enjoying the sunshine. And this is the time of year when all the flowers on many varieties are still hoping to be fertilized. If the weather isn't warm, dry, and windy, the pollen can't travel through the air and do its job.

On the bright side, though, if you recall from the first half of this book, 2004 was a massive year in terms of grape tonnage, to the point that anyone who experienced it firsthand will be recovering mentally and physically well into 2010. Some vineyards were overcropped and others came on stream for the first time, leading to huge volumes of wine and the New Zealand export market essentially doubling overnight. And if you think back even further, 2003 was a frost-affected year with low volume, so really an event such as a poor flowering in 2005 shouldn't have come as a shock to anyone. The person who was least surprised by a natural crop-lightening event was Dominic Pecchenino at Matador Estate.

"New Zealand will never have big back-to-back years," he told me. "We have a really big governor here called Mother Nature that Australia and California don't have." He would know, since he still works with or owns vineyards in all three places. "In 2002 we had frosts, so the 2003 crops were low; 2004 we had a big crop; and then in 2005 we had rain during bloom, so we have reduced crop levels."

Jeremy didn't seem all that concerned, either. "The cold and wet weather has caused a staggered flowering," he said. This results in hen-and-chicken, as it's called when a bunch has fully formed grapes as well as tiny, poorly developed ones scattered throughout. This isn't necessarily a bad thing overall, since it ultimately means a lower crop without having to pay people to go through the vineyards and thin the fruit.

However, "the conditions were good for disease," Jeremy added. "It was quite wet and humid. Some people put on a spray, and it just washed off the next day. And there's some wicked vegetative growth out there." Sure enough, one end of the new planting at the Millstone vineyard was overflowing with weeds—but nothing that couldn't be handled once the weather dried up and the spray program got back into gear.

For the moment, Bart, the viticulturist at Seresin, didn't seem all that concerned, either. Not just because he'd welcome a lower crop in 2005, but because in winegrowing there's no sense in counting your chickens before they hatch. All he needed to do was look back at the year before.

"The whole thing can change a lot in a short space of time," Bart explained to me a couple of weeks after the cool, wet weather had passed and summer started to live up to its name again. "Last year December was really hot, and you knew there was gonna be a huge crop out there—there was a huge amount of fruit hanging," he recalled. "And then all of a sudden you could see the guys with huge tonnages thinking what color Range Rovers they were gonna have this year after vintage, and then February was a dog. All of a sudden, the whole atmosphere changed, and everyone's saying, 'Oh my God, what're we gonna do now?' How we're looking at it now may be totally irrelevant come harvest time."

That was refreshing to hear at the time, because if you happened to read the local paper or any wine publications that keep an eye on this sort of thing, you'd think Marlborough's cold December was cataclysmic. All the headlines were about the crop size dropping as much as 20 percent from 2004 to 2005 and people screaming bloody murder, as if there were a single person who could be blamed and then dragged through the streets and stoned to death. It was at this point that I realized I'd stumbled across a relatively unusual dynamic in winegrowing that I'd never encountered in any other industry: Everyone, simultaneously and in harmony, seemed to need to have something to complain about.

If your memory's good you won't need to flip back ten or eleven chapters, to where I spent a lot of time asking around if the 2004 harvest in Marlborough was indeed The Big One. What you may recall was that it was really The Big Finger-pointing, with so-called "experienced" wineries having sensible crop loads and the new guys and growers all carrying heavy crop loads that the vines couldn't ripen. But really, anyone who harvested a single grape in 2004 had some sort of crop-loading issues to deal with, even if they didn't want to admit to it on the record. Which led me to wonder why, now, with lighter crops, nobody was saying that the quality might be better?

"Winegrowers just need something to complain about because we're farmers," John Belsham said to me when I asked him why everyone was griping. "That's just part of the deal."

"That's probably true," Allan said when I asked him the same question. "I've never known an industry like it, where people just like to pontificate on the merits and otherwise of what the crop's going to be like."

Dominic at Matador Estate put it this way: "There's probably no agricultural product in the world that's scrutinized as much as wine grapes. I was in a consultant firm in California for a while, and we had guys who consulted on cotton. And I said, when's the last time you sat in a room and said, 'Well, the cotton in my underwear came out of Arizona'?" (You don't talk about your underwear this way, but if you did, I'd have written a very different book . . . and the research for the thong chapter would've been one of the great joys of my life.)

Undeterred, I started asking around if the quality was indeed looking better, and I got some reluctant nods toward the end of January and some definite yesses as Marlborough headed into March. During that stretch, for the most part, the weather was warm, dry, and sunny. And even when it did rain, no one seemed to panic.

"Our biggest plus in Marlborough is the Nor'west," Uncle B told me.

"Because even if we get a rain, it turns around and blows about four or five hours, and it'll dry the vines out quick enough before any botrytis action."

But as for the quality of the crops themselves, "It really comes down to what you consider to be an acceptable yield," John Belsham explained. In other words, some producers might hack off bunches of grapes even after a poor flowering, just as he, Hans Herzog, Hatsch, and several others all claimed to have done—it's just what they do normally anyway. And others might not drop anything.

"My crops aren't that low," Dominic said to me of his vineyard, which is mostly Sauvignon Blanc. "If your crop level is too low," he went on, "your quality is not going to be good, either. I do not believe in the theory that you take a vineyard that normally produces four and a half to five tons to the acre and, say, pin it down to two tons to the acre and say it's gonna get better fruit quality. It doesn't work. If it's balanced in crop load and in canopy and in nutrition management, that's the highest-quality fruit you can get. You've really got to get your vine balanced."

Which is why, even in a good year (as 2005 was shaping up to be), wineries and growers often cause each other a fair amount of stress. In the case of ASW, it was with its longtime Chardonnay growers, who I'll call Jerry and Edna Jones. Unlike the other growers ASW buys fruit from or even in its own vineyards, the Joneses refused to prune and wrap their Chardonnay to two canes, and instead went with four—two on each side of the vine—to keep their tonnage and income both as high as possible.

"They're just farmers," Josh told me after a series of meetings with the grower that had gone in circles. With a two-year escape clause in the contract and neither side coming to an agreement they could live with, ASW finally suggested that the Joneses try to find someone else to take their Chardonnay. But they couldn't. No one wanted it, and it looked as though ASW would be stuck buying the grapes for the next two vintages—all forty-five tons of them, according to Jeremy's early estimates for 2005. In 2004 the Joneses delivered 68.69 tons over nine acres, which is more than 7.5 tons per acre (four tons per acre is really the maximum acceptable level for good-tasting, commercial Chardonnay, and that's really pushing it).

"Yield is relative to quality," Allan told me of the situation. "It's not everything, but it's a strong factor. We tried to make the payment relative to the yield. The better your fruit, the better your price was. They wouldn't accept that." They didn't even attend the ASW Christmas party.

All the meetings were held while everyone else was shoot-thinning, but the Joneses wouldn't budge. "They said there wasn't enough time," Allan recalled, shaking his head a bit. "If they did things the way we work, it would have cost them a hell of a lot less viticulturally to do the work in their vineyard—less risk and better returns. But still they saw growing grapes for tons."

From this I could really only conclude that the stalemate was a result of the Joneses being solely interested in sucking as much cash from the Scotts as they possibly could before the parties went their separate ways in a couple years' time. The Joneses certainly didn't seem to hold the long-term view that if they provided lower volumes of better quality, the wine would improve over the long term and command a higher price—in turn, so would their grapes. But I'll never really know for sure. During the research and writing of this entire book, the Joneses were the only ones who refused to be interviewed.

Dominic Pecchenino, however, was more than happy to sound off about such problems, and growers—because he is one, and has been for twenty-four years.

"Let's face it," he told me. "There are grape growers and grape farmers. There are a lot of grape farmers, unfortunately, who got into it because economics forced them there."

Before they planted grapevines, most of these guys either grew apples, the biggest moneymaker in Marlborough even up until the mid-nineties, or they had sheep and cattle. So far as they knew at the time, their land was worth NZ$1,500 per acre, tops. But when the wine industry became the biggest business around, that land was going for NZ$35,000 or more, and as much as NZ$60,000 today. It made them all millionaires practically overnight, and while that much money will change a lot of things, in many cases it had no effect whatsoever on the farming mind-set: The more you produce, the more money you get.

"They don't understand the industry. It's a grape, you pick it," Dominic went on. "When I came down here in 1993 to look at Matador, the nice breath of fresh air was the relationship the growers and wineries had. Now you're starting to see a bit of animosity . . . which is sad to see . . . because let's face it, in New Zealand there's no reason to grow grapes other than to make wine. No brandy production. No table grapes. No raisins."

For what it's worth, though, the Joneses seemed to be the exception to the rule so far as ASW's growers were concerned. Everyone else had signed up to the new era of grape-growing, where high-quality fruit resulted in fatter paychecks, and most other growers or wineries I spoke with claimed to have resolved any such problems they encountered.

"With that last season, we enforced a pricing schedule for the first time in a long time on one of the blocks that I considered to be excessively cropped, and due to that cropping, it came in at below-target Brix," Al Soper said of Highfield, which buys Sauvignon Blanc from several growers. "If we didn't, that grower was going to earn more per acre than the guys who were doing a good job. We needed to send a signal.

"We want to be fair," Al continued. "So we don't want our growers to be hurting. We want them to be making good money, but we need to be making good money as well."

The trick for the future lies in the wineries convincing the growers that there's no element of subterfuge involved, that quality really is paramount, and that everyone suffers if you just grow as many grapes as you possibly can. What it really comes down to, then, is just laying down the law, which seems to work well for some wineries, such as Nobilo.

"If you're going to grow fruit like that, you're only going to get NZ$600 per ton," Darryl Woolley said of his policy—that's about one-quarter the going rate for good-quality grapes. Even though Nobilo buys the lower-quality grapes, they don't find their way into anything labeled "Marlborough Sauvignon Blanc." They do, however, go into a lower label or supermarket blend. "We have a product in the U.K. called White Cloud, which is really just a blended product at an entry level," Darryl added, and I informed him that White Cloud is a brand of toilet paper in the United States. The irony wasn't lost on him. "We're quite comfortable picking up that kind of fruit, but I don't think that's the long-term future for Marlborough. We should be discussing quite seriously with our growers about their harming the Marlborough brand."

Cloudy Bay seems to think it's found a way around that problem: good communication. "The growers come in on a relatively regular basis, and you can just talk to them about what's going on in the winery and the markets," Dog Point's James Healy explained to me. (Not only did he work at Cloudy Bay for several years, but Cloudy Bay buys most of the grapes off Dog Point's eighty hectares of vines.) "It's not to make them buy into it, but to make them understand that some situations are more difficult than others."

And sometimes situations are just plain ironic.

After all the meetings and disagreements between ASW and the Joneses, the Chardonnay from their vineyard appeared to be of relatively high quality. Because of the poor flowering, their crop was reduced naturally, providing the very balance between fruit and leaf canopy that Allan, Josh, and Jeremy were begging of the Joneses from the very beginning. "Their stuff actually looks really good," Josh humbly admitted, but certainly not to the Joneses themselves.

However, the cool flowering period in late 2004 and early 2005 had affected just about everyone, which meant that there was all of a sudden a shortage of Chardonnay on the market rather than a surplus. As a result, the Joneses found another winery to buy their fruit, resolving the issue once and for all—but actually leaving ASW short of the volume of Chardonnay it would need by the end of the '05 harvest, to the tune of about 80,000 liters. For months ASW had more Chardonnay than they knew what to do with, and all of a sudden they didn't have nearly enough.

Allan just shrugged it off, possibly because he was relieved to have the situation over and done with, and because he knew he'd probably be able to find the juice he'd need on the open market. The Joneses and the headaches they'd caused were now someone else's problem.

What a relief it would be, too, if this were the only one.

There is that sort of stigma that because someone drives a tractor or works with their hands, they don't have the intellect to understand what happens in a winery. And it is simply a stigma. It's understanding the process that's rewarding.

—John Belsham, owner/winemaker of Foxes Island

23

Labor Pains

Vineyard work sucks.

I thought I'd just mention that again in case you'd forgotten since the first time I mentioned it.

I have no idea why, but many people who drink wine think that making it is some sort of relaxed, cushy lifestyle. And I don't understand it, because I've never eaten a juicy steak and imagined how romantic and luxurious a life I'd have if I started raising cattle in Wyoming. Similarly, I've never met anyone who got a massage and moved to Sweden or shot heroin and moved to Afghanistan.

People just seem to have wine all wrong. In fact, just as I began writing this chapter I called an airline in the United States to book a couple of flights for my return home. When the customer-service agent asked what I'd been doing in New Zealand, I told her that I'd been working at a winery.

"Geez, you've got it easy!" she said.

If it were possible—and I knew I could get away with it—I'd have reached through the phone and strangled her. Especially since I'd spent most of my time, of late, in the vineyards doing everything from bud-rubbing to shoot-thinning to lifting wires to replanting. By no means had I done that much compared to the average, everyday vineyard worker, but so far as I was concerned it was more than enough. In fact, every time I saw Uncle B coming I pretty much ran for cover, for fear that he'd give me any one of several vineyard jobs, each more miserable than the next.

He also has this uncanny ability to disappear when you're working hardest and return the very instant you take a break—and he makes you feel about the size of a two-year-old with the tongue-lashing he doles out. On the morning that I helped Fred's crew plant new vines at the Millstone vineyard, it was so hot that Fred told the guys digging the holes to stop, take a break, stretch their backs, and drink some water. As soon as they put their shovels down, however, Uncle B pulled up in his silver pickup truck, popped out, and let the verbal assault begin.

"You'd think he was paying our wage out of his bloody pocket," one of the workers muttered to me after the fact.

Whatever your opinion of Uncle B, however, the job gets done with only a minimal amount of complaint from the full-time and contract workers alike. "Abrasive" might be a bit too kind a word to describe Uncle B, but Fred, ASW's labor contractor, seems to be able to handle him pretty well, not just because ultimately they both want the same thing (to do a good job), but because Fred's been around the block a few times.

Fred's a jolly, gray-haired guy with a leathery face, a big smile, and a deep, dry smoker's voice. Fred was pretty much the first and only vineyard contractor in Marlborough when he started in 1991 (though he'd been working in the area on and off since 1979, around the time he thought he'd retire). He built up a workforce of roughly 120 people shortly after a freezer works south of Marlborough had shut down.

"All they knew was butchering. They were just laborers—they knew nothing else," Fred told me of the workers who'd been let go. However, he thought about it and realized that butchering wasn't all that different from vineyard work: repetitive and mundane. And if you did it right, a hell of a lot less bloody. So he put up a notice saying that he was hiring new hands. "They adapted very well to the vineyard," he said.

The downside, though, was that Marlborough wineries were only really able to offer Fred and his crew about four months' worth of work, mostly pruning, "then they'd go away and pick garlic or apples." Eventually, however, the wineries "started to find out that by putting more time into the vines they were getting better-quality juice. So we created other jobs for ourselves—fruit-thinning, leaf-plucking. Now it's really eleven-month employment on a casual basis," with that twelfth month being the wait for the fruit to ripen before picking.

These days Fred has a workforce of around forty on-and-off laborers (for pruning and picking that number usually doubles). Though he once had several clients all across the valley, he's since trimmed the business down to a more manageable size, and only works with ASW, Morton Estate, and Blue Slape.

"He's probably four to five dollars an hour cheaper than a lot of vineyard contractors around," Uncle B told me of his arrangement with Fred. Of the total sum paid Fred by ASW each week, more than 80 percent goes to the workers.

"There are some contractors who believe they need five dollars an hour per worker to run their businesses, which is crap. I'm on two dollars an hour coming back my way," Fred claimed. "Sixteen to twenty dollars per person per day is more than enough to run your business." In other words, Fred not only cares about doing a good job, but also respects his clients by not overcharging them, and he looks after his workers, whether they're backpackers who stay with him for two weeks or locals who stay with him for two or more years. He's so good at training people, in fact, that many of them have been hired by other vineyards to be permanent staffers. Some have even gone on to become vineyard managers.

Fred also takes on students during summer break from school. "I show them what they should never do," he said, almost as if he's running the Scared Straight program. "It's just hard labor. Stay in school and become a viticulturist rather than take the hard slog down these rows."

Great as that may be, by spending as much time with Fred's crew as I did I wasn't getting a sense of the industry standard—which couldn't have been especially high, considering the coverage in the local media. In August, at the height of pruning season, the *Marlborough Express* reported—and not for the first or last time in 2004—on a police raid that had resulted in the capture of fourteen illegal workers. Most of them were from China, Thailand, and Brazil, all working to send money home. One raid found eighteen workers squeezed into a small house with only one toilet for all of them to share.

While I imagine many of these people were pretty desperate, there was no question that the vineyards were even more so, considering the nation-wide labor shortage. Dominic Pecchenino, who serves on a number of local boards and organizations, saw how bad the problem was when he went to a meeting and found out that "there were fifty-seven unemployed people in Blenheim, and of those fifty-seven only five were physically able to do vine-yard work."

In other words, you'd think that the wineries and vineyards would be rolling out the red carpet for whatever transients they could find. Unfortu-nately, wherever there are desperate workers there are people willing to take advantage of them. There are rumors everywhere throughout the valley of contractors and subcontractors who charge upward of NZ$19 an hour per worker they employ, and pass on less than NZ$10 per hour to the people actually sweating it out in the vineyards—especially those without legal sta-tus. James, a British guy working in Seresin's new vineyard in the Omaka Valley and a brief tenant in Josh's house, told me about the predominantly Chinese crew working in another vineyard nearby.

"If they don't finish their row before they go on break or to lunch, they have to start a new row when they come back so they don't waste the time actually walking down to where they left off," he told me. "They also have to be at their plant the very minute they're supposed to start again, or they're docked a quarter of an hour. They're not allowed to talk to each other or take phone calls. The sad part is, it's still probably better than what their lives were like back home."

As I wondered how and why this could happen in a place so desperate for workers, a vineyard contractor named Linton Francis Brydon was sentenced to six months in prison for nearly NZ$400,000 in unpaid tax. The guy didn't even keep a company checkbook and paid all of his workers—whoever they were, since there were few records—in cash. Where there's smoke there's fire, so it doesn't take a genius to figure out what kind of workers this guy was hir-ing and the sort of rates he was likely paying. The Marlborough Contractors Federation (MCF) chairman told the local paper that this problem is "huge in Marlborough," with contractors such as Brydon undercutting legitimate ones. Sadly, Brydon was "not the first and not the last" to work in such a man-ner, the MCF chairman told the *Marlborough Express,* though Brydon cer-tainly won't be doing this sort of thing again—he died only a couple of months into his prison sentence (reports were that it was natural causes, though I like to think that it was death by salad tossing).

"Linton worked for me at Montana," Fred said to me when I asked about the situation. "He was arrogant and uneducated, and he was doin' it for someone who knew exactly what was going on—he was paying him to do it. 'I'll just pay you NZ$10,000 a week, and you pay them whatever. But keep it quiet.' And he kept it quiet, and he got himself in the crap.

"Vineyard people are a funny lot," Fred went on. "A lot of them are uneducated. They're just laborers, and they don't want to do any more or better, but a lot of them try to be contractors. There's no course set up for anyone to start as a contractor, and say, 'This is what you must do.'"

Someone who's especially outspoken on this issue is Dominic from Matador Estate, possibly because he worked in California for so many years, where the vineyard workforce is predominantly Mexican and has a long history of being mistreated.

"What really makes me mad is that the wine industry has been very good for Blenheim in a lot of ways," he complained to me. "Unfortunately, in New Zealand, you can become a labor contractor overnight. You go down and you pay a couple of hundred bucks and get a business license, and bingo, you're a contractor. In California you have to take a test. You've got to apply."

Fred was a bit more damning in his assessment of the problem. "Now they tell me there are about 120 contractors here in Marlborough. I'd say forty percent of them don't have an idea what they're doing," he said. "Half a dozen this year are already gone—they were charging too much and then not doing the job properly."

But who was to say for certain how bad the situation actually was? Of course, no winery wants to see workers treated or paid poorly, but no one seemed particularly eager to take the bull by the horns, either. For the most part, every winery I met with told me that they're quoted a price by the contractor, and it's pretty much a leap of faith from there—what the contractor pays his workers or how they're treated is between the contractor and the workers, whether those people know or not that there are other options available to them or can speak and read enough English to scan the help-wanted ads. Dominic was the only one who told me that he wanted to see his contractor's books to find out what he was paying his workers before he'd make any kind of agreement.

And still, the presses kept rolling with one story after another of housing raids, illegal workers, underpaid workers, or poor working conditions. So far as I could tell there didn't seem to be a union or any other organization with enough power to help address the problems. Just from reading the local paper it sounded as though the vineyards ranked right up there with North Korean prison-labor camps. I figured that the only way to come to any sort of conclusion was to find out for myself. I decided to pretend that I was a backpacker passing through, in need of some work to finance my travels, and I started answering the help-wanted ads placed by vineyard contractors.

Though it sounded like it'd be easier than getting hit by raindrops in a hurricane, landing a job proved to be a bit more difficult than I thought. The first ad I responded to, a couple of days after it ran in the paper, had generated enough calls that the contractor no longer needed more workers. I didn't hear back from the second one I called, but the third agreed to take me on.

The contractor offered to meet me outside the convenience store in the center of Renwick at 6:45 A.M. "Just follow the white van," he said to me over the phone, which turned out to be a bit like someone in Beijing giving you street directions and telling you, "When you see the Chinese guy on the corner, turn right." Standard practice for Marlborough contractors is to provide transportation to anyone who needs it, and I think they all went to the same dealership together and got some sort of group discount on white vans. After the first three or four passed by without stopping it was already 7:30 A.M., so I said, "Fuck it," aloud, turned the car back on, drove home, and went back to bed.

I had no luck on the fourth ad, either. I began to wonder by this point if the reason I was striking out was my fairly good command of the English language. I contemplated using a heavy accent from then on, but I realized that the only one I could do was a really bad impression of Borat on *Da Ali G Show*. Even if I could pull off the fake Kazakhstan accent to get the job, though, I couldn't imagine that I'd be able to keep up the charade for an entire week.

As luck would have it, though, the fifth contractor I called agreed to take me on. Over the phone he was a soft-spoken guy, and he turned out to be even more so when I met him in person at a grower's small vineyard, just as the sun was rising on a warm Monday morning. The voice didn't really match the appearance of the man, who I'm going to call Mr. Clean, since that's pretty much who he looked like—bald head, earring, stocky build. When we spoke over the phone he asked me if I had a work permit (I did), and if I needed transportation (I didn't). He also asked if I'd had any experience, and I told him that I'd had a little—pruning, dropping wires, bud-rubbing—and that sounded like more than enough so far as he was concerned.

We spent the first morning lifting wires, and I was paired on a row with one of Mr. Clean's longtime workers, a friendly and chatty former employee of the freezer works who everyone called Snooks. As we lifted wire after wire, I asked him where the grapes on this particular vineyard would wind up.

"Cloudy Bay, I imagine," he said, though it seemed like that was really the only winery in Marlborough he'd heard of even though he'd lived in the area for years. "Some of the wineries here are quite big . . . *national* even," he told me.

"You don't say," I responded, realizing that if I told him that New Zealand would be exporting about four million cases that year, I'd be blowing my cover. So I asked Mr. Clean who was buying the grapes, and he said, "Uh, I can't think of it just now . . . I should really know, though."

We finished lifting the wires before lunchtime, and I remember thinking to myself at the time, "This ain't so bad." But my spirits would be shattered over the next four and a half days.

We all piled into our cars and headed to a thirty-acre vineyard in Taylor Pass, at the southeastern end of the valley. The block had been planted by hand by Mr. Clean's crew just the year before. I have no idea how, since the entire vineyard, if you could call it that, was just rocks. It looked more suitable to be a gravel quarry than a vineyard, but since grapevines are resilient plants, they seemed to be growing just fine—along with the weeds.

Our job, as Mr. Clean showed us on the first couple of vines in the row, would be to kneel, open the plastic cartons that protect the base of each young plant from sprays as well as frosts, and strip off all the shoots and leaves on what would eventually become the trunk. After closing the cartons we'd then have to stand up and snip any tendrils that had grown off the top of the vine, and then twist the stalk around the wire so it'd eventually become a cane out of which the following year's shoots would grow. Then move on to the next one. And the next one. And the next one. And the next one.

"Young plants are a killer," Fred once told me, and I now believed him. If I thought this was going to be hard on my back (it was), it turned out to be especially rough on my knees from squatting or kneeling at each vine. By the end of the week my hands were covered with scrapes, scratches, and cuts from the cartons as well as the weeds that had to be yanked out. I also managed to snip my fingers a couple of times instead of the tendrils.

Stupid as that may sound, you tend to lose your focus when you're working under the scorching sun for eight hours. I started at 6:30 A.M. each day with the only skinny Samoan I've ever met, Levi, another of Mr. Clean's long-time workers. By 9:00 A.M., the sun had risen over the hills and begun roasting us under thirty-degree-centigrade-plus heat (that's the high eighties, low nineties, Fahrenheit) until quitting time, 2:45 P.M. Though there was no natural protection from the sun or sunscreen provided, there was a water tap at one end of the vineyard that was hooked to the irrigation (but could be used as drinking water), and a port-a-potty that, for port-a-potties in general, was pretty clean. I'm not saying you'd want to have a pizza delivered to you in it, but you'd be more than comfortable doing the sort of thing in there for which it was designed.

After I took note of the conditions I turned my attention to the people, and it didn't take long to realize that most of what I'd heard to this point about vineyard workers was pretty much true—they have little interest in what they're doing and just want the paycheck at the end of the week. Each one also has a relatively boring life story, so I decided that it was best that I have an uninteresting cover story as well. On my first day I happened to be wearing a Boston University T-shirt, so I just told everyone I was from Boston. There was only one other foreigner, a guy from Turkey named Sultan, and the rest of the crew comprised a few longtime vineyard workers, a couple of mothers with small kids, a few teenagers, and one guy who claimed to be a former policy advisor in Parliament (I avoided the temptation to ask him, "Whose secretary did you bang to wind up here?").

Though the work was painful, repetitive, and mind-numbing, the monotony was occasionally broken by someone asking me a question about America.

"Hoy, bro," one of the teenagers said to get my attention. "Where you from?"

"Boston," I told him.

"Ah, cool, bro. That's near Seattle, right?"

Okay, so the kid doesn't have a bright future in geography, but he seemed nice enough and was relatively hardworking. My favorite questions, though, came from Snooks.

"Is it true that the bread doesn't go moldy over there?" he asked me after about half an hour of silence among the workers.

"What?"

"The bread," he said. "It doesn't go moldy in America, does it?"

"Huh?" I asked him. I mean, I knew that many people in faraway places often consider the United States to be the Promised Land . . . but it never occurred to me that it might be because of the baked goods.

"Yeah, I had some friends who were over there once, and they left bread in the pantry for about two months. When they found it, it wasn't moldy. How do they do that?"

I just shrugged my shoulders, fighting off the temptation to tell him that yes, it is indeed true that American bread doesn't go moldy, and hasn't since that visionary kid Jack changed agriculture forever when he planted those magic beans.

Needless to say, most of these guys are not exactly members of Mensa. Hell, I don't even think they'd make it as members of AAA. But one thing's for sure: They understand the value of a hard day's work, and they put it in and then some. They can even work a few hours on Saturday mornings if they need to pull in some extra cash, and mothers can drop their kids at school, work until it's time to pick them up, and earn an extra three hundred dollars or so per week.

Overall, the workers seemed to be nice, genuine folks. And Mr. Clean was out there with us each and every day, doing all the work alongside us, and even telling us what to do if we were making mistakes. On Friday morning I lied and told Mr. Clean that I'd gotten a job as a cellar hand, and he thanked me for helping him out for the week. I left the vineyard on that last day mildly sunburned, very sore, and with a whole new appreciation of what has to be done to grow grapes for winemaking. The filth didn't come out from under my fingernails for more than a week, and only a good commitment to stretching saved me from another trip to the chiropractor.

I also left with some idea of what makes for an acceptable working environment so far as vineyards are concerned, much as the work itself may suck. But I decided to leave it up to the experts, and I listed Mr. Clean's strong and weak points with several winemakers and viticulturists and asked them to give Mr. Clean a grade.

You've probably already gotten a good sense of Mr. Clean's strengths, like working with the crew every day and providing transportation to anyone who needed it. However, he never told me how much I was being paid (though about NZ$400 appeared in my bank account at the end of the week, which I used to buy myself an iPod); he never asked to see my work visa; and he had no idea where the fruit was going to go on that first block where we lifted wires. Never mind the fact that he'd probably done much of the other work there throughout the year, since no vineyard owner would call in a contractor to lift wires for one day, then cut him loose.

"It's really important that if you have people working on your property they understand what you're trying to achieve," John Belsham told me, and gave Mr. Clean a score of two out of ten.

Allan failed him, too, but most people I spoke with gave Mr. Clean a passing grade, though not one to write home about. When I spoke with Dominic Pecchenino, however, it became clear why the vineyard-contracting business is plagued with so many problems even if, in my particular case, the experience wasn't all that bad. Any misery I experienced was simply from the nature of the work.

"This is a problem with some of the responsibilities of labor contractors, and what they think they're responsible for," Dominic explained. "If you read New Zealand law, I, the grower, am responsible for your toilet. Sunblock is the labor contractor's responsibility."

And he, too, feels that the pay rate is something the workers should figure out with the contractor rather than the vineyard owner butting in. Similarly, James Healy said of his contractor, "I don't think it's our job to check his people to make sure they have valid work permits," much the way the president of the company you work for shouldn't have to check that the people who empty the garbage bins from the cubicles every night have Green Cards. Though it often may not seem like it, he probably does have better things to do.

I wondered, too, if part of the problem stemmed from the fact that the workers have a relatively low interest in what they're doing, since they don't get exposed to the final product as part of the job. Mike Just, however, told me that "anyone who's worked a couple days in my vineyard takes a bottle of wine home." He wants the people who work in his vineyard to taste the fruits of their labor.

This was certainly the case when I spent a day helping Mike do some grafting at Clayridge. It took us all day to do just one row, but after we finished his wife, Paula, fired up the BBQ and bottle after bottle of wine was consumed. I staggered out at 1:30 A.M., and while this was probably exceptionally special treatment, I was certainly tempted to come back and work in Mike's vineyard again. So I started asking around how important it is for the workers to understand that connection between high-quality vineyard work and good-tasting wine.

"The more you get that going, the better," Whitehaven's Simon Waghorn said to me, using the guys who work on a Tohu vineyard in the Awatere Valley as an example. "They got a gold medal for the Tohu Sauvignon Blanc," a wine he'd made. "They knew they'd done all the work from planting to training, all the way to handpicking the fruit. They're hugely proud of that."

However, Simon's the first to admit that the vineyard guys prefer a beer at the end of a long day. "Some wine styles they haven't taken to like ducks to water, but they still try everything, even if it's not to their taste. They still take some time to try it and think about it. You've got to have a bit of a sense that you're all aspiring for the best-quality product you can make."

Simon's had them all come to the winery for a tour to see how everything works and even taste samples out of barrels. "We've spent a small amount of time trying to get them more interested in what they're doing. A lot of them are getting more educated and more excited about it."

Similarly, Dominic holds tastings of Nobilo wines that were produced with Matador's fruit, part of the reason being that Matador does a completely different type of pruning called Scott Henry (conveniently, it was invented by a guy in Oregon named Scott Henry). It's essentially the same as vertical shoot positioning (flip back to Chapter 21 if you forgot what it is), with two canes on each side of the vine, only the top two canes grow their shoots up while the bottom two canes grow their shoots down, making the row of vines look more like a row of shrubs. What this does is get more light exposure on the fruit as it ripens, and also makes it easier to get sprays into the leaf canopy—but it's harder work for the pruners.

"The guys had never done it before, and when we tasted the wines, they tasted the differences between the Scott Henry and the VSP . . . they all had a better appreciation of it and why we did it," Dominic said to me when I asked him how important it is for vineyard workers to understand what they're doing and why. "It's very important that the lowest man on the totem pole knows what the end product is like . . . make them feel proud of that bottle of wine."

This is not standard practice by any means, and one winemaker essentially told me that he doesn't think it's important at all for the vineyard workers to know about the end product.

"So, you can work on a car assembly line and take the subway to work every day because you don't have a driver's license?" I asked him.

"Exactly," he said.

Similarly, James Healy told me that while he thinks it's important for people to have a general idea, "I've seen people who don't care, and they still manage to do a great job. The taste of the wine is not their driving force, it's to do a good job. Some people don't even like alcohol."

I'm not sure who these crazy people are of whom he speaks, but one thing seemed certain: Problems the likes of which grabbed the local headlines and got people talking are probably the exception rather than the rule. Try as I might, I couldn't find a contractor who was malicious or ill-intentioned—just one who didn't know he was supposed to supply water and sunscreen, as well as be diligent about checking the visas of any foreigners on his crew. Even if Mr. Clean had been just like all those unprofessional, cold pricks I'd read about in the paper, all I needed to do was flip a couple of pages deeper to the help-wanted section and find a new job. Every industry has cowboys who want to operate outside the rules and take advantage of weaker or less-fortunate people for their own benefit, but they're probably outnumbered by those who not only want to do a good job, but want to share the spoils.

Marlborough's labor problems won't get resolved any time soon. Many people suggested to me that they'll get far worse before they improve as more and more uneducated laborers make themselves contractors overnight in order to satisfy the demand for workers and make a quick buck. But just as I discovered during the winter pruning season that the wineries and growers who put in the effort in the vineyards and treat their people well are the ones who make better wine, the same holds true for the rest of the year, through all the other vineyard jobs that need doing. Good-tasting wine involves not only TLC with the vines, but also with the people who tend to them. Mother Nature will then take care of the rest.

It'll be nice to have just a normal harvest.

—ALLAN SCOTT

24

Starting All Over Again

Just as the grapes were going through veraison and the bird nets were in place, ASW began to undergo a cosmetic change as well. The concrete ramp that had been damaged to commence the 2004 vintage was ripped out and rebuilt where it'd be easier for the truck to back up it. The presses and receival bin were moved with a crane, a conveyer belt was installed beneath the presses for removal of the marc, and several tanks were moved around and new ones added, along with catwalks constructed above them.

"We were going to be a five-hundred-ton winery, then a seven-hundred-fifty, and max it there. Now we're at one thousand and focusing on quantity rather than quality," Cathy complained to me a couple of months before the construction began. It was more the heat of the moment talking, since she was concerned about costs—Allan had already spent NZ$50,000 getting the gravel paved over without telling her beforehand. But as the construction work kicked in and the new crushing area began to take shape, it appeared Allan had taken both quality and quantity into consideration, mostly because his winemakers were more than happy with the way things were looking. "Allan just wants to make sure we're as modern and equipped as we can possibly be," Jeremy told me of the several hundred thousand dollars' worth of improvements.

Allan had taken the same approach in the vineyard, where Uncle B had received roughly NZ$500,000 worth of new equipment, including a new harvester (that can be converted into both a trimmer and a leaf-plucker), new tractor, new sprayer, and brushes for sweeping under the vines after pruning—all things that could get the work done better and faster and, in the long term, for less money.

Back in the winery, though, Allan was seeing to many of the improvements personally. He was jackhammering away at concrete only minutes before he was scheduled to be interviewed by a wine writer from a German gay magazine. The joke wasn't lost on him, either. He even sang a Village People song aloud as he yielded control of the jackhammer and sprinted to his office to make the appointment on time.

The weather was bright, sunny, and warm, and had been for weeks—perfect for ripening grapes, as well as just being outside waterskiing, diving, fishing, hunting, hiking, camping, you name it. I even joined a cricket team, despite the captain's warning me that it can be a lot more dangerous a sport than it looks—by pulling out his two front teeth, then popping them back in. "To my credit, I didn't go down after the ball hit me," he said proudly. Nothing like that happened to me in the couple of matches I played, though I imagine some of my teammates wished it had, considering how limited a contribution I was able to make, having been raised on backyard baseball. (Which, I should note, doesn't last seven hours, as cricket does. Of course my mind was gonna wander now and again over the course of the game.)

But what New Zealand seems to do best throughout the summer is one-day festivals. On the first two Saturdays in February were the annual Blues, Brews & BBQs Festival and the Marlborough Wine & Food Festival, respectively. A Mormon with his jaw wired shut couldn't walk away from one of these events sober. The good news is, if you go, you just might meet a hot, drunk girl and take her back to your place. The bad news, though, is there's a possibility that she might wake up in the middle of the night, pee off the edge of your bed, then crawl back under the covers and start snoring again as if she'd never budged. Not that I would know from personal experience or anything . . .

My favorite festival, though, the biggest and boldest of them all, came toward the end of the summer: the Wildfoods Festival in Hokitika, a small town on the South Island's west coast. If a giant frat party and an episode of *Fear Factor* could get together and have a baby, it would look like this festival.

Though I'd only had one beer, I decided for my first snack I'd try the sheep testicles, which came in sizes small, medium, and large (this is one time you seriously don't want to use the words, "Supersize me"). They were a bit chewy, but I've eaten worse things. Like the huhu grub, which came next. These little suckers are about two inches long and look like the sort of thing that would attack on *The X-Files*. Some people ate theirs live, but for a couple of bucks extra mine came floating in a shot of moonshine. Everyone asked me if the grub tasted like peanut butter, which is the commonly held opinion, but I really think it just tasted like a worm. At least the moonshine gave me the confidence to try the possum pie . . . which I thought was outstanding. Sure, I griped about the meat pies before, but this was earthy, gamey, smoky—delicious!

And then I tried the cow udder, which was sold at a booth called "Tasty Titties." Titties, yes. Tasty, no. Just awful. I then moved on to Kowlua and milk which, just as you'd expect, was coffee, vodka, and milk that came from the cow, fresh that morning; a stuffed seagull heart, which was probably the most disgusting thing I've ever let cross my lips; and a pig-penis sausage on a piece of white bread. Now, being an American raised on the occasional hotdog composed of multiple ingredients, I asked the people if they use anything other than pig penises in their sausages. They seemed horrified at the notion. So then I asked how many pig penises were required to make my sausage. The woman sitting there said, "Well, we used about thirty or so, ground 'em all up, and put them into casings."

"So, right now I have about thirty different pigs' penises in my mouth?" I asked her as I chewed, then swallowed what tasted like any other pork sausage. (Yet looking at the tip of it made my stomach turn.)

"Yeah, I guess you could say that."

"So," I asked, "shouldn't you be paying me five dollars to eat this?"

I decided to finish off with a roasted grasshopper and a kidney-and-tongue kebab before deciding that I'd had just about enough. Everyone was still talking about the previous year's hot seller, the shots of bull semen, but I couldn't find them this time around. To tell the truth, I didn't really look that hard. Though one guy did complain to me, "It's like five dollars for this little tiny amount. It's just not worth it," as if for that much money he'd want a full pint. But I think five dollars for a shot of bull semen is a pretty fair price, seeing as how some poor bastard had the job of extracting it. And you think your job sucks.

The festival ran into the wee hours with a couple of cover bands and a seemingly endless supply of beer. There was nowhere to stay, so I wound up passing out in the front seat of some chick's car at about 2:00 A.M., and slept until about seven with the gearshift doing an impersonation of a proctologist.

Brief discomfort aside, the festivals couldn't come at a better time, really, because in the vineyards the fruit-thinning, wire-lifting, and all the other jobs were done. Fred's crew, like every other across the valley, could only wait for harvest. And once the full-time vineyard guys finished spraying, they were left with only odd jobs here and there. I saw Uncle B in the break room at the winery, making himself a cup of coffee very slowly, almost as if he was trying to draw out the process as long as possible.

"There's nothing to do right now except wait," he said as he watched the kettle work its way toward boiling point.

For the winemakers, however, there wasn't a moment to lose, since they needed to not only clean the winery, move tanks, and organize the barrel halls to get everything ready for the upcoming harvest, but take this opportunity to get a real sense of the quality and quantity of fruit they'd get. Jeremy's crop estimates from early in the year were just that—guesses based on the fact that he knew what tonnages ASW got the year before, and that they'd be significantly lower in most of the vineyards. But nothing was certain.

So Jeremy dispatched Susan to do sampling across all the ASW and contract-grower vineyards, and I joined her for a couple of days of the work. As with all other tasks in the vineyard, I found it best to avoid this one as much as possible once I got the hang of it, but I did help her a couple of other times she needed to gather data quickly.

On each block we visited, Susan and I zigzagged up and down the rows and picked ten vines randomly. We'd then count the number of bunches on each vine. On the first block my counts varied from twenty-eight all the way up to fifty-eight, and Susan even managed to pick some vines with upward of seventy bunches (though most of them were quite small). Like every other vineyard task, this turned out to be repetitive and tiresome, and since the vines had grown so many shoots and such healthy leaf canopies from the December rain and long stretch of sunny weather afterward, getting an accurate count involved kneeling, reaching in, and digging around as if I was a kid trying to find the baseball after it rolled into the prickly bushes.

One grower's block was especially interesting because it was old and beautiful, each vine with a big, fat trunk. But beauty's only skin deep, as they say, since the root systems were infested with phylloxera, a nasty little insect that snacks on the roots of grapevines. This problem isn't very common in the world's vineyards anymore, since most plantings in the past thirty or so years have been done by grafting classic winegrowing varieties—such as Sauvignon Blanc, Chardonnay, or Pinot Noir—onto any one of several different American rootstocks that are resistant to phylloxera. Once upon a time phylloxera almost wiped out the entire French wine industry, since for decades the growers there, true to national identity and history, chose to eat lots of cheese, smoke, fuck each other's wives, and pretend that the problem didn't exist until some Americans came in and saved the day.

On this particular block, however, the infestation was so deep that there were huge gaps in the canopy and even yellow leaves in the fruit zone, as if autumn had begun two months early. Some of the healthier-looking vines had no fruit whatsoever, while the uglier ones had plenty. I found one vine with sixty bunches while Susan found one with as few as twelve. The only consistent thing we discovered here was tiny bunch sizes, with grapes that looked like peas. Put simply, the roots of the vines were so decimated that relatively few nutrients could be sucked from the soil and transferred to the fruit.

Fortunately, this sort of thing is pretty uncommon in Marlborough, and these particular vines never represented more than a blip on the radar in terms of ASW's total grape harvest for any particular year. On this block, like all the others, we picked one vine randomly and stripped off all its fruit, counting the bunches as we did so and weighing all the grapes once we got them back to the lab at the winery. With a little multiplication, you get the total weight of the grapes on that block (understanding, of course, that the grapes increase in size over the course of the growing season). Susan continued collecting samples all through the next several weeks to help the winery get a better idea of how much and how fast the grapes would mature in future growing seasons.

ASW was also, for the first time, using a software package that would help determine its volumes as well as automatically graph the vineyards' ripening progress as Susan entered the results of the Brix, acidity, and pH tests she'd conduct later on. Some wineries, like Highfield, take it a step further and even bring in an independent consultant to do their crop estimates.

"We want the advice to be independent for the growers because if there are potentially large crops, we would be using that information to be able to say, 'You need to go and thin fruit,' and trust that we're not manipulating it," Al explained. And like ASW, his preliminary results showed that the winery's volume would be considerably lower than 2004's.

"Our estimates tell us we'll be down fifteen percent to twenty percent, but I'm still not convinced that will happen," he said to me during the wait for the grapes to ripen. "In the past few years we've seen berry weights compensating by getting big. It wouldn't surprise me if the numbers come in close to normal or average. We're looking at about six kilograms per plant as an average on our blocks this year, and in a normal season it might be seven."

Even with the potentially lower volume, excitement was starting to build, perhaps because as the grapes grew and swelled, that meant my time in Marlborough was coming to an end, and every winemaker would finally be done with answering all of my stupid questions. Or maybe they all just got more excited as the sun continued to bathe Marlborough in its rays, ripening their grapes.

"We had seven days in February above thirty degrees, which is about consistent with the long-term average," John Belsham told me at the beginning of March, just as the weather was starting to cool off a bit. "Now that we're having cooler nights, the average temperature's going to drop, and we like that because that's going to condition the fruit. If we have a normal Marlborough autumn, we're looking for a really good year."

But he wasn't about to count his chickens, either.

"There's a really famous line by the chief winemaker at Montana at the end of January 1995, in which he said, and was quoted in the British tabloids, 'The quality and quantity of the vintage was looking the best [he'd] ever seen it.' And at the end of January it was. And I'm sure you've heard all the '95 stories . . . a total disaster."

Ten years later, however, Dog Point's James Healy was optimistic about the vintage to come, even though the harvest seemed as though it would commence a bit later than normal. "Late vintages," he explained, "often give the best flavor—they give a bit more intensity of flavor because you get that final ripening at the cool end of the season."

What he and everyone else was concerned about with a late season, though, was disease. You can spray to prevent it, but once there's an outbreak, there's really not much you can do. "This sort of year, you do have a risk of botrytis," James went on. "Some people think that it gives complexity, but botrytis is not something you want in just about every variety."

In other words, wet weather is the enemy this time of year, but not if it dries up quickly. However, at the end of March, just as Marlborough was welcoming vintage workers from around the world as it had the year before, the rain came pouring down for about a week straight. And the Nor'west wind was nowhere to be found, swooping in and saving the day from botrytis as it was supposed to. Good Friday wasn't so good at all, and rain fell more or less continuously through the Easter weekend. Allan was at the winery for much of that time, doing last-minute concrete-pouring, welding, and tank-cleaning to make sure everything would be ready should there be any picking to do on the Monday after the holiday. But the more the rain fell, the less likely it was that any picking would occur.

For March 24 to 30, a local research service reported the average temperature as fifteen degrees centigrade (fifty-nine degrees Fahrenheit), when it had been warm and sunny the week before. Sixty-eight millimeters of rain fell slowly and steadily over that time, inviting botrytis into the vineyards like a flashing neon sign over a porno store on Eighth Avenue in New York. Even once the weather did dry up, the researchers advised that this was when the botrytis would start to appear at its worst.

"It was a brilliant growing season, and now this shit," Josh said to me on the only sunny day in the middle of the rainy stretch that would last for eight days total. "We're starting to get some botrytis, so we'll just monitor it and see what happens."

But it didn't get much better as time went on, just as the reports suggested. "There's heaps of botrytis out there," Josh told me the Monday after Easter. "We can only hope it'll dry up over the next three or four days. Otherwise, this could be a short, sharp harvest, just like 2003," meaning they'd have to pick fruit that wasn't as ripe as they expected it to get.

A couple of days later I tagged along as Josh drove through the vineyards so he could make a better assessment, but the rain had set in again, forcing him and Jeremy to rethink whatever picking decisions they'd already begun to pencil in based on the Brix tests Susan had begun to report over the last couple of weeks. The Pinot Noir, fortunately, didn't seem to have a botrytis problem at all. But some blocks of white varieties appeared to be overwhelmed by rot, with purple, soggy, wrinkled grapes hanging on to the vines about as securely as a Popsicle holds on to its stick at high noon in the Kalahari Desert.

Fortunately, just as many or more blocks looked fine, having emerged from the cold, wet weather with nary a spec of infection or berry-splitting. The Pinot Gris and Gewürztraminer looked especially healthy, as did most of Marlborough's sugar daddy, the Sauvignon Blanc. The Chardonnay seemed to be hit the hardest, and the Riesling had a little rot here and there, but several blocks of these varieties had pulled through unscathed. Still, Josh didn't seem entirely convinced as we drove up and down more and more rows, his frustration mounting.

"Is everyone shitting their pants?" I asked him.

"Not really, it's just that it makes you pick before you want to and affects your volumes," he told me. I asked him, though, if a couple of days of warm, dry, windy weather would stop the botrytis.

"Maybe," he said, "but probably not. Once it sets in it just spreads. It'd be like hitting AIDS with antibiotics. It might slow it down a little, but that's about it."

When the weather cleared a few days later, though, so did the panic. Hope returned, just as it does at the end of the summer blockbuster movie with healthy-looking people, alive and well, having successfully avoided the meteorite, ice age, or aliens with ray guns.

The rugby season kicked off again, too, only without Josh and Jeremy, as they'd both decided to spend more time with the wines (though, somehow, I couldn't imagine that they'd ever give up rugby entirely, since asking a Kiwi to quit rugby is like asking an Italian to give up pasta). I went to watch the first Moutere game of the season even though the ASW winemakers weren't playing, and though it was a sunny day nothing had been declared ripe and ready for picking just yet, so the stands were full. Bart from Seresin happened to be sitting behind me in the bleachers, and I overheard him talking to a friend who asked him about how things were shaping up after the rain.

His tone of voice expressed displeasure, "But we haven't been forced to pick anything yet," he said.

Essentially, it seemed that the rain was just a smack in the face. A very hard one that would bring lower volumes, a later harvest, and, in turn, likely frost scares toward the end of it. But that's just the nature of the beast, and the sting seemed to have worn off quickly, since there were plenty of healthy grapes still hanging on the vines and working their way toward ripeness. Where there were questions about the quality of the 2004 vintage, 2005's was in little doubt even after a narrow escape from the jaws of disaster.

It was then that I realized there's no such thing as a normal harvest—at least not in Marlborough. Every one truly is different, with some varieties turning out better than others. The end of the 2005 season may have deflated expectations and even a few egos, but there was no reason to assume that anyone would put the Marlborough name—much less his own—on a bottle of wine that wouldn't taste good. And since the valley had finally dried up, sentiment improved once again, and the excitement of the buildup to a new harvest resumed.

A couple of days later, Josh and Linus were making last-minute fixes to the presses and hoses, as well as cleaning and sterilizing every piece of equipment they'd need to process the eight tons of Chardonnay grapes that had just splashed into the receival bin. It was fruit from the same block that had been harvested more or less upon my arrival the year before, and this juice would also be used for ASW's sparkling wine. The other varieties would begin to flow in slowly but surely over the next several weeks, and though it hadn't started with a bang and probably wouldn't finish with one (just like every one before it), the new vintage was finally under way.

I remember swearing to myself—and anyone who'd listen—that I would never work another harvest. The hours are too long, the days too cold, the nights too wet, and the work too messy and tiring. But soon after those first grapes started spilling into the must pump and splashing all over the new receival and crushing area, I could smell something in the air. I didn't notice it at first, but I was suddenly awash with exhilaration at the very moment that I realized what I'd smelled: fresh grape juice.

The scent hovered in the air for hours as if it were smoke in a jazz bar, sticking to my hair and clothes. The juice wouldn't take the form of a drug for months, but it was already having a similar effect on me, if only because I finally understood what this stuff was, where it came from, and what it would become. And the more I did the hard work involved with making it, the better the wine seemed to taste.

I wanted to get cold, wet, and dirty all over again.

Epilogue

Two thousand five turned out to be the year that Josh and Jeremy proved they could play with the big boys, at least so far as critical acclaim is concerned. The Allan Scott Sauvignon Blanc scored 91 points from *Wine Spectator* and won gold medals in several competitions. And the Gewürztraminer not only won a gold medal, but took home the trophy at the Air New Zealand Wine Awards.

And Josh's beer, Moa, really took off. Big time. He went from making a couple of brews a month and selling most of the beer locally, when things first got going, to several brews a week, and he even hired a full-time brewer from the Czech Republic. He also now makes the regular lager, a wheat beer, a dark lager, and a ginger beer. He even began exporting Moa to the United States and China. God only knows if Chinese people actually like the beer, but it turns out they associate red birds with good luck and, wouldn't you know it, the moa on the beer's logo is red.

Josh also had good luck with his girlfriend, Laura, who graduated from University of Otago and returned to Marlborough. For a short time they lived in Josh's house in the Omaka vineyard (which was renamed the Hares), and then bought a house together in Blenheim.

Jeremy and his girlfriend bought a new house in the Omaka Valley, where they planted a vineyard with Sauvignon Blanc, Pinot Gris, and Pinot Noir. Having been the guy behind the guy for what he probably felt was far too long a time, in mid-2006 Jeremy left ASW to become a winemaker at the Marlborough facility of one of New Zealand's biggest and most reputable wineries. The parting with ASW was amicable, as it was only a matter of time before he outgrew his shoes. Maybe they'll fit his new son, Finn Nico McKenzie, born October 26, 2006.

Josh and Jeremy both played another season of rugby for Moutere, which made it to the finals (unfortunately, they lost there to a team called Pelorus, which is so far in the backwoods between Blenheim and Nelson that I think the players emerge from the forest for the game, then disappear for another week—combined tooth count on that team is about three and a half). It was Jeremy's final season, and afterward he had long-overdue operations performed on both his worn-out knees. Josh, however, had a breakthrough season and was called up to play for the Marlborough Red Devils.

Josh's younger sister, Sara, returned to Marlborough from England in late 2005 and joined the family business full-time, focusing mostly on the vineyard. She quickly helped redesign the spray program, and ASW now is a member of the Sustainable Agriculture initiative. She and Josh have become extremely competitive athletically, regularly taking each other on in everything from triathlons to road races to bike races. In early 2007 they even did the 243-kilometer Speights Coast to Coast race from the west coast of the South Island to the east coast.

Allan and Cathy bought a house in Queenstown and began spending more and more time relaxing there. They tried to buy their nearby Central Otago vineyard, Mount Michael, from their investment partners, but since they didn't want to sell, Allan chose to sell his share to them instead. He hopes to plant a new vineyard elsewhere in Central Otago and hand off more of the day-to-day business in Marlborough to Josh.

All of them still call me Eric the Eel, or just Eel for short. Each time they do—whether it's over email, instant messenger, or a phone call—I can't help but think about going back to New Zealand to help make wine again, and maybe break less of their shit the next time around. After the 2005 harvest I moved back to Brooklyn and took a job at *Wine Spectator* magazine. Though I have yet to show up to work on time, I'm still employed there as the news editor. The job is great and I've learned a lot, but I'm sure I'll return to New Zealand at some point, since these days I never get to pick grape skins out of my underwear. I kinda miss it.

Acknowledgments

Telling a down-to-earth wine story turned out to be much more difficult a proposition than I expected. With my approach—actually doing the work in the vineyards and winery, potentially learning nothing *and* breaking lots of other people's expensive stuff—I opened myself up to a hell of a lot of scrutiny, potential factual error, and downright embarrassment. And that doesn't even include the time I had a bit too much to drink and pissed on the Cloudy Bay sign. But what concerned me most about writing this book was eventually being viewed as or even becoming one of those writers who waxes poetic about wine and claims to pick up hints of "leathery violets" (whatever the hell those are) or "velvety tannins." I don't know about you, but I've never licked the sofa cushions and told people they taste like Merlot.

However, before all that, a book like this does not come to fruition when some numbskull packs a bag, gets drunk, and hops on a plane to New Zealand. It certainly starts that way, but it has no chance of getting past the first sentence unless the writer has an ability on par with that of history's most feared and psychotic dictators to convince people to believe in his ideas and, in turn, provide unquestioning assistance and make ridiculous sacrifices. Among those who have done so are my family members who supported this project in more ways than one, but more important were quick to tell me when I was doing a good job and even quicker to tell me when I wasn't. They are my parents, Tom and Carol Arnold; my grandparents, Maury and Judy Colman; and my uncle Warren Colman. Special thanks are also due my sister-in-law Lori and my brother Bill, an associate professor of civil engineering at the University of Minnesota who cast his expert eye over Chapter 21. The true believers who championed this idea from day one are Fred Ordway of

Uniqco Imports and David Strada of New Zealand Winegrowers. Thanks, guys, for making this possible in the first place.

During the research and writing, Tom Matthews, executive editor of *Wine Spectator,* provided regular doses of encouragement. As did esteemed New Zealand wine critic Michael Cooper, who may look like a retired seventies porn actor but is actually just a nice, kind-spirited fellow who loves tasting and writing about wine.

A debt of gratitude I'll probably spend the rest of my life trying to repay goes to my agent, Bob Lescher; my editor at Scribner, Beth Wareham (who will spend the rest of her life trying to out-disgust me . . . not a chance); the insightful/helpful/encouraging Scribner assistant editor Anna DeVries; and publicist/drinking-buddy-extraordinaire, Kate Bittman.

Thanks also to my friends who either read early drafts of the book or simply helped keep me sane during some of the tougher times in which it was written. There are too many of you to list here, but the ones I couldn't have made it through this without are Carl and Meghan Berglind, Laura Warrell, Jennie Rose, Ella Garnett Hoskins, Seth Fox (for sending bagels from New York), Eddylicious, Madmat, and Genevieve Poirier. Carly Tushingham, for your work on the drawings in this book as well as your support in the run-up to its publication, I can't thank you enough. Caroline Levchuck and Michele Drohan, thanks for teaching me a long time ago to just go for it. I also must thank Spencer Watkins for introducing me to Marlborough wine in the first place, as well as Timur Kibar, James Shearing, and Tiffany Wilkinson, and the smartest and toughest boss I ever had the privilege to work for, Jonah Bloom.

Thanks are also due each and every winemaker in New Zealand who took the time to show me around, educate me, provide the odd favor, and give honest answers to all of my questions, no matter how idiotic they may have seemed at the time.

But most of all, thanks go to everyone who worked at Allan Scott Wines during all or some of the time I spent there: Jeremy, Kevin, Elisha, Murray, Victoria L., Brent, Liz, Uncle B, Geoff, Ann Marie, Ra, Terry, Brian F., Gerald, Peter (RIP), Little Peter, Kosta, Joe, Linus, Danny, Allan M., Phillip, Jemma, Susan, Tim, Marine, Frenchie, and everyone from Russell Viticultural Services. And especially the Scott family: Allan, Cathy, Josh, Victoria, and Sara, thank you for welcoming a complete stranger into your lives and making him feel at home from day one. I hope this book is only the first step toward repaying the kindness and hospitality you so willingly gave to me. I still have a long way to go.

A L L A N
SCOTT
FAMILY WINEMAKERS

marlborough
SAUVIGNON BLANC
WINE OF NEW ZEALAND

Glossary . . .

. . . of all those winemaking terms I used throughout, which you're welcome to flip to at any time. Don't feel bad about it, 'cause most people who claim to know a lot about wine will have to flip here just as often as you. They might know the difference between Beaujolais and Bordeaux, but that doesn't mean they know how to make wine in either place any better than you.

Acetic acid: A contaminant in wine that makes it smell like vinegar or nail polish. Usually only occurs with wines that are aged in barrels. Some people think a barely detectable amount of VA (volatile acidity) in a wine adds complexity, and for whatever reason, some people think that really high amounts of it make a wine taste great. Mostly just French people though.

Bentonite: A clay substance added to white wine to help drop out proteins. Also has multiple industrial uses, but I have no idea what they are.

Biodynamics: An environmentally friendly grape-growing philosophy that involves not only organic farming but working in harmony with Earth's natural forces, cosmic rhythms, and the phases of the moon. Most people believe its ultimate affect on wine quality is debatable at best. I tend to agree, though I've never had a truly awful biodynamic wine, either.

Block(s): Part or all of a vineyard.

Botrytis: A mold/fungus that grows on grapes in warm, moist weather conditions. Not at all good for the production of table wine, but essential in the production of dessert wines ("late harvest" dessert wines are the same thing). The mold sucks the water from the grapes and concentrates the sugars so the alcohol level is roughly the same as in regular table wine, but the sugar level is much higher.

Brix: A measure of natural sugar content in grape juice. Each unit of Brix equals roughly ten grams of sugar per liter of juice. Measuring Brix is a way to indicate how far along the ripening of the grapes is, as well as an indication of what the alcohol level will be if the grapes are picked, crushed, and fermented into wine at that moment. Fermentation involves the yeast converting the sugar into alcohol, so if you know how much sugar you have, you know roughly how much alcohol you'll have in the finished product.

Bud-rubbing: By far the worst vineyard job of them all. Involves rubbing your hand up and down the trunk of the vine to remove any buds or shoots that have grown out of it. These are removed in springtime, since you want the vine pushing its nutrients into the shoots that will grow grapes, not into the little ones close to the ground.

Cane: A branch on a vine. When the vines are pruned, a cane on each side of the plant is twisted and tied down to a wire that runs along the entire row. In the spring, the buds along the cane will burst and grow shoots, from which the new season's grapes will grow.

Cold soak: Period of time that crushed red grapes and juice are held together in the tank, kept at a low temperature, before fermentation starts.

Cold stabilization (cold stab): Process through which the tartrate crystals are dropped out of wine. Temperature on the tank of wine is dropped to minus one degree centigrade, and then cream of tartar is added.

Cream of tartar (aka "cot"): Same stuff as what's in baking powder. Helps drop tartrate crystals out of a tank of wine.

Cross-flow filter: Expensive, complicated piece of equipment that employs membranes to filter a large tank of wine in a matter of just a few hours.

Diatomaceous earth: Fine powder made mostly of silicon that's used to filter wine. Using an earth filter is considerably slower than using a cross-flow filter, and also produces more waste, but is just as effective.

Downy mildew: A mold that can infect the leaves of grapevines, inhibiting their ability to capture sunlight.

Ethyl acetate (EA): A contaminant that makes wine smell like glue. Usually only occurs with wines that are aged in barrels.

Fermentation: Process by which grape juice is turned into wine. Yeast, once added to the juice, eats the sugar and converts it to alcohol, releasing carbon dioxide as a by-product.

Filtering (also see diatomaceous earth and cross-flow filter): Process of removing unwanted particles from wine, particularly proteins.

Fining: Process of clarifying, purifying, and stabilizing wine by adding egg whites, skim milk, fish guts, or a collagen-based substance.

Free run: Best-quality portion of juice from a load of white-wine grapes. When the grapes are loaded into the press, the weight of them all pushing down on one another makes juice run out freely, hence "free run."

Lees (juice): Solid particles that fall to the bottom of a tank of juice after a couple of days.

Lees (yeast): Dead yeast cells that fall to the bottom of the tank or barrel during fermentation. Generally, the longer the dead yeast cells are left in or below the wine, the better the finished product will taste.

Macerate/maceration: The mashing together of grape flesh, skins, and seeds, particularly in red wine. This extracts tannins from the skins and seeds and puts them into the wine.

Malolactic fermentation: Process of converting the wine's natural malic acid into softer-feeling lactic acid. Will occur naturally over time, but is usually accomplished with the addition of a dried bacteria culture (often called a "malo bug").

Marc: The grape skins, stems, and seeds that are left inside the press after all the juice has been squeezed out. ASW loads it into a farmer's truck, and he then drives it home and feeds it to his cows. But in Italy, this is what gets shoveled into big distillers and turned into grappa.

Must: Slushy combination of recently crushed grapes and juice.

Organic farming: Form of agriculture that eschews the use of man-made chemicals and fertilizers. People who practice organic farming usually shop only at Whole Foods or Trader Joe's. And they smell like tofu.

Overcropping: Term used when the vines are carrying too many bunches of grapes. If the vine is growing too much fruit, it can't get enough nutrients into all of it for the grapes to ripen fully by the end of the season.

Phylloxera: Nasty little insect (*Daktulosphaira vitifoliae*—say that five times real fast) that eats the roots of grapevines. Most vines are grafted onto a kind of rootstock that's resistant to the little fuckers. Until an American horticulturist figured out that you could do this, phylloxera nearly wiped out the entire French wine industry. Yet again, an American had to save the Frogs.

Plunging: Act of pushing grape skins and seeds at the top of a tank back down into fermenting wine, using what looks like a giant toilet plunger. The process helps keep the color of the wine consistent and helps extract a small amount of tannins from the skins and seeds.

Powdery mildew: A fungus that eats away at the leaves of grapevines.

Pressings: Juice that comes from pressing on the grapes. They couldn't come up with a more interesting name.

Pruning: Process of hacking unwanted branches/canes off the vine during the fall and winter, after harvest. Anywhere from two to four canes are left intact for growing the next year's grapes.

Pumping over: Pumping wine from the bottom of a tank of red wine up onto the skins and seeds floating on top. Process keeps the skins moist during fermentation, and is an easier, faster method than plunging by hand.

Racking: Process of pumping clear juice or wine off the top of cloudy juice or wine, resting on the bottom of the tank or barrel.

RDV (rotating-drum vacuum): Piece of machinery that takes juice lees and separates the solids from the liquids. The recovered juice is turned into wine, and the solids are thrown away.

Residual sugar (RS): Sugar in wine that the yeast has yet to convert into alcohol (during fermentation), or leftover sugar in finished wine (after fermentation).

Scott Henry: Method of pruning in which two canes are kept on either side of the vine. The top two canes grow shoots up, and the bottom two canes grow shoots down. Makes the row of vines look like a row of shrubs and better exposes the grapes to sunlight, since they're in the middle of the shrub, and the leaves are above and below them.

Shoot-thinning: Process of ripping new shoots off the vine's canes, partway through spring, to reduce the number of grape bunches grown per vine (and the total crop load), so they can all ripen fully by the end of the season.

Sustainable Agriculture: Program that helps wineries and grape growers use only the minimum-needed amount of chemical sprays to better protect the environment, yet still produce a healthy, good-sized crop.

Tannins: Naturally occurring compounds in the skins and seeds of grapes. In red wine, tannins give you that drying, cottonmouth feeling.

Tartrates: Crystals that form in a tank of wine, removed by adding cream of tartar. Even if they're not removed (some winemakers leave them in red wine), they won't hurt you. So drink up.

Terroir: A French term that refers to the piece of land on which the vines are planted, and the resulting unique flavors in the wine—basically why Sauvignon Blanc from one part of Marlborough tastes a little different from the Sauvignon Blanc from another part, because the nutrients in the soil and the microclimates are slightly different. But I didn't use this word anywhere in the book, mostly because people sound like assholes when they say it. Kind of like when someone tries to sound French when they order a croissant at Au Bon Pain. Also, in European wines, people often think contaminations like VA and EA are unique characteristics in the wine imparted by the soil the vines were planted on, and they call it *terroir* rather than contamination to make themselves sound knowledgeable. Assholes.

VA: Stands for volatile acidity. See "acetic acid."

Veraison: Later stage of ripening in grapes, when the red varieties actually start to turn red (they start out green). Basically when the grapes stop growing and start ripening.

Vertical shoot positioning (VSP): Method of pruning in which all the branches/canes on the vine are snipped off, except for one on each side of the vine. The canes are tied down to a wire that runs the length of the entire row of vines. Come spring, the buds on the canes grow shoots straight up. Two bunches of grapes will grow at the base of each shoot.

Vintage: Synonym for "year," when referring to the date on a wine label. Also a synonym for "harvest," when referring to working at a winery. If you say that you "worked the harvest at Winery A," that's the same as saying you "worked the vintage at Winery A."

People

Marlborough winemakers (and others) who were kind enough to be interviewed or share their thoughts and opinions, instead of telling me to go fuck myself:

Allan Scott: Cofounder and co-owner of Allan Scott Wines.
Cathy Scott: Allan's wife, and cofounder/co-owner of Allan Scott Wines.
Josh Scott: Allan and Cathy's middle child, and winemaker at Allan Scott Wines.
Victoria Scott: Allan and Cathy's oldest child; helps run the winery's restaurant with Cathy.
Sara Scott: Allan and Cathy's youngest child; helps in the management of the winery's vineyards.
McKenzie, Jeremy: Winemaker alongside Josh Scott at Allan Scott Wines; left in 2006 to become a winemaker at one of Marlborough's largest wineries.
Funnell, Jemma: Assistant winemaker under Josh and Jeremy; was replaced by Susan van der Pol.
Hopkins, Geoff: Manager of Allan Scott Wines' bottling operation.
Kenny, Brian: Vineyard manager at Allan Scott Wines (also known as "Uncle B").
Hebberd, Ra: Vineyard supervisor at Allan Scott Wines.
Marks, Kosta: Chef at Allan Scott Wines' restaurant.

Allan, Mike and Claire: Owners/winemakers of Huia Vineyards.
Arnst, Bart: Viticulturist at Seresin Estate; left in 2005.
Belsham, John: Winemaker at Wairau River and owner/winemaker of Foxes Island; left Wairau River in 2004 to focus on Foxes Island.
Bicknell, Brian: Winemaker at Seresin Estate; left in 2006.
Digger: aka Bill Hennessey, winemaker at Mount Riley.
Duke, Gary: Winemaker at Hunter's.
Glover, Ben: Winemaker at Wither Hills.
Healy, James: Winemaker at Dog Point.

Hedley, Andrew: Winemaker at Framingham.

Herzog, Hans: Swiss immigrant, founder/owner/winemaker of Herzog Estate.

Judd, Kevin: Winemaker at Cloudy Bay.

Just, Mike: Winemaker at Lawson's Dry Hills; left in 2004 to work as a consultant for other brands, as well as focus on his own brand, Clayridge.

Kalberer, Hatsch: Swiss immigrant, winemaker at the Fromm Winery.

Le Brun, Daniel: French immigrant, owner/winemaker of No. 1 Family Estate; founder, but no longer owner, of Cellier Le Brun winery.

MacKenzie, Ant: Winemaker at Spy Valley.

Marris, Brent: Managing director and head winemaker at Wither Hills; left winery in early 2007.

Michel, Georges: French immigrant, owner of Domaine Georges Michel.

Russell, Fred: Vineyard labor contractor for Allan Scott Wines.

Sinnott, Jeff: Winemaker at Central Otago winery Amisfield.

Soper, Alistair: Winemaker at Highfield Estate.

Thomson, Matt: Consultant winemaker for St. Clair, Mud House, Cape Campbell, Lake Chalice, and Delta.

Waghorn, Simon: Winemaker for Whitehaven, Tohu, and Astrolabe.

Woolley, Darryl: Head winemaker at Nobilo.